BRAZIL

BRASÍLIA

The
PANTANAL
Brazil's Forgotten Wilderness

RIO de JANEIRO

SÃO PAULO

MW01012914

The Pantanal

The Pantanal

Brazil's Forgotten Wilderness

VIC BANKS

SIERRA CLUB BOOKS

SAN FRANCISCO

Copyright © 1991 by Vic Banks

Library of Congress Cataloging in Publication Data
Banks, Vic.
The Pantanal : Brazil's forgotten wilderness / by Vic Banks.
  p. cm.
Includes index.
ISBN 0-87156-791-1 :
1. Pantanal (Brazil)—Description and travel. 2. Natural history—
Brazil—Pantanal. 3. Marsh ecology—Brazil—Pantanal. 4. Banks,
Vic—Journeys—Brazil—Pantanal.
F2585.B36 1991
981'.72—dc20   91-12668
                                                                    CIP

Production by Janet Vail

Jacket design by Bonnie Smetts

Book design by Seventeenth Street Studios

Map Illustration © 1990, Bill Peterson

The text of this book is printed in the United States of America
on acid-free recycled paper.

10 9 8 7 6 5 4 3 2 1

Acknowledgments

When you work in a place the size of the Pantanal over several years help comes from many gracious people. Among them I am particularly thankful to:

Renaldo Araugo, Benedito and Oizes Falcão de Arruda, Dr. Nilson de Barros, Biatriz Biancardini, Gizela Bojikian, Dr. Newton de Carvalho, Jerry Emory, The Hon. Fabio Feldman, Vivianne Ferreira, Mario Friedlander, Prof. Jośe de Godoi Filho, Tony DiFiore, Roberto Klabin, Dr. Carlos Leite and family, Dr. Robert Lipgar, Miguel, Gaspar S. Rocha, Alexandre da Silva, Arne Sucksdorff, Dr. Octavio Vaz and family, Carlos Yamashita, Janice Blanck-Wiles, Eurípedes Alcêntra, Prof. Helmut Sick;

Andrés Foto Lab, Center for New Television, Datavue Corporation, Embratur, Embrapa-Corumbá, Fazenda Caiman guides, IBAMA, Lineas Aereas Paraguayas, Lider Cine, The Max McGraw Wildlife Foundation, Mstur, Sema-MS, Teddy Roosevelt Association, Turimat, Varig Brazilian Airlines, Zenith Data Systems;

The John D. and Catherine T. MacArthur Foundation;

And for Lu who made things abundantly Claire.

The rest is my fault.

Contents

Contents

Nay, they are ignorant of the greatest part of America,
which lies betwixt Peru and Bresill . . . some say it is a drowned land
. . . others afferme there are great and flourishing kingdoms . . .
—*Acosta, In Search of El Dorado, 1590*

The Pantanal has the greatest concentration of fauna in the
Americas. . . . People outside Brazil know only the Amazon . . .
it's a shame because the Pantanal is a very important ecological place.
—*Dr. Maria Tereza Jorge Pádua, former director of Brazil's
national parks, 1982 Getty International Conservationist*

one

Flying Down to Rio

Of the gladdest moments in human life . . . is the
departure upon a distant journey into unknown lands.
— *Sir Richard Francis Burton (December 2, 1856)*

The big Varig plane with its above-average service — illustrated
menus in three languages, china, and surprisingly tasty meals
with Bordeaux wines — can't keep me from getting restless on
the flight. It takes eighteen hours from Los Angeles to Rio
with a refueling stop in Lima.

No matter how nice the crew is, the plane is still a tin can
hurtling through space. I would much prefer knockout drops
and having them stow me with the baggage below, a "Wake in
Rio" tag dangling from an ear. Instead, I muscle through the
long night watching old television sit-coms and blurry, in-
house productions on how to buckle up and kiss your ass
good-bye should we go down in the jungle.

Nose pressed up against the window, I'm mulling over how
lucky I was just hearing about the Pantanal, let alone falling in
love with it. I had finished a long Smithsonian project in Thailand, interpreting the remains of a prehistoric Bronze Age culture found beneath the village of Ban Chiang. I was tired and
in need of a new vista. It was then that I met Lúcia, a Brazilian
foreign-service officer working in Chicago. She urged me to
take a break in her country — not in the Amazon's imposing

1

forest, but in the Pantanal, a spectacular wildlife sanctuary few foreigners know.

The Pantanal—which means "swampland" in Portuguese—is an immense, kidney-shaped lowland comprising the Upper Paraguay River Basin in western Brazil, eastern Bolivia, and northeastern Paraguay. Two Brazilian areas are officially protected: a remote national park near Bolivia and a small ecological reserve in the state of Mato Grosso. The balance consists of huge, privately owned cattle ranches. Each year, torrential rains inundate up to 70 percent of the Pantanal, merging rivers, lakes, and ponds into a vast inland sea. Five months later, the powerful tropical sun and a north-south outflow transform the region into a verdant grassland with many water holes populated by great numbers of trapped fish, tall wading birds, and crocodilians. It is indeed a different vista, alluring in its bountiful, exotic wildlife and refreshingly easy on the spirit.

Since then, I've made eight trips in seven years to this all but forgotten wilderness at the very heart of South America. It's been nearly a year since my last visit, and in a country with such rapid industrialization, great debt, and runaway inflation, that's a lifetime. What I'm hearing from friends about the Pantanal is distressing.

Illegal hunters, miners, and commercial fishermen are doing their best to take a precious fortune in skins, gold, fish, and rare birds for pets in the face of dubious enforcement efforts. In the high plains surrounding the Pantanal, farmers are said to be using enormous amounts of agrochemicals—some banned in the United States—to raise soybeans. And with so much attention directed at the Amazon, many miners are seeking gold in and around the poorly patrolled Pantanal, using toxic mercury freely. Some of them are now bringing malaria where there had been none.

Along with the outcry over the Amazon has come an awakening in Brazil about the country's incredible natural wealth. According to one straw count, there are currently more than five hundred conservation groups in Brazil that are attempting to protect everything from the Amazon and great Atlantic forest to many native tribes. As one observer of the blossoming conservation movement put it, what oil is to Saudi Arabia, nature is to Brazil.

Except for Pantanal Alert, a group of artists and musicians in São Paulo who produce popular media events about this wetland, there are few effective national organizations dedicated to scientific investigation and conservation of the Pantanal. In the last twenty years, as the exploitation and pollution of this seasonal wetland has grown exponentially, scientific response has been woefully inadequate. Even the most fundamental animal and plant surveys and water-quality baseline studies are virtually nonexistent. Ghillean Prance of the New York Botanical Gardens, one of the few botanists to have worked in the Pantanal, wrote in 1982 that "the vegetation of the Pantanal remains one of the least known in tropical America." It's still true today.

The Pantanal has never figured high in the priorities of well-endowed international wildlife or conservation groups either. Last year I was talking with a foreign diplomat familiar with environmental issues in Brazil. I was baffled why the long-decimated Atlantic forest was receiving so much funding and not the Pantanal. He said, "If you had two bank accounts, one with 4 percent of its original deposit and the other nearly full, which one would you save?" A good question, indeed.

According to cultural geographer Jerry Emory, who has worked in the Pantanal, this disregard has deep roots. Despite an advancing, interconnected world, the exquisitely isolated Pantanal has "a legacy of use and exploitation that hasn't changed much . . . " for nearly three hundred years. Emory theorizes that in the seventeenth and eighteenth centuries, Spanish, Portuguese, and English explorers found the region nearly impassable. Perhaps the hard going encouraged considerable tall tales, earning the Pantanal an early reputation as unconquerable and dangerous—a place to carefully pass through on the way to somewhere else.

From 1580 to 1780 most cartographers chose not to venture into such formidable swamplands for their own observations. Instead they were content to copy each other's errors, depicting the Pantanal as a great permanent lake called "Lacus Eupama" or, more commonly, "Sea of Xarayes." In the map collections of Chicago's Newberry Library, I've seen notations on these early maps informing that the region is "terra incognita," "poorly known," or that the "people here have much gold and silver."

In the early 1900s the British adventurer Lieutenant Colonel Percy Fawcett believed this lore of riches and fielded a major expedition searching for an El Dorado, a "lost city of gold." He entered Brazil's western state of Mato Grosso, traveling through the Pantanal's heartlands. Fawcett was presumed killed by Indians 300 kilometers northwest of the Pantanal. The lure of "much gold and silver" continues to have a life of its own, attracting prospectors there to this day.

Oddly enough, on my first visit to the Pantanal in 1983, I arrived two weeks after Jacques Cousteau's film crew had done extensive shooting there. I thought he had been profiling the Pantanal and its fabulous wildlife for a major documentary. But, in fact, the film crew had been frustrated trying to find animals in the Amazon's dark forests. The Pantanal's bright light and easy-to-see animals proved a blessing. The wildlife footage was incorporated into Cousteau's Amazon River documentary series, especially in a short sequence of the "Legacy of a Lost World" episode. The program showed Pantanal footage and talked mostly about the Amazon, giving the distinct impression that the Pantanal lies within the Amazon Basin. This further perpetuated the Pantanal's obscurity at a time when international pressure could have helped deter its exploitation.

What I see from my window is a fairyland of cumulonimbi illuminated by a lightning show high above the Amazon. Before dawn a lovely wake-up film gives passengers a glimpse of sylvan Brazil and its many types of birds, with "good morning" translated into a dozen tongues spoken by hordes of incoming tourists. Do authorities realize this wonderful avian sampler is rapidly becoming an ironic record of the endangered?

Extensive flooding in the Pantanal has delayed me from arriving sooner. I had first heard about it on my shortwave receiver one sleepless night in Chicago. In the spring of 1989 so much rain had fallen, said the announcer, that the Paraguay River, the main river running north to south through the region, had long since left its three-hundred-meter-wide streambed. It was a bloated sixty kilometers across. A card from a friend said, "The floods are going down. It's okay to enter the Pantanal." And I can't wait.

It's incredible the kind of pull the Pantanal exerts on me. I have missed the place and friends badly. And that's funny because the Pantanal doesn't bowl you over at first. There aren't any snowcapped peaks, fierce mountain streams, or even neck-craning stands of kapok or cotton-silk trees. It's just the wild west of South America: marshlands, cowboys, a few Indians, and perhaps the most spectacular gatherings of animals that can be seen on this continent.

Maybe this time I'll see my first anaconda or be able to study increasingly rare hyacinth macaws or giant river otters. The nesting season is well under way, providing the best chance to study some of this wetland's great wading birds up close. But there won't be much time. Soon the rains will come in monsoon strength, making photography and travel difficult. I have my work cut out.

I'm not traveling light this time. In previous trips I've gone in and then wished I'd brought some other piece of gear or a spare. I can't bear the idea of not being able to record a sound and an image after such a long trip. What would I do if I got close to those big, blue hyacinth macaws without a long lens?

I've narrowed my baggage down: three still cameras and a 16mm movie camera; 28mm, 60mm macro, 135mm, 300mm, and 560mm superlong lenses; 2-x extender, filters, lens cradle, stereo recorder, microphone, tapes, film-changing bag, laptop computer, rechargeable battery packs, nearly two hundred rolls of still and movie film, flashes, tripod, remote camera release, portable spotlight, pesticide-testing gear, bird identification book, three novels, binoculars, repair kits, mini-shortwave receiver, thirty batteries, medical kit, fishing equipment, and gifts of dry flies, Swiss army knives, photo prints, Balkan Sobranie pipe tobacco, clothes, three bottles of Stoly, and one Chivas. I've managed to cram all of it into three innocuous bags. But they weigh a ton.

Like modern-day Baron von Münchhausen, we glide gently from the sky into tropical light so bright it hurts my eyes. Low clouds break open to reveal Rio's Atlantic forest and dramatic skyline.

Readying to deplane, I'm nervous about clearing all my gear through customs. I've heard it can be a random business. Some seasoned travelers to Brazil say foreigners zip right through. Others recount horror stories. Rumors abound that from the moment passengers disembark, customs agents are scanning them, eager to catch returning nationals or visitors with contraband electronics. Not that I'm out to get away with something.

Even though I have proper credentials and customs registration (most of the gear has been well used), it's up to the individual officer if he wants to hassle me or not. He can impound my equipment and make me go into Rio (thirty kilometers) to put up a cash bond that guarantees I'll leave the country without selling my gear. It can take hours.

I put the bags on a cart, suck in my breath, and wait in line for customs inspection. Each passenger is confronted by a post with a black button. It's my turn. A green light means go through without inspection. Red means get out of line and open your bags. I get a red.

The agent is surprisingly young, with a beard, hair close cut, and wire-rim glasses. He digs through the cases and unwraps some pants, revealing a tripod. A softball-size roll of underpants hides the fluid head. A shoulder bag's packed full of camera gear. But it's the carton of several hundred rolls of film that seals my fate.

"What are you doing with all this?" the agent asks. "I'm a photographer," I say. Without a blink he says, "I'm sorry, you'll have to leave your equipment here and go into the city to post a bond." As I plead my case, an older official comes over to the agent and they confer, blowing cigarette smoke at each other while speaking. "Where are you going with so much gear?" the older man asks. "The Pantanal," I offer. For added credibility, I unzip a long bag and pull out my collapsible fishing rod, and in a snap of the wrist I've extended it, pretending to have one on the line. "See, I'm going for *dorado*." These big, green-and-yellow fish resemble salmon and fight like tarpon; they're much esteemed by fishermen. I've dreamed of catching one.

The men confer again, half hidden by their cloud of smoke, incredulous a gringo wants to venture into the world's biggest swamp. They figure if I'm telling a story just to get in with all that stuff, it's pretty good: they haven't heard that one before. They turn to me, smile, and shoo me through the sliding doors. Two words have set me free: "Pantanal" and "*dorado.*"

My friends, Dr. Octavio Vaz and his wife, Evelene, arrive to pick me up. They've opened their house to me until I shake my jet lag and arrange for my next leg up to Brasília, the high-plains capital. There I'll get permission to travel to the Pantanal's remote national park.

Rio is a mighty enticing place with its unbeatable physical setting: green Atlantic escarpment, expansive Guanabara Bay with its many soaring frigate birds, and the two-legged "wild-life" at those famous beaches. Unfortunately, this great beauty is marred by a litany of unmanageable urban problems: pollution, sprawling hillside slums, crime, and a failing infrastructure. Of late, the mayor has declared the city government bankrupt, cutting or curtailing many municipal services. Octavio is a surgeon who recently finished a specialist course in throat surgery in Chicago and now races between three jobs to keep up with a crushing 80 percent inflation a month.

For all its humanity—the city's Copacabana section is said to have a population density greater than that of Hong Kong—there are parts of Rio where the jungle literally comes to a high-rise window. Evelene's charming mother, Dona Mariinha, decries the fact that years ago birds used to come to her house. Because of the high crime in Rio many families have given up their homes for the safety of apartment buildings. Now that she lives above the street, "the birds aren't here anymore." I install a hummingbird feeder the next afternoon, and she's pleased to see green-and-rose hummingbirds hovering at the feeder outside their fourth-story condo.

Gilberto Ferrez, a well-known writer who lives in Rio, swears small monkeys still come to his backyard to take bananas set out for them. They live in the remnants of the once great Atlantic forest that stretched south from the northern state of Ceará to Rio Grande do Sul for five thousand un-broken kilometers. Today, the Atlantic forest has shrunk to less than 4 percent of its original size. But it's taken the better part of five hundred years of steady exploitation.

The Pantanal—approximately 210,000 square kilometers, arguably the largest wetland in the world—may well succumb in less than thirty.

two
/ / /

Bird Paradise of the Americas

/ / / / / / / / / /

The birds alone are worth the arduous
trip across Mato Grosso . . . to the Pantanal.
— Dr. Jean Dorst, South America and Central America, A Natural History

*I*t's August, springtime — a wonderful, contradictory time to
see the fabulous birds of the Pantanal. Nearly all of those inun-
dating rains that fell from October through March have either
drained south or evaporated under the relentless tropical sun.
Rain hasn't fallen since April. In spite of this seasonal drought
trees have blossomed, and millions of great wading birds have
surrendered to an ancient call, courted, and built nests together
forming immense *viveiros,* or colonies. They are a fabulous nature spectacle to behold — that is, if I can find one. People in
the know say they reside deep in the Pantanal. It's going to
take some serious reconnoitering.

Getting into the region is nearly as difficult today for
foreigners as when French ornithologist Jean Dorst traveled
there forty years ago. It's one of the reasons why the Pantanal
remains one of South America's best-kept secrets.

To facilitate backcountry travel I have flown seven hundred
miles from Rio to Brasília, the futuristic-looking capital. Here I
want to find out if I can get the guiding expertise of a wildlife
officer named Gaspar. I worked with him seven years ago
when I first went into the Pantanal, and he proved invaluable.

And, I'll obtain permission to enter restricted national park lands far to the west adjoining Bolivia.

Brasília will also serve as a hub. Extra gear, bags, film, clothes, and spare cameras will be stored safely at the home of Dr. Carlos Leite, a good friend. I'll be able to travel more quickly, and should I damage a camera, I can call in another.

I learned a precious lesson long ago. To get something done officially in Latin America, you have to be a political archeologist: start at the top and work down. Otherwise you'll be at the mercy of the formidable bureaucracy. I think it will take only a couple of days to set up meetings with some officials, but they seem in perpetual motion, going to meetings or traveling. My political rooting about in the ultramodern government edifices takes longer than I thought: ten days pass before I've made all the arrangements and have the necessary documents in hand. Still, I have good luck. My friend Gaspar Saturnino Rocha—who works for IBAMA, the newly formed Brazilian environmental protection agency, and manages the remote national park—is going to help. And before one of Brazil's many holidays I book the last seat on Varig's domestic flight 490 to Cuiabá, northern gateway to the Pantanal.

Those planes are always full; this one is packed with ranch hands, warm-eyed mulatto women—some with crying babies— pinstripe executives, bearded young entrepreneurs, and a few foreign tourists. The aging Boeing 737 lifts easily into the clear blue sky above Brasília and heads northwest. Before the wheels are up several businessmen light cigarettes, filling the plane with a strong, blue haze, and fish through their leather briefcases for papers. Cuiabá is also the gateway to the southern Amazon, and many of these people are going there.

The flight across Brazil's *planalto,* the central high plain, seems suspended above an immense checkerboard of brown-plowed fields and yellow-green pastures. It's so large that at more than 550 knots an hour the terrain changes little in the ninety-minute flight that takes us into another time zone.

Despite the morning hour, a grilled steak lunch is served on china, and a liquor cart with expensive imported whiskies and tasty domestic wines is pushed up and down the aisle, soothing the cowboys and impressing a few German tourists in the back.

Suddenly the plane shudders, bouncing the luncheon service around. Everyone cranes out their windows wondering if our old Boeing is breaking up in a storm—except there isn't a cloud in sight. The sky above is clear blue. But we are flying into this black line on the horizon. About the only feature on the ground I can make out is the sun glinting off a bend in the Cuiabá River.

The Germans are getting boisterous, seemingly enjoying the rough ride: every time the plane drops, tugging at our stomachs, they let out a squeal of delight as if on a roller coaster. One of them unpacks a quart of schnapps, takes a pull, and passes it around.

The pilot explains that our descent into Cuiabá is turbulent because a mass of warm, smoky air is rising from thousands of range fires set by cattle ranchers. They do this each dry season to burn off undesirable vegetation and to promote fresh grasses for fodder. In fact, he adds, we're lucky to be landing there at all. This is August, he says, the peak month for these fires. The airport at Cuiabá had been closed for two weeks, canceling scores of flights and forcing travelers to take a five-hour bus ride from the nearest open airport.

The steward announces it's 35°C in Cuiabá. That's 95°F and it's not even 10:30 A.M. By 2:00 P.M. the mercury will soar to 40°C, maybe 41°C—106°F in the shade. *Bem vindo*—welcome—to Mato Grosso.

Cuiabá, Mato Grosso

Mato Grosso means "thick brushwood country" in Portuguese. This enormous region was Brazil's largest state until officials realized that more than a million square kilometers—an area one and a half times the size of Texas—was too large to administer. A sister state, Mato Grosso do Sul, now occupies the lower third of the region and contains a little more than half of the Pantanal's territory.

Cuiabá is Mato Grosso's capital and jumping-off point for the Pantanal. It's also a booming frontier town sprawling along the banks of the Cuiabá River, one of the major feeder streams of the northeastern Pantanal. The city is currently in the throes of its second settlement in two hundred years. And this one is tumultuous.

The first came in the early eighteenth century when *bandeirantes* (explorers) set out from São Paulo in search of diamonds and fist-sized emeralds rumored to exist in Brazil's forbidding interior. They found placer gold here on the banks of the Cuiabá—enough to start a small gold rush that lasted about thirty years. And when the gold ran out most of the prospectors moved on; for those who stayed, sugarcane plantations and huge cattle ranches provided a tidy profit, enough to attract interest from the king of Portugal. He established a captaincy in 1719 to rule and collect taxes.

The region remained undeveloped for well over a century until the impossible dream of unlocking the Amazon's riches began. Then, twenty years ago, the construction of the Cuiabá–Santarem and later the Cuiabá–Porto Velho highways changed Cuiabá's fortunes dramatically. While Manaus and Santarem provided major Amazon River access points, Cuiabá opened northwest Amazonas along the land route. And it's still true today.

Government engineers planned those roads expecting Cuiabá to reach a maximum size of 150,000 residents. But thousands of would-be entrepreneurs were spellbound by the promise of great wealth locked up in the hinterlands. Lumber mills, charcoal kilns, rubber plantations, gold mines, cattle ranches, diamond mines, kaolin mines, whorehouses, and exorbitant flying services deep in the jungle were planned; much of the supplies and manpower would pass through Cuiabá.

Moreover, policy makers in Brasília looked upon the Amazon Basin much like North Americans viewed the Far West and Pacific Northwest: it was Manifest Destiny and a great relief valve for crowded coastal cities. Once those roads were in, desperate people from the drought-ravaged northeast and the *favelas* (slums) surrounding Rio and São Paulo were encouraged to seek their destiny by homesteading the jungle. They, too, would pass through Cuiabá.

Today no one is sure how many people live here. Estimates range from 750,000 to maybe a 1,000,000, up from 100,000 in 1980. Town boundaries now spill across the Cuiabá River to the village of Várzea Grande, built upon the river's old flood plain. A new burden of silt freshly eroded from extensive corn and soybean fields along its watershed has made the river shallow. Local people complain that their river has lost its bed, and it is taking away their beds too. Officials agree that each rainy season the floods are becoming an aggravation.

The main highway from the airport is hopelessly clogged with all kinds of vehicles, many unmotorized. Donkey carts, bicycles, and commuters on foot try to cross the road or hail a bus. Buses stop on the highway to pick up riders, halting the traffic that stretches for miles outside town.

Much of this traffic consists of zany trucks decked out in Christmas-tree running lights, chrome hubs, yellow-and-red pinstripes, and plastic holy families jammed on the dashboard. They spew black clouds from huge, unmuffled side exhausts. As we drive by, I feel the exhaust settle on my sweating skin. The trucks are jam-packed with cooking-gas tanks, brown Amazon logs, and Fanta and Coke bottles; some have a shabbily dressed kid or two bouncing around in the back.

As we get closer to town, Chevies, Fords, and VW Beetles (all made in Brazil) play tag with Vespa scooters and Yamahas. This motor-vehicle bumper derby is very Italian—no one stays in their lane; weaving and cutting each other off are expected, with only a perfunctory raised palm offered by the offender. Double and triple parking in the street slow us further. Taxi drivers in yellow Volkswagens utter *"Merda"* and other oaths under the breath, taking it all in stride. They'd be champs in L.A.

In town, the sidewalks are crowded with casually dressed Cuiabanos. Everyone is informally dressed: jeans, slacks, summer dresses. Most are nut brown from the eternal sun or the mix of African, Indian, and European blood over two hundred years. The women have an elegance that belies the stifling heat. They walk with their upper body steady, while their hips navigate with eye-catching allure. A few unwashed hippies hang out in the Praça de República—the old main square—under the shade of sprawling fig trees. They play guitar and hammer silver wire into earrings with ceramic beads and feather decoration. Behind them many of the public buildings sport red and black political graffiti suggesting alternate forms of employment for the mayor.

From my ninth-story room at the Hotel Excelsior I can stare down at the old church on the plaza. City hall is to my left. On a nearby hill there's a twelve-story white television tower. Right next to the tower is the alabaster minaret of a Moslem temple, evidence of the large Arab community living here.

I call my friend Gaspar and talk over arrangements for pulling the expedition together. He's coming to get me at 6:00 A.M. tomorrow. We'll repack at his headquarters, then head out for the Pantanal.

One of the local papers—*Jornal do Dia*—carries a front-page story today about how some Italian investors paid a visit here and were very impressed with Mato Grosso's undeveloped natural resources. They were proposing to put together a ten-billion-dollar project for agricultural development. What would be the impact on the Pantanal? Why were state officials having so much trouble developing tourism programs—especially those so-called "ecological" tours that had been so successful in other regions?

The article quotes Jota Alves, *secretário extraordinário* to the governor. He's the man in charge of encouraging foreign investment in the state—sort of a Mato Grosso rush chairman. I call his office and am able to arrange a meeting in the afternoon. I carry along the newspaper article, thinking that the ten-billion-dollar story will be a good opener.

Secretário Extraordinário

Jota Alves works in the governor's palace on the outskirts of town. Palacio Paiaguas is a modern, low-slung office complex built around a shaded atrium filled with luxuriant tropical plants—the same kind we see in better offices in the United States, except these come from their backyard, and they're much bigger.

Alves's office is on the second floor and adjacent to an immense meeting room. There are many doors, none with numbers or name plaques. I guess wrong, several times. Embarrassed, I ask an aide, who guides me through the proper door into the office.

The room is spacious, decorated in stylish off-white, and shaded from the bright sun. Alves is writing with a fountain pen on a very small piece of paper at a large, empty, glass desk. He's in his late forties, slight of frame, and casually dressed in open sport shirt, linen pants, and chocolate Gucci loafers. I pull out the Italian investment story and show it to him.

"Oh yesss," he says, not looking up. "The Italians are very interested in Mato Grosso. And so are the Chinese, Soviets, and Japanese. You see," he says in heavily accented English, "we are the only state in Brazil with normal climate and good land . . . for so many different plants: soybeans, cotton, coffee, and cacao. We need investment here to develop these crops. But our federal government is in such debt we have to seek our own investment money."

He shuffles through some papers on the credenza behind him and continues, "That's why I created 'Mato Grosso Convida'— Mato Grosso Invites—program. Businesses that start up here are given many incentives . . . waiving 70 percent of taxes during the first five years. Maybe some land too. We are particularly interested in agro-industry . . . processing our many crops here instead of having to send them down to São Paulo and lose money."

But what of the Pantanal? "Oh, the animals are wonderful," says Alves, "but we're not so experienced in being able to market that abroad. The Pantanal is mostly for the domestic market—fishermen and sightseers from the big cities. We want to bring in more international groups. French, Germans, and Japanese already know about it, and we want to try what we call ecological tourism. But our infrastructure . . . ah, it's *muito fraco,* weak. We can't offer the luxury to attract Americans, who insist on deluxe accommodations. Maybe soon. A group of investors are building a five-star hotel here in Cuiabá—the Eldorado—and they will have cabanas or chalets in the Pantanal.

"Our sister state of Mato Grosso do Sul has developed this ecological tourism with a good measure of success, largely because the governor there wants it. They are closer to São Paulo and Paraguay trade routes. For us in the north it's coming a lot slower. You see, we are just emerging from more than twenty years of dictatorship in Brazil. And our last governor was closely associated with the dictatorship. Only now are we opening the state's resources for the people.

"In such a climate it's hard for us to protect the Pantanal. There are many *bandidos*." Alves makes a pistol with his hand and waves it in the air, smiling. He hands me a newspaper story telling of a major shootout in the south between skin hunters and police. After the fire fight the police received an anonymous call saying that for every man killed, a son of a policeman would be killed.

"We have [special state] forest police here now too. But we can't cover such an immense area by ourselves. We need international support for equipment. And more. But there are too many things going on for us. The *garimpeiros* [gold miners] are at the door of the Pantanal. We fight their mining, close them down, but they come back at night or go somewhere else." He shrugs. "We're helpless.

"There's a great division between rich and poor here. We need to have other choices [than hunting and gold mining]. In our country only now is there a Brazilian conscience for the land."

I ask Alves how he got into the business of selling Mato Grosso abroad. "I grew up here," he answers. "The governor was a childhood friend of mine. When he decided to run for office, he asked if I would manage his election campaign. After he won, he asked if I would be interested in attracting business here. I'm off to your country. It's Brazil Day in New York City on Saturday. Mayor Koch is going to open the party." He hands me a copy of *The Brazilians*, a newspaper for expatriates in New York that he founded twelve years ago.

It was nearing 5:30 P.M. by the time I left his office. The sun was still well above the horizon, yet it looked dim, as if sundown—but that was almost three hours away. Although there wasn't a cloud in the sky, I could stare directly at the dark-orange disk without any irritation. Looming over the entire region was an ash-gray cloud, the same cloud that I saw from the plane. It was smoke. Smoke from thousands of range fires burning off the *cerrado* (grasslands).

At first I didn't feel it. But walking from Turimat, the state tourism office on the town square, I felt the sting, something like when you cut raw onions.

Gaspar

In the morning Gaspar comes up the hotel stairs looking the proper Pantaneiro. I shake hands and he gives me a bear hug, Brazilian style. I haven't seen him in ten months and am relieved to see he hasn't changed a bit. He's five-feet-nine and built like a bull, his muscular physique making him look larger. A swarthy complexion, wavy black hair, faded jeans, worn cowboy boots, and the ever-present smokes complete the picture.

Gaspar grew up on his father's small dairy farm just outside the town. For not having much formal education, he's has done surprisingly well. He married his childhood sweetheart, Sebastiana, and they are raising two boys and two girls.

Before the forestry service, Gaspar was a construction worker on BR 165, the Cuiabá–Santarem road that cut through virgin forest in northern Mato Grosso. Along the way, the crew made an astounding discovery. By sheer chance they had made contact with a much feared, Stone Age people, the Kreen-Akrore Indians—the same group that Brazilian anthropologists had been racing to find ahead of the road. Gaspar's level-headed manner and resourcefulness throughout this contact, as well as his knowledge of wildlife, made him a good man to have in the field. Shortly after the encounter, he joined IBAMA in Cuiabá.

But I've worried about Gaspar. Over the years, his IBAMA patrolling has been a sticking point for skin hunters, as well as for competing enforcement agencies. No one would mind seeing him removed or even shot.

Gaspar and I dump my gear in a tiny, white Fiat with "IBDF-MT" (the former environment agency) stenciled on the door. We're going over to the forestry service headquarters, where we'll pick up our truck.

At the ranch-house-style headquarters, Paulo Beneditc Siqueira, Gaspar's former boss, hears about my interest to adventure in the Pantanal and finds it contagious. He says he'd like to take me to the remote national park bordering Bolivia. It would be interesting for him, too, since he's always stuck in his office in Cuiabá. "Sure," I agree, thinking that this impromptu invitation is half-serious. "Just let Gaspar know."

Gaspar ushers me down the hall and opens a photo album showing his new responsibilities. There's a picture of him on a pearly white *praia* (beach) scooping up little turtles and putting them in an aluminum boat. From October through March he guards turtle breeding grounds on the Rio das Mortes (River of Deaths) during their hatch-out. Another picture shows him sitting in a boat completely filled to the gunwales with turtles. He and his men transfer them to a secluded lake where there are fewer predators: *urubus* (vultures), caracaras (scavenging hawks), jabirú storks, coatis (raccoon relatives), *tucunaré* (bass-like fish), *pintado* (large, carnivorous catfish), and turtle poachers.

He points to a map and says, "We can only protect three nest grounds, but there are many more. We just don't have the money." The locals also know where and when to catch the turtles. A few take the eggs for food. But most sell the eggs and baby turtles "to the cosmetics industry in São Paulo," he says "An ounce of their extract costs U.S. $160." During the rest of the year, he manages the guards at the Pantanal National Park.

Heading Out

Our vehicle for the trip is a four-wheel-drive Bandeirante, named for seventeenth-century prospectors who explored Brazil's forbidding interior. It's made by Toyota in São Paulo and has a four-cylinder Mercedes diesel. It has no pollution-control devices, nor safety glass or seat belts; nevertheless, it's built like a tank and regarded by Pantaneiros as the ultimate swamp buggy, if you can pay U.S. $16,000 and wait a year for delivery.

We drive south from Cuiabá on Mato Grosso 060, the last paved road we'll see for a long time. It's 120 kilometers from Cuiabá to Poconé, the village where the Transpantaneira Highway begins. That road is the only major access route south into the Pantanal.

The landscape opens into savanna, a pre-Columbian name describing treeless plains. Here the grass-dominated country is called *cerrado*. It has clumps of grasses, brown weeds, squat woody bushes, occasional gnarled dwarf trees, dende palm trees, and low, rolling hills bristling with quartz rocks. To the uneducated eye it's scrub country. But there's actually a rich array of genera *Axonopus, Andropogon, Hemarthria, Panicum, Paratheria, Paspalum, Reimarochloa* grasses, *Bulbostylis* sedges, *Cassia, Desmodium, Galactia* herbs, and more.

A few *Caesalpinia* and *Acacia* trees rise barely ten meters above the red dirt. Scientists believe it's not only dry-season stress that stunts them, but the incredibly impoverished soil; *cerrado* soil has been found to have even less of key elements— calcium, phosphorus, sulphur, zinc, and nitrogen—than does Amazon soil.

According to Dr. Guillermo Sarmiento, a tropical grasslands expert, part of the reason this dry-season vista appears so barren is that the *cerrado*'s scrub plants have evolved an economy that concentrates much of their biomass close to the ground. In fact, a great deal of it lies buried within twenty centimeters of the surface. As a result, many scientists have literally overlooked this habitat's ecological significance. While much of the world's media and conservation groups have been caught up with the demise of rain forests, some 700 million hectares of tropical grasslands a year go up in smoke. According to a United Nations' Environment Program study, "Tropical grasslands have as much to do with stable global climate as do the rain forests."

The day is stunningly hot and clear. In the distance I notice several dirty little tornadoes. I point them out. "Uh-huh," says Gaspar, "we call them *Lacerdinhas,* named after a short politician the people didn't like." Each morning they form by the rapid heating of the air. They swirl around near the road, picking up dust, paper, and debris.

Amidst the savanna vegetation there are pockets of forest

called *capões,* similar to the mahogany hammocks in Florida's Everglades. Gaspar says termites are the first colonizers, throwing up the earth in tall mounds. Then birds pass seeds in their waste, establishing a thriving microhabitat of dense brush and woody plants. Many *cerrado* animals take refuge in these *capões* during the heat, and when high water comes, large ones become life-saving islands for capybaras, snakes, nine-banded armadillos, giant antbears, and even jaguars. During flood time, I once photographed a small capybara and a two-meter-long caiman sleeping less than two meters from each other on one of these islands.

Brilliant yellow and purple blossoms of *ipê* and *paratudo* trees (*Vochysia* species) add a welcome dash of color. In this perpetual tropical climate, these flowers are one of the few signs that let you know it's springtime. Yet the trees haven't a single green leaf on them. Botanists theorize that they have an underground storage system allowing them to complete the reproduction cycle. So when the rains do come, seeds can be germinated and dispersed in the waters.

"*Tucano,*" says Gaspar, pointing to a black bird leaping from a palm branch. As it flies parallel to us, we can see the outrageous beak — long, yellow, black, and red. One naturalist described the toco toucan as a crow pushing a banana. It's an awkward flier too: beat, beat, beat, then the wings are folded to the body; for an instant the bird starts to fall before picking up the beat again. Further down the road, we spot nearly a dozen more perched in bushes and trees surprisingly close to the highway. This impoverished-looking brushland is deceptively rich.

A road sign indicates Poconé begins to the left and Cáceres straight ahead. Less than five kilometers ahead is Poconé, a picturesque colonial village dating back to the mid-eighteenth century. There are many white and pastel stucco homes. Around the tidy *praça* (town square) there are general stores, snack shops, the *prefeito*'s (mayor's) office — all dominated by a large, sky-blue church that looks new. Schoolgirls in uniform walk home wearing small backpacks; others bicycle. A horse drawing a wagon clip-clops by a café where we've stopped to drink some cold pop.

I'm about to say something about how quaint Poconé looks

when a heavy rumble shakes our metal table. A huge, yellow bulldozer clanks around the narrow corner. "KOMATSU" is stenciled in big, black letters on the engine cowl; it's followed by a dump truck filled with red earth.

"*Garimpeiros,*" yells Gaspar above the diesel. Gold miners. Here in this sleepy village? He nods yes. He assures me I'm in for a surprise. We walk down several side streets to take a closer look. A general store that used to cater to the local cattle ranchers now sells picks, ore hammers, and huge, wok-shaped pans. Across the street are two stores. One has a sign that reads "*Matto Metais, Compra-se ouro.*" Buy your gold. And next door, "*Associação dos Garimpeiros de Poconé.*" I count three more gold-buying stores closer to the square. There are some hardened-looking miners hanging around in front of the stores. They're wearing straw Stetsons, sweat-stained shirts, worn-through jeans, and beat-up cowboy boots.

Later I piece together the story from Gaspar and several local people. Three years ago gold was rediscovered here, just as it was nearly 150 years ago. The town went crazy. Many miners in northern Mato Grosso and Amazonas heard "Gold in Poconé." And when their grubstakes ran out in the north they came here. Some could barely afford to leave Amazonas. They brought just the shirts on their backs and a flickering dream of striking it rich.

That increasingly rare fantasy is kept alive in the media. The popular magazine *Manchete*—a combination *Life* and *National Enquirer*—often features glossy pictures of lucky *garimpeiros* and their coconut-size gold nuggets. Invariably they are being hugged by a big-breasted model in a string bikini.

Poconé's *prefeito*, Sr. Guido, told me the gold fever was so uncontrollable that the *garimpeiros* remembered the charming church was built during the first gold rush. They wondered whether there might be gold still in its earth walls. Somehow they managed to sell the idea to the padre, and they tore down the walls, sifting every clump for the yellow dust. They found enough to pay for constructing a new church on the same site, he says.

Sr. Guido has his shirt unbuttoned, revealing a gold chain made of large bracelet links with a three-inch gold cross. Pointing to it, he says, "This is Poconé gold." I'm curious if he thinks the wildlife in the Pantanal could bring money here, too, through tourism? He looks at me, outraged. "Tourists don't even stop to buy gas here." He hoists the cross from his chest and declares, "This is our future."

It's late in the afternoon, and we decide to get a room and leave Poconé before dawn. A short time later, we decide to get something to eat and walk to the motel's dining hall, an ambitious room with vaulted beams and nearly fifty tables. Every one has a dirty red tablecloth. Sixty-year-old frontier tools, now antiques, are placed around the room: spears, a wicker fish trap, a foot-powered sewing machine, and milk and water jugs. On the walls hang large color photos of Pantanal animals — caimans, jaguars, rhea (the South American ostrich) — and a few old photos of Indians in feathered headdresses.

Gaspar mumbles repeatedly about his jaw, holding it in obvious discomfort. A toothache? No, he shakes his head. He senses I don't understand what he's complaining about. In frustration, he nudges me to get my attention and spits out a full set of dentures dripping with saliva. Aw jeez, Gaspar, at the table? He opens wide his mouth. There isn't a single tooth in his head, and the gums are swollen and reddened. What the hell happened? I ask.

"I worked on my father's farm in 1975," he explains. "A cow swung around, butting my jaw with its horns, knocking me out. When I woke, all my teeth were broken. The dentist said he could fix my broken teeth, but it would cost a lot of money — and I didn't have enough. So he talked me into pulling out all my teeth and making me dentures — bad ones." He winces at the painful memory. "And they are still killing me."

We go back to the room and I fish through my medical kit for hydrogen peroxide and an analgesic cream. Maybe they will help until we can get to a pharmacy. We return to the dining room and I order the closest thing on the menu to baby food — puréed potatoes — for Gaspar and a little piece of fried catfish — *pintado* — swimming in butter for me. Gaspar pops out his choppers and sets them neatly on his napkin next to his plate. Instantly his youthful cowboy face ages twenty-five years as he gums his soothing potatoes.

In the morning we buy sacks of frozen chicken legs for the trip — just in case fishing is bad — toss them under our gear in the back of the truck, and hit the road. The Transpantaneira Highway leading out of Poconé is easy enough to find: just turn right at the gas station on the edge of town and keep on going. It's the only road south into the Pantanal.

And hit the road is indeed what happens. Just past town the road runs out of asphalt and becomes what the Mato Grosso map euphemistically refers to as an all-weather highway. Which is no good in all weather. There are bomb-size craters that would accommodate a Buick. Granite rocks poke through the red dirt, forcing Gaspar to steer the Bandeirante drunkenly. There are smoother stretches, though, which can best be described as washboard, setting up a fierce shimmy reminiscent of those fat-jiggling machines found in old health clubs.

The countryside is becoming easier on the eye, when I'm not seeing double from the vibrations. Stretched before us are great, open vistas of scrubland fringed by squat clusters of trees and drying pools. It's hard to believe that just four months earlier this place was an inland sea. A primitive barbed-wire fence lines both sides of the road, but there are fewer buildings, mostly ranch houses set well back from the road. Range cattle — Indian zebu, the gray ones with a hump — lie in the grass and seek shade among the trees.

A donkey-drawn cart with two nearly naked black kids at the reins pulls to the side to avoid our rooster tail of red dust. We slow too. In the back of their cart is a freshly butchered cow resting on palm leaves, the severed head sitting indignantly on its hindquarters, eyes open, tongue askew.

Ahead there's a checkpoint barring our way. Above it is suspended a wooden sign — similar to those I've seen marking the entrance to Texas ranches — chiseled with words marking the beginning of the Transpantaneira Highway and the Pantanal.

A couple of men wearing ten-gallon hats and holstered pistols emerge from a rough-hewn guard house. They're Gaspar's *campanheiros* at IBAMA. We're greeted warmly, then splash our faces with cool water and drink a *cafezinho* from a thermos. That's the demitasse of friendship: strong, sweet coffee proffered to friend and stranger alike to say "Welcome."

In short order we're back in the Bandeirante, the men lift the barrier across the road, and we officially enter the northern end of the Pantanal. Just down the road the dry scrubland melds into weed-choked marsh, making it clear that without that road, even with our trusty four-wheel drive, we'd have one hell of a time getting in—and out.

Gaspar nods in agreement. Before there was the road, he says, ranchers made the perilous journey by canoe and horse. And airplane. As early as the 1930s German-made seaplanes, based in Brazil's southernmost state of Rio Grande do Sul, pioneered air routes deep in the Pantanal to Porto Joffre, where wealthy hunters and fishermen used to fly in from big cities to bag game along the Cuiabá river. Less than a decade later, single-engine planes—mostly Cessnas—revolutionized life in these hinterlands.

The *fazendeiros*—ranchers—thought nothing of stepping off their horses and jumping into their planes to fly several hundred miles to do their shopping and banking. In fact, one *fazendeiro* later confirmed that in the 1940s there was a fly-in emporium right in the jungles of Mato Grosso. Pilots could buy hard-to-find imported items: American cigarettes, French wines, Scotch whisky.

Today general-aviation aircraft are as important here as the bush plane is to remote Alaska, except here practically all the well-to-do *donos* (owners) have their own. I remember the Cuiabá airport and the squadron of light planes crowding the landing apron.

Nevertheless, for decades major goods, equipment, and livestock were brought in by the slow, difficult water route and oxen pack train to reach those isolated ranches. According to one regional historian, the military dictatorship that held power in the country between 1964 and 1985 managed to do one decent thing. They made a concerted effort to link together this vast and diverse land by improving and expanding postal service and telecommunications and constructing roads.

The Transpantaneira Highway was one of Mato Grosso's better legacies from that dictatorship. The road was originally planned to cut through the entire length of the Pantanal, more than four hundred kilometers of formidable terrain. But they ran out of money and interest halfway through. Today the road stops where it meets the Cuiabá River.

From a plane the area looks pancake flat, but that's illusory. In fact, there is an impressive array of topographic features:

permanent rivers and shallow lakes, many seasonal streams, gallery forest, and low, rolling hills. And the place floods to a size greater than England each rainy season. It was enough to uncivilize the best civil engineers.

Their solution was to elevate the road between two and three and a half meters above the surrounding floodlands throughout its length, interconnected by no less than 114 separate wooden bridges in the northern half alone. It was constructed from materials found within the region. Clay-bearing soil was dug alongside the road, leaving great rectangular trenches.

What planners couldn't possibly have foreseen was that the road construction would greatly alter the natural ecosystem of the area. Perhaps the most spectacular effect of the road was to create a de facto animal reserve right beside it. In the rainy season, the Transpantaneira becomes a linear refuge, offering many animals respite from the high waters. When the flood waters recede, millions of fish are trapped in the roadside trenches, offering a veritable smorgasbord for predator and scavenger alike.

Caimans and the great wading birds didn't take long to figure out that those artificial pools were the perfect waterholes to wait out the dry season. Seeds borne on the wind and in the guts of birds created the landscaping. And, in very short order, those trenches were transformed into a very natural-looking habitat that resembles parts of East Africa.

three

Down the
Transpantaneira Highway

The Transpantaneira is not only a road.
It's *the* national park of the Pantanal.
— *IBAMA official*

*D*riving this road is a filthy experience: the surface is an inch deep with loose, red dirt. Each time we stop to look at animals, a stern wave of dust sweeps over us, seeping into the cab. After only three stops there's a crunching noise in my mouth from grit.

To complete the dust bath, vehicles coming toward us also generate a rooster tail, forcing us to roll up the windows and kick shut the floor vents quickly before we pass, making it an oven inside. My 560mm telephoto lens is cushioned on my lap and held tight by my left arm. Each bump and bang sends beads of sweat trickling down the inside of my arm to pool on top of the long lens. A small reservoir is forming in the crook of my arm, mixing with the dust and making red mud along the long, black lens barrel. After we wind down the windows and open the floor ventilators, the mud cakes.

Out in the fields small herds of cows seem stupefied by long hours in the broiling sun. They're zebu—those fatty-humped, gray-skinned cattle from India—brought here in the 1920s. They're the favored species today because they're able to survive this sweltering heat and adjust to the annual flood waters.

But a little further down the road it's clear this isn't a complete success—a cow has toppled over days ago. Gaspar explains it's a tough time of year for cattle. Water is scarce, and despite the extensive yellow-green vegetation around us, those plants provide poor nutrition that isn't easily digested. That's why so many ranchers torch the countryside each year. It's become an easy way to clear off old pasturage for the price of a match. And, say locals, it's only a matter of weeks before the scorched earth is sprouting tender, green shoots that cows relish.

Pantaneiros generally don't burn down forested regions for pasture as the new colonists are doing in the dense Amazon. Even before ranchers came here fire was a natural phenomenon of the tropical grassland ecosystem. Along with seasonal drought, fire keeps large tracts of forest from becoming established.

The cow's carcass is shriveled, with numerous white bird-wash stripes, giving it a botched zebra paint job. A small flock of crested caracaras (*Polyborus plancus*), those raptor-scavengers, pick at the bones through a tear in the hide. In fact, they look more like hawks: pale blue-and-red sharp beak, cream-colored neck, brown body and wings, and thin, black, horizontal stripes across a cream-colored tail.

Eight of the birds feast on the dried maroon meat, each working up the shoulder, the highest point on the carcass, to claim dominance. Each time one reaches the top it utters what can only be described as a yuk . . . yuk . . . yuk . . . yuuuuuuuk victory call, tossing its head back. The victory is Pyrrhic, lasting only a few seconds until a more aggressive one flies in, flapping aside the previous victor and issuing its own nasal trill.

Not far ahead is the first bridge. I'm not sure what I was expecting, but as Gaspar slows the Bandeirante for the approach, I can see the "bridge," and it's a disaster: a concoction of bird-washed boards, weather-beaten planks, and split timbers. There are no rails or other barriers to prevent driving off. In its present condition I wouldn't want to peddle a bike across, let alone drive our vehicle, which has the weight of an armored personnel carrier. "It's okay," says Gaspar, sensing my rising fear. "That wood is jatuba and ipê—hard like steel."

The bridge spans a twenty-meter gap in the raised road, allowing flood waters to flow across the dike during the rainy season. But this is the dry season, and there's a plant-choked pool below—full of trapped piranhas. Before I can protest going across, we've left the safety of the high dirt and I tense up at the thought of crashing through the boards and being chomped on by a horde of frenzied fish. Scenes from the sixties' cult film *Mondo Cane* reel through my head: Venezuelan cowboys drive a cow into a river, where it's devoured in seconds by a roiling wave of those fish. (Pantaneiros don't use *boi de piranha*—a sacrificial cow.)

The bridge timbers jut out to meet the road—or at least they did once upon a time. Now they're jagged-ended, badly worn, leaving a toilet-size hole between land and bridge. As we start over I crane out the window and see pebbles and dirt falling into the water below.

Gaspar has aimed the Bandeirante for two planks running the bridge like rails, but the right front wheel rolls into the hole, rocking the truck back and forth and bringing us to a stop. Stuck. Without reaction, he revs the engine and gingerly engages the clutch, pulling us onto the flimsy structure.

We ride up on the left plank. It's warped at the other end like an old cross-country ski and pops up eight centimeters from our weight, revealing a bolt hanging from the other end holding onto absolutely nothing. It jingles like a dinner bell as we inch out to the middle. Are the piranhas listening?

An Amazon kingfisher (*Chloroceryle amazona*) sitting on the bridge signals displeasure, twitching its tail up and down nervously at our approach. When we get within five meters, the iridescent bird with big eyes takes to the air in protest, chattering in its looping flight.

Ka-chunk. Our big rig drops off the planks onto the other side. I open an eye. Gaspar laughs, lighting up a cigarette, and says, "Have only 113 more."

As we pick up speed, I notice barbed-wire fences lining both sides of the road. They're primitive, with four rusted, bristling wires stretched taught between sun-bleached timbers, some very crooked. Between the fences and the road are thick, brown weeds with pea-size white flowers and tall, green umbrella plants—I think they're Araliacae family, relatives of schefflera houseplants, but here they grow ten meters tall.

The fence and bushes along the road are used as perches for an impressive variety of birds. There's a big, rusty brown savanna hawk (*Heterospizias meridionalis*) sitting on a post. It doesn't fly off so quickly—just when I creak open the truck door to take a shot; then it hops several posts away. We creep up further in the truck. I again poise to take a shot, and the hawk eases over a few more posts. It's a strange kind of leap-frog we're playing. Obviously this bird is skilled in dealing with gawking photographers.

There are several softball-size earthen mounds atop fence posts too. They're the handiwork of ovenbirds (*Seiurus auro-capillus*), little, burnished-brown mud architects with big mouths. Each oven-shaped house is a remarkable construction. Mud and wet clay have been daubed and shaped with great skill, resulting in a perfect miniature of the clay-domed kiln used throughout the region for charcoal production. The birds even fashion a curved entryway with a rounded top.

These ovenbirds are so incredibly loud for their puny size. When one lands next to its house, it opens wide its mouth and belts out a two-part call that some people swear says "tea . . . cher." It hops to the left, then the center, repeating the noise. I can't tell what it sounds like, but the ovenbird puts so much energy into making that ear-splitting sound that its tail shakes.

There are also many cuckoos (*Coccyzus* species) sitting on the fence. These long-tailed, beige birds have wide little eyes and head feathers wildly askew, making them look disheveled or worn to a frazzle and badly in need of a rest. And there are coal-black birds with long tails and thick beaks like puffins. They're called ani (*Crotophaga* species). They hop, without spreading their wings, into the protective foliage of an umbrella plant, away from the camera.

I'm getting wild with frustration. Making notes, taking pic-tures, changing lenses and film, observing. Although we're go-ing down the road under fifteen kilometers per hour, it's clear I can't keep up. And while pulling some gear from the back seat I start swearing up a storm. I'm having a tough time adjusting to this awful—and awful good for wildlife—Transpantaneira.

It gets worse. As we bump along it's obvious there are countless glimpses, flits, twinklings, snatches, and flutterings that I can't follow up—for now. I want to spend weeks watch-ing and getting to know these animals. I also know it will probably never happen. I've decided to go with the flow, to let the road trip and the wildlife determine the time—not the other way around.

Thankfully, we drive by a large hawk and it stays put, the first bird to let me get pretty close. It's a charcoal-gray raptor that has just landed with something in its grip. We back up.

Flipping through my handy *Birds of Venezuela* (an authoritative paperback that covers much of Brazil's birds too), I find it's a snail kite (*Rostrhamus sociabilis*), the same bird that's struggling for survival in Florida's Everglades. There are several more kites perched on yellow-flowering bushes across the marsh. The magnificently streamlined raptor balances on top of the fence post with one talon. The other grips its favorite food: a golf-ball-size apple snail (*Pomatius* species). The kite tries to pry open the operculum—the trap door that protects the soft body within the shell—using its scalpel-like, hooked beak.

On the road there's no use in stalking: there's nothing to hide behind. Creeping up in the truck is apparently something the birds will tolerate, and we're able to pull within seven meters. He's on Gaspar's side, so I edge out the door; at first the kite utters a high-pitched warning hiss and then puts its head down, working on the snail. Just as I'm pulling my long lens to my shoulder, he takes flight, carrying the snail with part of its innards dripping out, disappearing in the overhanging leaves of a nearby tree.

"Damn," I say under my breath, "that's a rare bird." Gaspar shakes his head no. "It's not Florida [where they are endangered]. We have many here, like bananas."

About an hour down the road, we pull in at a small gas station and roadside restaurant. Gaspar says it'll be the last public facility; we should take advantage to top off the diesel and get a pop. The two wooden buildings have peeling white siding; in the uncut grass near the gas pump lie empty cans and discarded auto-care products. Spilled oil stains the road in front, and several black handprints on the pump-house wall lend a traditional outback charm to the place.

The restaurant is built on stilts away from the road and is reached by a long boardwalk. A weed-choked pond lies under the building, and a branch of the Cuiabá River runs about fifty meters behind the place. In April the river floods, lapping against the diners' seating area five feet above the ground. Water stains prove it.

Inside there are unpainted picnic tables. One has three men in T-shirts intently putting away lunch; four large, stainless-steel platters are constantly, silently, being passed around. They're filled with fried meat and onions, french fries, pale canned peas, sliced plum tomatoes, white onions, and steaming, oily rice. Three large, frosty bottles of Antarctica beer catch my eye. I raise my eyebrows to Gaspar, but he shrugs it off, "A long way to go."

We walk around sipping our Fanta orange and Guaraná— Brazil's ginger ale, made from an apricot-size fruit rich in caffeine. We stare at several beautiful Pantanal wildlife photographs hanging on the walls.

One picture is absolutely arresting. "Jeez, Gaspar," I say, "look at this." Seven men in various stages of undress are lined up across the photo struggling to hold on to an enormous snake. The man on the left has the head end draped over his shoulder, holding the smallish, triangular head as if it were the nozzle of a firehose.

Except this hose gets fatter and fatter as it runs across the picture so that the shirtless man in the center has both arms wrapped around the snake's girth, which at this point has the diameter of a large watermelon. A tall, shirtless man at the right end is holding up the snake's tail with one hand and is smiling.

"That's a giant anaconda [*Eunectes murinus*]," says the guy behind the wooden counter, "eight and a half meters long." He adds that it weighed 227 kilos, almost 500 pounds. It was caught in the northern part of the Pantanal.

Back in the truck, I tell Gaspar about the hair-raising story I read before coming to Brazil about a large ranch in northern Mato Grosso. The owner raised fine horses and loved to ride the boundaries of his property on his favorite, a gelding with Arab and Spanish bloodlines. One day his stable boy came to him and said his horse was missing. A search turned up nothing—that is, until a number of weeks later, when several cowboys came across an enormous serpent in a marsh and killed it. Inside they found the crushed horse, partially digested.

That snake had a head that measured more than half a meter on a side, so the anecdote went, the girth of an oil barrel, and a forty-meter length.

Gaspar shakes his head. "Not possible," he says. "The biggest *sucuri* [anaconda] I've seen was seven meters." Then he shows me his right hand. Running from his upper palm around the index finger and diagonally across the back of the hand are two lines of tiny white dots. "That's where an anaconda bit me," he says. "*Sucuri* don't have fangs; they kill by strangulation. But they've got teeth, rows of little needle ones angled back toward the throat. A few years ago I captured a three-meter one, and I didn't have a tight grip on the head. Wham." He grabs his right hand with his left, remembering the attack and the pain.

That fuels our conversation about snakes for the next few kilometers. The giant anacondas are generally regarded by naturalists and herpetologists as the largest snakes in the world on a weight and length basis. There is still some argument about Southeast Asia's reticulated python, listed by the *Guinness Book of World Records* as being the longest snake. But the giant anaconda gets first place as heaviest. One Asian python, just over 8 meters, weighed about 104 kilos; the same length anaconda was more than double that weight, nearly 227 kilos and a girth of 1.1 meters. "I'm dying to see one, even a baby," I plead.

"Last week," pipes up Gaspar, "I was driving down the Transpantaneira and saw one crossing the road, but it was small—only four meters." "Oh, sure!" I complain. "You said that to me the last time I went with you." He smiles, inhaling his cigarette deeply. It's a running joke I think the locals like to play on visitors, especially gringos.

Every time I come to the Pantanal and take this damnable road, cowboys and farmers that I meet invariably say, "You shoulda been here yesterday. There was this big _____ [you fill in the blank with anaconda, jaguar, jungle pig, rare parrot, etc.] right where I'm standing," and I grimace in frustration. Fish stories like these abound, and when someone starts showing me how big a supposed animal was, I go crazy.

The second bridge is longer and in better condition. It spans a long, weed-choked waterway, maybe a seasonal river. One side is alive with cormorants—hundreds of them—roosting in low, sturdy shrubs sitting on mud banks. Many have wings outstretched, drying off in the sun. They're a water circus performing in front of us—and making noises like people with severe indigestion. Some leap from the shrubs and glide into the water, flapping their wings and skiing to a stop with their orange, webbed feet. In the water they paddle vigorously, look this way and that, and then execute neat rolling surface dives one right after another in a perfect synchronous swim.

Peering over the bridge, I see the water is chalky but not cloudy enough to obscure the movement of three fish rising to the surface among the weeds. They're big and oval with black mottled stripes and what looks like an orange dot near the base of the stubby tail. A light turns on in my head: these large-eyed fish are tropical oscars (*Astronotus ocellatus*); pet stores back home sell adult pairs for a hundred dollars.

Despite their third-of-a-meter-long, stocky bodies, they glide effortlessly with a flick of the pectoral fins up to a floating, broad-leafed plant; they appear curious, tilting their heads up out of the shadows to see my rippling face from another world. We stare at each other in a peculiar encounter. I'm convinced that the way they hover there, they, too, ponder what I am; then they dart away into the deep.

A very beautiful, stark tree comes into view not far off the road on Gaspar's side. Its barren, gray limbs seem enormous, made more so because it stands by itself in the middle of a field. In the crotch of a big branch is a thicket of twigs covering an area the size of an easy chair. In the middle of that nest are three ungainly jabiru stork fledglings (*Jabiru mycteria*) standing about a meter tall.

"I've seen that tree before, but where?" I say to Gaspar. "That's one of the most photographed scenes in the Pantanal. You could have seen it anywhere," he replies. I remember now. It was one of those large photo blowups that hung in an office of the forestry service in Brasília where I got permission to come here. Other photos of it were hanging in the Cuiabá airport, the regional headquarters of the forestry service in Cuiabá, and on the wall of my room in the Hotel Excelsior. Was there some Johnny Appleseed of the Pantanal anonymously spreading the marvels of this place?

"You're probably thinking of Sr. Sucksdorff," says my knowledgeable companion. Sucksdorff? What kind of Brazilian name is that? "It isn't. He's from Sweden, and he lives in Cuiabá. He has photographed the Pantanal for many years. You should go and talk to him when we go back. He knows a lot about this place."

Circling in the wind high above the nest are a dozen big birds riding a thermal. There are black-headed vultures and two great white jabiru storks with long, black beaks. The storks soar with barely a beat of their wings against the pale blue sky. When we approach the tree, one of the soaring jabirus cuts away from the formation and glides down to the nest, settles in, and touches one of the fledglings reassuringly. Then it sets to clacking its beak, nervously warning us away.

They're nesting in a dead tree; not a single leaf remains on those gray branches to protect the flightless birds from the heat or possible predators. This is an *ipê* tree, Gaspar points out; this is August. *Primavera,* springtime, is still more than a month away. The *ipê* tree will soon blossom with brilliant yellow flowers, even before there is a single green leaf.

In fact, Gaspar says the nest's location close to the road draws many tourists and fishermen to see the jabirus. Those disturbances haven't deterred the great birds from returning year after year to nest, making us feel that we don't have to tiptoe around the tree. In a way, that's the beauty of observing and photographing in these wide open spaces.

Just past the forty-seventh bridge, the fencing ducks behind a small stand of forest and comes out again, only much further back and interrupted by a huge, wooden gate with a carved sign above it reading "Fazenda São João." Saint John Ranch. It has a gatekeeper's house and a windmill next door, the only signs we're passing a ranch.

Gaspar tells me that São João is one of the biggest ranches in the entire Pantanal. He says the man who owns it, Sebastiano Camargo Correia, is the richest man in Brazil. Many big politicos come here, and past presidents of Brazil have visited. And many powerful military men from throughout South America visit, too, including recently deposed Alfredo Stroessner of Paraguay. There's an airstrip big enough to accommodate a Boeing 727 jet. General Stroessner used to land his Lineas Areas Paraguayas jetliner there.

But Gaspar won't go in. He says they've done some things to the land—converting it to intensive agriculture and somehow keeping back the annual flood waters—and the owner doesn't want the forestry service snooping around. Of course, this peaks my curiosity, and I leave a note with the gatekeeper asking permission to visit the ranch on our return.

At bridge fifty-four, an oncoming cattle truck forces us to pull over at the lip of the bridge and wait until it passes. The span is identical to others we've edged across, but the main support beams have sunk unevenly in the muck below, making the surface undulate up and down and tilt like a rickety roller-coaster track. Yet the truck driver doesn't hesitate and runs the bridge, rocking left and right, at times uncomfortably angled a few degrees too many toward the mud below. And then he guns the powerful, unmuffled engine on the other side.

Beneath the bridge a big, furry head pokes up through a mat of green plants. A capybara (*Hydrochoerus hydrochaeris*)—a kind of large, aquatic guinea pig—is taking a cooling bath in the midday heat, leisurely munching plants. A yellow and black bird the size of a sparrow lands on its back and pecks at things crawling in that huge rodent's fur.

As the truck passes by, I stare at its overloaded cargo area. Steinbeck couldn't have created a more ramshackle land schooner. Cooking pots, oil lanterns, folding lawn chairs, plastic water jugs, and spare fuel tanks are lashed to the cattle siding; so, too, are gym shoes and underpants. Midway there's an opening between orange tarps, and peeking through are three ragamuffin men, one playing a boom box, gaping at me the same way I'm looking at them. On top of the truck are several small craft: two aluminum runabouts, outboard motors, fishing rods, paddles, and one fiber-glass kayak that looks like a genie's slipper.

The rear end of the truck is open. Two more unshaven men are stretched out, their feet resting on brown boxes and silver, bottled-gas tanks. Another guy is smoking while leaning against two very large white-enamel kitchen appliances. Fridges? I can also see buckets, vinyl suitcases, bags of charcoal,

and cases of amber bottles—beer or *cachaça* (distilled sugar-cane spirits).
"What the hell's that, Gaspar?" I ask. "Sportsmen," he replies. I can't believe it. He tells me these trucks—called *frigoríficos*—and their "sportsmen" are from big cities. They're quite common in the dry season. The men pack up the household and friends and head out for the teeming waters of the Pantanal. They often stay weeks, shooting up the place for fun, filling up those gas-fueled freezers with everything they catch, and watching television run by generators. Gaspar says thousands of kilos of fish are taken out of these waters by such visitors and sometimes sold commercially.

Such wholesale catches are illegal. There are laws on the books governing the size of individual fish as well as the total catch of certain species. But we see no patrols.

Another tree is cause for stopping. It, too, is leafless, but this one has an enormous, spreading crown full of birds. The afternoon sun is right behind it, silhouetting the animals. Most are big; I make out the hunched-over shapes of vultures. At least a dozen sit on the right side of the crown. To the left, there's a large nest with a gray ibis (*Treskiornithidae* species) popping up to see what's making the clattering sound (our engine).

Through the binoculars he's a funny bird indeed: narrow, down-curving beak, orange eyes, and several long, loose plumes trailing from the head in the wind give a frenetic, nervous appearance. The ibis stands up and cries out plaintively. At that moment the sun declines exactly behind the nest, creating a corona that surrounds the bird in a brilliant halo of yellow sunlight.

Below, several other peculiar nests hang perilously off this tree's limbs. They're long, pendulous baskets, woven by orapendola birds (*Icteridae* species), a crow-size black bird with yellow beak and striking blue eyes. At first glance the nests resemble Spanish moss dressing the tree in enormous, dark teardrops. But they're much too large for Spanish moss: one to two meters in length and coming to a bulbous end. Through the long lens I can see the remarkable work of their winged architects. Grasses, pliable twigs, and fibers stripped from large-leafed plants have been interlaced in a tight mesh quite capable of taking the weight of the birds, their young, and just about any storm that rumbles out of the Andes.

Unknown to the ibis above, an adult orapendola flies to the bottom of the ibis's nest, where a blade of grass is waving in the breeze. The bird yanks it out and makes off with the construction material in its beak. At its own nest, it climbs down to the bulbous end and sets to weaving the grass into the thick mesh.

What are the vultures waiting for? And why are these other birds tolerating them in such close proximity? Dense bushes in front of us block the answer. As we move away to get a different angle, I can see that those scavengers aren't interested in the small birds after all. Twenty more of them are gathered on the carcass of an unfortunate cow that had become mired in shoulder-deep mud and lost a race between the drying effects of the sun and its struggle to free itself.

The cow died stuck in the mud right up to its shoulders. The vultures are huddled so close together that they form a black drape over the head and neck. When they see our truck coming, several take flight, and a few hop over to stubby bushes rising from the mud. One flies straight up, carrying away the eye and optic nerve, which looks like a long pull of pink bubble gum.

It's awful inside the truck now. We're swigging lots of water, eating oranges, and munching salty biscuits. This heat normally lays me out like a rag, but I'm stimulated by the astounding number of animals here. I tell myself people would have to trek weeks to see what I'm seeing next to this road. It's an unintentional wildlife park.

I notice that Gaspar's tired, and while he doesn't admit it, I insist on driving a bit. In minutes he's snoring away, his cap over his eyes. The Bandeirante is fun to drive, kind of like the British Land Rover I'd driven from Belize across the Maya Mountains to Tikal, but much more reliable. A real land yacht.

I think about our situation. Here I am, this stranger, falling in love with a region that Gaspar knows like the back of his scarred hand. I'm a city guy with an outback sense of adventure, totally unfamiliar with the place. I know where I've been and don't know where I'm going.

And there's Gaspar. I depend on him and trust him. Though he's seen this part of the Pantanal before, my enthusiasm has rubbed off, and his incredible ability to spot what I can't see is making the trip great.

My earlier exasperation, urged on by years of hurried projects with short deadlines, is giving way. This road is becoming a rite of passage for me. What will I be like when this is over?

We've settled into the pace. The truck is a platform not only for spotting animals, but for framing through the windshield or open door simple vistas of grass, waterways, and big sky. Here there's none of the forest's bewildering lack of direction. Only the road.

A dark blotch on the road. A snake? It's a caiman that's been steamrolled by a vehicle; it looks like a huge, green, flattened toothpaste tube. Guts burst the skin along the sides.

Gaspar's awake, but quiet, smoking thoughtfully and spotting animals. The dead caiman's changed his mood. He bemoans the damned road, bringing in strangers who take so much from the place and kill for fun.

The seventieth bridge. Large common egrets, wood storks, and cormorants fill the squat bushes surrounding the water. In the short grasses are caimans (*Caiman yacare*)—called *jacarés* here—and they're all over the place. Maybe a hundred of the two-meter-long reptiles lounge along the water's edge, many with jaws open.

Several float in the water like tiny islands, with only the bumps of the eyes and plated skin showing. One cruises the middle of the pond, exhibiting no bodily movement except the powerful drive of the tail swishing side to side, snout pushing a bow wave. Yet this is an oddly peaceful scene. These *jacarés* show remarkably little aggression. Is this caiman sunstroke?

In fact, on a finger of land strewn with water plants is a striking demonstration. An eighteen-kilo capybara is resting in the sun, absolutely relaxed, not more than a meter away from an adult caiman, jaws agape. Both are clearly aware of each other; in some other place they would be mortal enemies— predator and prey. But there seems to be an understanding that this afternoon isn't the time for a fight.

This isn't the dark and forbidding jungle where it's catch as catch can. Even during the dry season there's plenty to eat for all. That is, as long as there are fish. Maybe I'm getting cooked in this tin can or being lulled by the endless open landscape that's easy on the eyes and spirit. But the Pantanal seems a garden rather than a wilderness.

The wind wafts in, carrying the message of something dead ahead. We both wrinkle our faces as the acrid smell of rotted fish registers. There's nothing. A little more than a kilometer further, in the middle of the road, twenty or so black vultures (*Coragyps atratus*) flock around the bloated body of a capybara. It's inflated with putrefying gas, like a deep-sea diver brought up too fast.

I have a good chance to see nature's street cleaners up close. They're not as flighty as the other big birds here. As long as there's something to munch on, they just hop back away from me. Through my long lens gray skin around the head appears heavily wrinkled and loose, without a feather; they make no noise except the whoosh of their big, black, flapping wings and the ripping of decaying meat. No matter how judicial their appearance, their meal, its smell, and the heat make me a little nauseated. I put down the lens and climb back in the truck.

Soon, the long shadows from nearby trees reach across the road, painting black patches on the red surface. Big, black birds with long tails, ruffled crowns, and yellow beaks scurry from embankment to embankment—skinny wild turkeys? Another one explodes into flight, coming to rest on the limb of a tree set back from the road. They're currasows (*Crax alector*).

The Falcão Brothers

We're somewhere around the eightieth bridge. This one's over a pretty little pond surrounded by tufted water plants. A pair of gray ibises work the edge, and on a small island near the pond's center are turkey-size northern screamers (*Chauna chavaria*), who, when they see us, live up to their name and utter a trilling scream, putting all creatures within a kilometer on notice that strangers are approaching. A couple of Amazon kingfishers dart overhead.

Well ahead of us two stubby-winged Amazon parrots (*Amazona* species) dash across the sky heading for an open area, where they disappear in the leaves of a palm tree near a small farmhouse. They've landed at the farm of Fião, a good friend of Gaspar's. A VW Beetle is parked in front. Chickens and domestic turkeys scratch the open ground.

Gaspar honks the horn and pulls off the road in front of Fião's shuttered little refreshment stand on the opposite side of the road. It's situated at the edge of a grove of short palm trees that have great clusters of egg-size, green coconuts hanging from them.

Fião and his brother Tutu come out to greet us. The Falcão brothers are in their late forties, slender, unshaven, and wearing faded jeans. About the only difference between them is Fião is showing gray hair and walks barefoot. Tutu wears old shower thongs, one black and the other yellow. Fião complains that the family VW is sick and raises up his greasy hands.

The refreshment stand has rows of dusty *cachaça* bottles. Fião opens the fridge for pop; there are also bottled water, a coconut, and a big, oval fish taking up the entire lower shelf. "That fish looks like a piranha with a thyroid problem," I say. Fião doesn't laugh, but his eyes twinkle. "The piranha here are only so big," says Gaspar, holding his hands almost half a meter apart. "This is a *pacú*. It eats fruit, not people." They caught the fish the day before, in a river not far from where we're going to stay, twenty kilometers ahead.

The *pacú* (*Colossoma* species) is a relative of the razor-toothed piranha and ranges up to twenty-seven kilos. Oddly enough, this large fish is completely vegetarian, lacking the sharp teeth of the piranha. In its mouth, the *pacú* has evolved flat teeth adapted for crushing nuts and fruits—and they look surprisingly like little human molars.

Fião pulls out the fish and gives it to me, gesturing to his mouth with his free hand, eating fashion, "This is a good one." Gaspar rolls his eyes in delight, anticipating the taste of such a fine, fat fish.

Gaspar says he'll see what's the matter with Fião's car—that is, after drinking the fridge dry. Soft drinks and mineral water are guzzled. Fião cleaves the top of the coconut and passes it around. Fresh coconut water, cold enough to mask the sweetness. Then Gaspar, Fião, and Tutu walk off toward the house.

I'm slow to follow. I'm going to find those Amazons, which

turns out to be surprisingly easy. They're less than fifty meters from the farmhouse, sitting on a palm leaf and bobbing in the hot breeze. I'm thrilled and take my time, slowly stalking them with my long lens like an African big-game hunter, amusing everyone at the house. Later I find out the parrots live here, and although not pets, they're used to people. I could have walked right up to them.

An enormous dead tree rising nearly thirty meters above the cleared land near the house is an odd site. A flock of big muscovy ducks (*Cairina moschata*) is perched in something of a cross configuration up the trunk and out several broken limbs. Despite a powerful, gusting wind, they're secured by sharp nails extending from the webbed feet.

In another palm tree right beside the farmhouse is a laundry-basket-size nest. About twenty green birds have set up a communal nest. The birds are smaller than the Amazons but a lot louder, constantly screeching and chattering. These are monk parakeets (*Myiopsitta monachus*). They are much larger than common parakeets that come from Australia and are native only to South America. They've got a grass-green back with gray forehead, throat, and belly. Nevertheless, with their yellow beak and black eyes, they do resemble budgies.

These feisty birds are famous for their adaptability. In fact, there's a famous nest full of them surviving blissfully along Chicago's lakefront, even during the horrible winters. No one knows how they got there. The birds are endlessly chattering and socializing: locking beaks, pecking one another, and sitting close together, bodies touching, in what must be bird snuggling.

Then, in a flash, they take flight en masse. The formation—a noisy puff of green, with wings making the sound of rustling crinoline—darts to a tree and then flies back again, making it impossible to follow the birds through the long lens.

It seems one or another of them is constantly doing maintenance work on the nest: trimming, adding, tucking new sticks into the mesh, or keeping vigil. As I tiptoe closer, I must look ridiculous, an alien with mysterious hardware approaching the palm tree, hunched over to appear smaller. Then I start to giggle. One watchbird turns up the chatter. As I get within twenty meters, the little birds set up a surprisingly vicious shriek. I've come close enough to sound an alarm: invader. Then they're off once more, their ear-splitting chatter growing softer as they disappear into a tree several hundred meters away.

Gaspar has taken charge of the VW resuscitation, asking questions about the car's ailments while tinkering and removing various parts and harumphing to himself. The two brothers, sitting in chairs, are entranced by Gaspar's industriousness in the heat. He's pulled off the vacuum hoses and is unbolting the carburetor. Fião's wife peeks through the screen door, sees what's going on, shakes her head in disbelief, and moves back inside.

Suddenly, above the barnyard sounds, from the edge of the forest behind the house, comes an unearthly howling on the wind. What's that?

"Monkeys," says Fião. I'm like a kid in a candy store. Grabbing my lens and the gear bag with the tape recorder, I roar with eagerness, "Let's go! They're just over there," and point to the nearest trees.

They laugh at my foolishness. "They're far away, maybe a kilometer through the forest," Gaspar says. "That's not possible," I insist. "They're so loud."

Gaspar reassembles the carburetor and pours some fuel alcohol down its throat. Tutu jumps in the front seat to start the engine; a hiccough, a firecracker explosion, and the car's running. The household turns out to give Gaspar a well-deserved pat on his back, and he's grinning proudly from ear to ear. After washing up, Gaspar points to the sun low on the horizon, urging us to leave now so we can reach the *posto,* a remote IBAMA guard station along the Transpantaneira Highway, by dark.

While I have a chance, I mark down the birds seen on the ranch and scan my chicken scratchings to tote up the animals we've seen. What a mess! I've been writing in the truck, and it looks, indeed, like a chicken has been dancing with inky feet on my pages. What I can decipher is impressive, but I've missed a lot of animals, too. Just along the road today there have been:

Birds

savanna hawks	41
snail kites	33
black hawks	18
Amazon kingfishers	33
snowy egrets	28
cattle egrets	32
Maguari storks	6
toco toucans	7
swallows	4
black-headed vultures	65
great egrets	29
night jars	32
crested caracaras	34
wood storks	7
buff-necked ibis	17
gray ibis	4
ovenbirds	40
great blue and buff-necked herons	18
doves	35
tiger herons	5
curassows	6
Amazon parrots	4
ani	17
monk parakeets	40+
warblers	43
woodpeckers	5
southern lapwings	20
northern screamers	2
cormorants	45
cuckoos	14
unidentified warbler-size birds	56

Mammals

capybaras	34
coatis	3
marsh deer	2

Reptiles

caimans	125
iguanas	3
small lizards	15

In the dim light we drive toward the *posto*. Twenty minutes into our journey we come upon a capybara family in the middle of the road, bedding down in the dust for the night. They're unwilling to yield; it seems this road has become their kingdom too.

The Posto

We drive a stretch of flatlands where the road bends slowly in a big curve to the left. Gaspar slows and, at the end of the bend, points among a grove of fruit trees to an Alamo-style building—the *posto*. It's going to be our base for a number of weeks. From here we'll make exploratory trips off the road and investigate the surrounding countryside.

It's about 6:30 P.M. We're desert rats: coated in a thin film of red dust, thirsty, and exhausted. We pat each other on the back in congratulations, and little clouds of dust form above our heads. In the back seat the fine dust has managed to seep into everything despite our best efforts to seal it out with plastic bags. My right arm—the one that rested on the window—is sunburned on top; underneath, along the lower bicep, it's black and blue from the violent banging around. The top of my head hurts from hitting the cab roof, and a filling is loose. I'm curious if the computer survived. We're 101 bridges out and nearly three hundred kilometers down from Cuiabá. It's been a long, eventful day. The notes from the ride alone could pass as pages from a modern-day von Humboldt diary.

The *posto* was built in 1977–78 as a way for the federal government to control traffic along the middle part of the Transpantaneira. It rests on a little outcrop of landfill extending from the road about three meters above the surrounding field. On both sides of the road thousands of hectares of refreshingly open fields—naturally free of forest—stretch beyond my sight.

The place looks deserted, not a light or household noise. Just evensong Pantanal. Roosting birds and roosters welcome us. But there are two *rêdes* (hammocks) slung on the veranda that are thick like a snake after dinner. One comes alive and disgorges a heavyset man, tan, shirtless, rolled-up pants, barefoot. It's Sr. Firmo. A head peeps out of the other hammock. Gaspar says it's Maria, Sr. Firmo's *espousa* (wife).

Dona Maria and Firmo are in their sixties. They've been living here since 1983. Gaspar says I know them from an earlier trip here. Sr. Firmo . . . Sr. Firmo. Ah-ha! Now I remember. It was my second trip down the Transpantaneira. I was filming a rhea family working a field of mimosa grass when a long, Greyhound-type tourist bus pulled in front of the *posto* with a group of VIPs.

The bus drove a short distance up the road; then its passengers spotted the stork rookery in a marshy pasture, about a kilometer beyond the barbed-wire fence. Like tourists everywhere, they weren't satisfied with the distant view. They began hooting at the birds to make them fly. Several people became emboldened and crawled through the fence to approach the nesting trees in the rookery.

Sr. Firmo saw this through his binoculars, got fairly worked up, picked up his official IBAMA baseball cap, strapped on his utility belt with holster (no one was sure if he had *pistola,* but it looked good), sucked in his stomach, and marched down to stop them. The tourists were Paulistanos—natives of São Paulo—with an air of authority, like New Yorkers have. Firmo ordered them to return to the road. They paid no attention. Sr. Firmo was getting loud—and red in the face at this blatant affront—something Brazilians almost never do.

He was trying to open his holster when one of the group—a man dressed formally for the Pantanal in open white shirt and yellow slacks—stepped forward to identify himself as a *deputado,* a congressman, from Brasília. Firmo didn't care who the guy was; no one was going to disturb those nesting birds. Threats were exchanged. The congressman snapped his fingers; he was going to have Sr. Firmo's job just like that. And Firmo was going to charge him for crimes against nature. I took a couple of pictures, and all the words were jotted down by a journalist in the party.

A quick-thinking nature guide stepped between them. Her distracting beauty managed to keep a silly moment from becoming a tragedy in the woods. After all, the congressman was on a junket to see why the Pantanal was worth congressional attention. Once the confrontation subsided, efforts to have the men shake hands failed. The affront had been too great. They would not even cast an eye on each other again.

Their argument wasn't really about nature. It was a rare, head-on clash between a man of privilege and a minor official in a society having a lot of difficulty with democracy. Congressmen are *gatos gordos* — fat cats — says Gaspar. They're powerful people, not to be fooled with. The incident was reported in the *Estado do São Paulo,* one of the most important newspapers in Brazil. And Sr. Firmo had his moment of glory. But somehow the Pantanal had taken a back seat to the two men's intense personal differences.

Today, Sr. Firmo is just the caretaker here; he's managed to work a little *jeitinho* — a way around the bureaucracy — to permit his wife to live with him. Only sometimes does he tell strangers coming through to take care not to frighten the birds. But no one takes the *posto* seriously. There are never any surprise vehicle inspections, checking for skins or out-of-season fish or even drugs. He's happy to welcome locals he knows with cool, filtered water and a chat in the shade. And like a gas station sign I know in Indiana — "If you can't stop, smile as you go by" — he waves warmly from the veranda to any and all.

Gaspar hasn't seen the couple in several weeks and talks news of town and country while they go over to the generator shed to turn on the lights. Sr. Firmo's yellow hound dog uncurls and lopes to our truck, where I'm unloading our food and gear, and promptly sticks his snout in the gringo's crotch.

The *posto* is practically self-sufficient. The concrete cabana has a large rectangular room serving as office, radio shack, and dining room. There are also two baths — one inside for the Firmos and important guests, the other outside for cowboys and IBAMA personnel — and three bedrooms, each with two sets of bunk beds. There's a *cozinha* (kitchen), complete with stove and refrigerator run by bottled gas and a ceramic water filter by the sink. The filter is a common fixture in kitchens throughout the land.

Suspicious-looking, brown well water pumped into the *posto* is made palatable with that filter. It's got the heavy burden to remove not only visible sediments but to screen out amoebas and other microbes that bring on diarrhea, pernicious dysentery, hepatitis, typhoid, and whatever else might ruin the adventure. I remember the boxes of mineral water in the truck and sigh with relief. It'll be a bank account that I'll draw down while my guts get accustomed to the local bugs.

Cracks crisscross the kitchen walls in several places, but when I look closer, they're ants. Ants that know where the detritus of dinner is and march in formation to them. Dona Maria has reached a sort of truce with them. A cardboard box underneath the sink contains designated ant offerings, and the ants, in turn, honor the arrangement by not eating the people in their sleep.

Out back are the well, chicken coops, food-storage sheds, and a generator hut set away from the main house. All around are mango, cashew, and hot-pepper trees and lovely flowering vines and bushes. The place is a tidy little oasis in an immense, dry sea.

After carrying in the gear, Gaspar and I stretch our legs from the long, cramped ride. The air's grown cool with a touch of dampness. As we walk down the road, patches of ground fog rise off the marshlands, lending a touch of make-believe to the *campos* (fields).

With the sun gone, an easy peace prevails. The afterglow reflects like liquid mercury in the few remaining pools of water. The backs of *jacarés* glisten silver, and storks still working these waters cut a wake that sends rose-colored ripples around their legs.

A cow bellows in the distance; then a capybara barks like a wheezing dog, splashing into a safe water hole. Gaspar says something scared them. There will be a whole new cast of characters in the night. He sweeps the *estrada* (road) with the beam of his flashlight and looks for jararacas (*Bothrops jararaca*). Gaspar makes a V sign with his left hand and then jabs it at me. I get the message. They're real biters, aggressive pit vipers that can reach more than two meters long. And night hunters. My eyes are wide as doorknobs, but all we see is a smooshed giant toad.

A delicious fresh wind wafts in from the southwest, clearing the sky a bit. Right above the horizon I can just make out several stars in the Southern Cross, that familiar constellation, pointing down to the South Pole. It's the southern hemisphere's Big Dipper: easy to identify and comforting to see. For centuries navigators have depended on its reassuring bright points of light to guide them home. They're the first celestial bodies I've been able to see through the smoky sky since leaving Brasília. It seems increasingly difficult to get into the Pantanal. It's been an ordeal to get here—the fires, gold miners, politicians, clogged cities. But I'm very happy. Tears well up in my eyes.

The chill night air makes for an easy, deep sleep, and I'm barely dreaming before a raucous chattering makes me unglue an eye. It's 4:50 A.M., and my pocket thermometer reads 67°F, more than forty degrees down from yesterday afternoon. The trees around the *posto* are chock full of singing birds.

Out front, the purple morning sky is crowded with wave after wave of wood storks (*Mycteria americana*). Their formations course so low that I can hear the powerful wing beats as they glide straight over the *posto,* then bank into a broad turn and seem to land right behind the cabana. The roosters are already having a crowing contest, and the hens with their brood peck the sand as I run to the back.

Less than two hundred meters behind the house is a gathering flock of great wading birds literally filling a small pond. There are hundreds and hundreds. Many more are still arriving. They're in a feeding frenzy—white feathers, flapping wings, striding long legs—making it difficult to follow any one bird. Most are American wood storks that have come in from a nearby rookery.

Bigger still are the magnificent jabiru storks (*Jabiru mycteria*)—*tuiuiu,* pronounced to-yu-yu in Portuguese—standing nearly one and a half meters tall. They seem to be equal in number to the wood storks. Lesser in number are great egrets (*Casmerodius albus*), snowy egrets (*Egretta thula*), and a few little blue herons (*Florida caerulea*). The wood storks dominate prime fishing in the center. Back and forth, back and forth, they stride, driving their large, open beaks through the water to snap up fish.

By sheer force of numbers the storks have pushed the

47

smaller waders to the edge. Here and there, elegant tall herons—great blue (*Ardea herodias*) and white-necked (*Ardea cocoi*)—hunt by stealth, stationing themselves near water plants. Their frozen posture and legs lost amid the stalks help them spear unwary fish as they surface.

The pond is one of the few bodies of water left in this enormous field. And through some as yet to be deciphered signals these great birds have selected this pond for dining en masse today. Many kinds of hapless fish were trapped in the *baixa*—receding flood waters—weeks ago. Needle-nose *agulha*—miniatures of their ocean relatives, striped *carauacu*—pricey at pet stores; *cambuata,* little catfish; bigger, striped *pintado* catfish; and several kinds of piranhas await their doom in snapping beaks.

Or they'll suffocate in the increasingly warm, oxygen-poor stew of algae and muck. Most will succumb. A small number may be lucky to last until the rains begin again in October and free them from their pothole prison. Those that die before then do so in spectacular fashion. Thousands of suffocating fish break the pond's surface, gulping oxygen, giving the distinct impression that a light rain is falling.

Through my binoculars I focus on one jabiru who's working the shallows with particular zeal. The big bird pokes its half-meter, black beak deep into the cloudy water. Takes a step. Pokes. Looks around. Steps . . . pokes. Again and again. Despite its enormity, the beak is touch-sensitive and astoundingly quick to the slightest fishy bump. In a flash, the stork dredges up a beak full of muck, plants, water, and a meter-long, wriggling creature. A snake? No, a *mucum,* an eel, says Gaspar, who's joined me.

The jabiru hauls out of the water and walks a short distance away on the grass, where there are fewer rivals to pester him for his catch. He crunches the eel gingerly, tosses it into the air, and catches it near the head. Then he drops the eel and stabs it with his beak. But it won't give up. Several more crushing grips seem to have no effect at all.

The big bird now tries to muscle the prey down, tilting back his head trying to swallow the thing whole. That works . . . well, sort of . . . half is down. The protruding part continues to flail away at the stork's beak. Once more the jabiru's head goes back. And it's done. The eel's gone, but there's a distinct twitching bulge now in the stork's black-and-red neck pouch. Without hesitating, he returns to the pond, washes off the slimy residue, and wades into the shallows less feverishly.

Observing and documenting these great waders feeding makes the time go by quickly. It's now midmorning and the sun is blistering. In less than five hours my pocket thermometer has jumped to 112°F. In the distance, heat waves shimmer above the field. The feeding frenzy has slowed considerably. Many sated birds move out to preen and take refuge under the inviting shade of a fig tree.

A few have been absolute pigs. One jabiru, beak open and panting, has eaten so much I could probably walk over and catch it. The big bird's neck pouch is packed with fish, making it difficult to lift its head. It sinks to the ground from the weight and wilting heat. Out of sheer desperation one wing unfolds, bracing against the ground to keep the stork from falling over. I've never seen anything like it.

But I'm wilting too. Although a light breeze stirs the air, we retreat to the house to while away the midday. Dona Maria is preparing *lanches,* the main meal of the day. She walks out back to the laundry line, where a haunch of beef is drying in the sun. Sr. Firmo bought it fresh from a rancher down the road.

Picking at the meat and fat are nearly twenty red-capped Brazilian cardinals (*Paroaria gularis*). Although mostly seed-eaters, these regal-looking little birds, with glossy black back and wings and white belly, have learned to appreciate the *posto*'s riches, however foreign to their diet. Maria shoos them away long enough to carve a gristly chunk. As soon as she leaves, they're back.

She cooks *feijão* (beans) with pieces of sun-dried meat, rice with chopped-up onions and pieces of sun-dried meat, and spaghetti with — that's right — pieces of meat and sliced tomatoes; side dishes of fried potatoes and fried bananas complete the meal. In the Pantanal, with such abundant fish life, it's remarkable how much Pantaneiros insist on meat.

Dona Maria has salted the food way beyond my poor powers of appreciation. It's really hard to swallow. But Gaspar and Firmo shake on even more. Beans, spaghetti, rice, and potatoes are heaped together, forming an impressive starch

mountain in the center of the plate. Gaspar notices my reti-
cence and asks Maria for *pimenta* (pepper) for me. She returns
from the kitchen, not with a shaker, but an old whisky bottle
with a cork in it. That's *malagueta*—the native Tabasco. Maria
made it by picking the little, green peppers from the tree out
back, putting them in the empty whisky bottle with oil and
vinegar, and letting the liquid ferment for six months.

They all smile at one another, waiting for the gringo to fry
his face. The few drops sliding down from the cork transform
the glutinous mass before me into a Thai-like feast. I pop the
cork and eat two of the gray-green peppers; feeling their fire, I
smile, with tears welling up. The fire in my mouth reminds me
of time spent in Southeast Asia.

The meal is washed down with *cafezinho*. Spoonful after
spoonful of sugar is heaped into the tiny cups, convincing me
that there's something more to their love of these condiments.
Perhaps it's a socialization of the need for maintaining the
body's electrolytes in this unforgiving climate.

In any case, the food is nourishing and has done its job,
making us very sleepy. As if in a drugged stupor, everyone
quietly stakes out a place to sling a hammock on the veranda
and climbs in. One more glance at the fish fest out back. I'm
envious of the birds' lunch. They're very quiet too. More than
half have dispersed in the heat, with many more under the fig
tree. It's *sesta*—nap time.

four

At the Posto

Oh, the *posto* . . . is wonderful. Sooner or later
everything in the Pantanal passes there.
— *Zelito Dorileo, Pantanal rancher*

*I*n the coming weeks Sr. Firmo and Dona Maria reveal the
daily routine won from long years of marriage, six of them out
here. At 5:50 A.M. Firmo arises, slips on his pants, pours from
a thermos a *cafezinho* made the night before, and begins his
day. He grabs a broom made of local, tough, brown weeds
bound around a stick and starts sweeping the sand of newly
fallen leaves.

I had gotten up before dawn, ready to film a blood-red sun
rising through the smoky, gray horizon and the busy, early-
morning bird commute. I was enthralled by their tumultuous
morningsong. When I meet Firmo in the yard I mention having seen a flight of storks coursing low over the field and cutting across the sun. He pauses a moment, resting on the broom
handle pensively, twitches his head, and walks back to let the
chickens out of the coop. Ah, bucolic torpor.

Dona Maria joins him about an hour later. She does the
heavier domestic work — cleaning the house and washing the
clothes. At the moment she's setting the breakfast table for
us with eggs fresh from the coop this morning, water biscuits,
a big wheel of white farmer's cheese, marmalade, a pot of

51

Brazilian tea, and the familiar thermos of hot coffee. Bowls of sugar, grated manioc, and condensed milk are already there.

After breakfast Gaspar turns on the radio telephone to check in with his assistant, Beijamim, at the remote Pantanal National Park outpost about eighty miles southwest on the Bolivian border. Then he calls the headquarters in Cuiabá and reports that everything's okay. Except Firmo has not received his paycheck. He explains to me that Firmo recently learned that he has a heart condition, forcing him to leave the forestry service. But he explains further that one of the environmental groups in Brasília pays him the minimum wage to stay out here to have someone at the *posto* and that salary comes from headquarters.

Gaspar and I return to the field behind the *posto*. The morning's fishing frenzy has long since played out. Only a few storks and great blue herons stand guard at the water hole. A white line on the field, perhaps one and a half kilometers off, is this day's location for the moveable feast.

Through the binocs, I can see a long line of wood storks and jabirus tracing a stream's course. A number of caimans sit at the edge, absolutely still, some with their jaws agape. Between them gingerly step several kinds of shorebirds, some of which have traveled up from Argentina.

I'm especially taken with many pairs of southern lapwings (*Vanellus chilensis,* a large, crested plover). They're quite handsome. Buff-colored, lithe bodies are set off by black and white chest and belly feathers; long, red legs; and an elegant, long plume dancing at the back of their heads. Perhaps the most distinguishing aspect of their anatomy is large, stark, red eyes and black pupils.

Two caracaras set down on the far end of the water hole where some lapwings have taken up residence. The caracara is not a bird to take lightly. In the Pantanal it fills the niche of both vulture and hawk. It's a great opportunist and will eat carrion, baby chicks, and fish—live or dead. And it's about three times larger than the lapwing.

At first sight the lapwings fly off to intercept these territorial intruders. They go at the caracaras much the same way as blackbirds attack hawks and owls in the United States. They dive-bomb the intruders while constantly screaming.

These two fly a shallow arc course repeatedly, like a pendulum, nearly striking the caracaras each time they sweep low to the ground. It's a demonstration of precision flying that any top gun would appreciate. The caracaras duck down at each attack, with one actually being driven off by the faster, alarmed lapwings. The remaining caracara keeps looking around the shore, while the lapwings continue their screaming defense.

Then I saw what they are so upset about: bobbing here and there are four speckled lapwing chicks, and gauging from their awkward wobble, they can't be more than several days old. One seems oblivious to all the fuss, pecking and exploring the mud and what must appear to it as a great dismal swamp of water lettuce.

The adults think differently. When the remaining caracara won't fly off, they change strategy. They walk directly into the open grassland and sit down, squawking constantly and drawing attention to themselves. They are offering themselves as targgets so that the helpless little ones will instinctually freeze and go unnoticed. The ploy works, and within minutes the caracara leaves, winging low to the ground. For good measure, one of the adults actually dives on the caracara, making it falter a bit in flight.

In the late afternoon, Gaspar and Sr. Firmo disappear with their fishing poles while I pop open the computer and try to keep up the journal of the trip. The laptop survived the Trans-pantaneira Highway and has been the focus of much discussion with the folks at the *posto* and visitors who stop by. While Brazil has its own budding computer industry, it has yet to produce these laptop portables.

I slip a Marian McPartland jazz piano tape into my tape recorder and clack merrily away at the keyboard of my computer. In the fading daylight the screen casts a clean, blue glow like a backyard bug zapper. As I write, hundreds of flying and crawling insects smack into the screen. After a couple of hours it looks like a windshield after a summer's drive in Wisconsin. When I get back home I'm going to tell the manufacturer how well the computer performed, and I'm going to recommend that the company offer a couple of new options: a little windshield wiper and squirter.

At dusk Gaspar and Firmo show up with a string of strange fish called *trairas* (*Hoplias malabaricus*). I ask where they went, not seeing any large lakes around. They point to a water hole about the size of a swimming pool a kilometer away. They used enormous hooks that would be too large even for big northern pike in the midwestern United States. Bait was stew-size chunks of spoiled meat. No technique necessary here, they insist. Just dunk the baited hook into a weed patch and wham! *Traira.*

The thirty-centimeter-long *traira* is a very primitive hodge-podge of anatomical components seemingly lifted from other successful fish. The large head, occupying a good third of the body, is protected by tarpon-size cartilaginous scales. Four pugnacious canine teeth (two on top and two on bottom) jut from the fish's broad, hard mouth. Large, overlapping scales cover the body, much like carp; only one spiny dorsal fin rises from the back, reminiscent of arctic char; and, at the end, there's a stubby, brush tail.

Trairas are able to withstand the water hole's low oxygen and relatively high temperatures by becoming inactive, eventually resting in the bottom mud. However, they're not as successful as the local eels and crabs, says Gaspar, which actually burrow deep into the mud, surviving the entire dry season, even when the surface is pavement hard. But if there's water, adds Firmo with a flick of his wrist, "there are *trairas*, and you won't starve." Like piranhas, they're a lazy man's fish.

They clean the still-wriggling fish (as with piranhas, *trairas* can live out of water up to an hour or more) and toss the guts to the chickens, which fight eagerly to gulp them down.

The *trairas* bring to mind similar fish that I pulled from rice paddies when I was working in northern Thailand near the Mekong River. Many of those fish were full of worms, which I never forgot. Those rice paddies were many things to local residents: rice field, duck pond, fish farm, play ground, cess-pool, and who knows what else. I remember Lung Liu, our guide, demonstrating rice-paddy plowing. He harnessed up an enormous, pink water buffalo and began working the perimeter of a rice paddy. He paused a minute while the big animal relieved itself in the water. Then he bent over, cupped a hand, and drank from the same water. Kids speared fish from that

ntanal (center) labeled "Sea of Xarayes." English map, ca. 1740.

opposite page:
TOP LEFT: Cowboy
TOP RIGHT: Subsistence
fisherman
BOTTOM: Commercial
fishermen holding
pacú

this page:
Cowboy on cattle
drive, Mato Grosso do
Sul

this page:
RIGHT: Caiman: note how upper jaw accomodates lower teeth
BELOW: Patrolling Cuiabá river

opposite page:
TOP: Gasper with confiscated poachers' gear
BOTTOM LEFT: Arne Sucksdorff
BOTTOM RIGHT: Toco toucan

TOP: Fião
BOTTOM: Gaspar

TOP: Ranch hand with baby cascavel
(rattlesnake)
BOTTOM: Informant's wife

cher burning pasturage

TOP: Great egret feeding
chick

RIGHT: Cowboys heading
home

paddy that looked exactly like the ones Gaspar and Firmo are working on.

"Are they good eating?" I sheepishly inquire. Firmo clucks his tongue and rolls his eyes as if to say, "Are you crazy? These are delicious."

Dona Maria pours oil into a pan to cook up the *trairas*. But my mind dwells on the little eggs and parasitic worms that could be lodged in the muscle of those fish; I fear that meal can mean big bills for a gastroenterologist when I get back. So I make a feeble attempt to have her cook some more of the sun-dried meat hanging on a line. No luck. I go back outside.

"Uh, guys, can't we use them to catch some *pintado* [huge, predatory catfish]?" I jerk my arms as though fishing. Gaspar lights up with another thought. "Good idea! We'll go see some caimans tonight," he says, setting aside only four fish. "Make sure you bring your camera. You won't believe what you'll see."

The *trairas* are fried and served with rice and beans, fried potatoes, boiled manioc, and sliced tomatoes. We eat on the veranda, with the hound dog and the cat as an attentive audience. The fish has white flesh and lots of thin, sharp bones that Dona Maria warns are easily choked on. So the table falls into silence as we work on the crispy fish carcasses. The fish probably even had a delicate texture once upon a time, but Dona Maria spanked the life out of them in the skillet until they achieved the texture of greasy balsa wood. But come to think of it, overcooking the fish probably finished off any microscopic aliens seeking a fork lift to a new world.

When we finish, Dona Maria clears the table and Sr. Firmo takes the leftovers from our plates and makes two little hills on the sand for the dog and cat. But the cat races back and forth sniffing and sizing up the mountains, making sure all is equal, and hissing back the big-eyed dog. The dog, now drooling out both sides of its mouth, can maintain its sweet disposition no longer and raises its muzzle in a wild snarl, revealing a healthy set of teeth. Upon seeing this, the cat launches into a Halloween arch and is not seen again until morning.

The dog wolfs down the scraps with relish, and I look on in horror as it gulps all those needle-sharp fish bones too. I complain to Firmo, who replies, "We give him all the leftovers, chicken bones, fish bones. It's what we've got." I watch the hound and remember my brother's Dalmatian, Ivan. The vet operated on a blocked bowel and found a fistful of bone chips that would've killed it. Good luck, pooch.

Night Eyes

I pack up my camera gear and dig through my baggage for a high-powered spotlight that will pinpoint the caimans. Going into the starless evening is invigorating. Is it the chill air or the black night pregnant with possibilities of what could be out there that makes me smile nervously? I've had this same feeling before going deep-sea fishing. You could pull in a grotesque hammerhead shark, a shimmering sailfish, or nothing at all. The possibilities were wondrous, making my mind reel. Gaspar assures me that with the Pantanal's many types of habitat, practically any animal that roams tropical America could cross our path tonight.

We jump into the Bandeirante and drive south. I strain to peer into the darkness beyond the headlights while my mind projects animal images that aren't there. After only fifteen minutes we stop on the approach to a bridge. "Here?" I ask, deflated. No tromp through the jungle? No slog through the marsh? "Uh-huh," Gaspar says with a big grin on his face. "*Aqui.*" We tilt forward the driver's seat, remove the battery cover, and unwrap the spotlight cord.

The weak light from the Bandeirante's headlights barely illuminates the murky water beneath the bridge. It looks as if the bridge has fallen into the water. Actually, it's debris from an old bridge repair job, completed by a Mato Grosso state road crew when the bridge washed out years ago. Old planks, discarded timbers, logs, and nail barrels litter the shallows and mud bank.

Hundreds of small fish with long whiskers kiss the surface. *Cascudo,* small catfish (*Otocinclus* species or *Microlepidogaster* species), gulp air, doing a pretty good impression of light rainfall. Then Gaspar switches on the spotlight.

The 200,000-candle, yellow spotlight has a peculiar effect.

While it isn't exactly a klieg light, the wide beam is strong enough to reach out beyond a hundred meters, revealing hundreds of eerie, orange, marble-size lights floating in the dark. No water, field, or trees are recognizable, only those unsettling pairs of lights staring back.

As Gaspar plays the light back and forth, a wave of reflections lights up, then goes black as the light passes. At first my eyes aren't adjusted well; I have the distinct impression that I'm gazing into a star-studded night sky.

Gaspar says the eyes of caimans are orange-yellow, those of big marsh deer are green-blue, and a jaguar's eyes are red-orange. In fact, he contends that locals experienced in night hunting can accurately tell what animal is out there merely by the color of the eye reflections and their height off the ground.

Ophthalmologists call that the "red reflex" in humans. They examine the eye by sending a powerful light through the clear, vitreous liquid to the parabolically shaped retina. A sheer reflecting membrane behind the retina has tiny blood vessels that cast back a pale light, resulting in a red-looking eye. It's the same thing that happens when taking someone's picture with the flash straight on.

In nocturnal animals, anatomists have found a specialized reflecting structure, the tapetum, which is also behind the retina. Its epidermal cells reflect back stray rays of light through the retina, which acts like an image-intensifying lens. The tapetum is so efficient that when animals are hit by even a weak light, the eye gives off a spooky glow, appearing to have its own internal light source.

Deer and jaguar, capybara and caiman — the hunted and the hunters — have this adaptation. Different animals reflect different colors because of chemical variations in the pigment tissue. Whatever the anatomical details, people living here are well aware of this phenomenon. It is one sure way Pantaneiros successfully exploit their environment.

Gaspar points the beam close in, turning night to day. Most of the apparent logs aren't logs at all, but floating caimans waiting for fish. Gaspar hands me the light and I track the bank. As if in some overcrowded zoo, hundreds of the saurians lie shoulder to shoulder along the entire circumference of the pool. I count fifty-five in less than a tenth of the perimeter, with many more floating out in the middle. My guess is at least six hundred have taken refuge in the pool. Gaspar figures that's a minimum, adding he's never seen more *jacarés* in one place, alive.

"Aaaawwk. Aaaawwk." The light scares off a great blue heron that had been standing right between two two-meter *jacarés*. It apparently knows the reptiles are sated with fish, because the tall wader didn't vary its course a bit, stepping closely to their jaws.

Normally, in still water, a caiman herds fish to shore using its body and tail. But in these catch basins trapped fish are easy pickings, requiring little effort. Without relying on eyesight, the reptile simply glides among the surfacing fish and waits until one brushes the sensitive skin along its jaws.

They aren't successful every time. According to a study conducted here in the early 1980s, eighty-five caimans were observed on one water hole. Over a thirteen-day period they caught 10,208 fish throughout the day and night, averaging only one fish for every 6.9 tries.

To get a better idea of their feeding behavior, I retrieve the sack of fish from the truck. Gaspar tosses one onto the nearest bank. A large adult with dry weeds stuck to its back lifts up onto all four legs and waddles over to the sandy fish. In the water, a smaller caiman has seen the fish fall and hauls out after it too. When they are within a meter of each other the bigger one bellows out a frightening hiss that stops the smaller one dead in the water.

The large adult, unable to pick up the fish straight on, now turns its broad snout sideways to facilitate grabbing on to the fish with its long rows of teeth. This it does with a bone-crunching grip; then it crawls over a pile of half a dozen caimans and heads for the water.

Several more reptiles cruise over, showing a strong interest in obtaining a share, but the one with the fish submerges just before the others converge. Ten seconds later it pops up in the middle of the pool with the fish hanging out of its mouth. The caiman arches its body so that its head and tail are well out of the water. Then it tosses the fish to the back of its mouth and chomps it two or three times before assuming the rigid floating-log position.

The evening air has cooled dramatically from the day's high of 44°C (112°F), down to the mid-sixties. Eventually the caimans will wade back into the warmer water in an effort to regulate their body temperature. But Gaspar has the idea to give them a jump-start. He walks to the center of the bridge, cups his hands to his mouth, and begins making loud, guttural noises deep in his throat, barely opening his mouth.

"Ummmp . . . ummmp . . . ummmp . . . ummmp," he calls again and again, tilting his head back with each grunt.

Those reptiles closest to us on the shore start. They open their eyes, swinging their heads up off the mud, intent on locating that threatening, low rumble. Pretty soon hundreds of crocodilians have heard the call loud and clear and sit up, alert. An imposing adult is the first to crawl off the bank into the water. That initiates an immediate chain reaction, with the mass of caimans slithering into the water in great confusion, making tracks and splashing their way for the deeper sections of the pool.

Gaspar is laughing and having a great time. "What are you doing?" I ask. "The *onça* [jaguar] makes that noise when it's out hunting," he says. "It takes *jacarés* when it can." It's a peculiar sight indeed, seeing such fearsome-looking predators suddenly act like fearful prey because of a sound in the night.

Gaspar points the beam at several others sitting on a little island near us and pretends to shoot them like the skin hunters do, making rifle sounds, "pichoo . . . pichoo." He pulls out a special flashlight; it has a special focusing mechanism that makes it easy to spot caimans in the water. It's stamped "Made in Hong Kong." "I took it from a skin hunter I stopped," he says, "They get the equipment in Paraguay. They're paid in dollars—forty dollars for one skin. *Muito dinheiro aqui.*" Much money here, he says, pretending to shoot again, "pichoo . . . pichoo."

Is There a Bigfoot Here?

When we return to the *posto,* we're joined by Sr. Firmo and Dona Maria, who set up several hammocks on the veranda and light a candle on an empty condensed-milk can. I pass around a bottle of *cachaça,* take several pulls of the breaktaking liquid, and talk about that spectacular gathering of caimans. A couple more sips launch me into rounds of an old song, "I Want a Green Canoe."

Then Gaspar takes a sip and sings out a plaintive tune about tragic love—a love between a very rich girl and a poor boy. The girl's father didn't want her to marry the boy. She chastised her father, "Keep all of your money, except a little bit to place a wooden cross on our grave." The father saw them on a faraway hill. He ran to the top and found them dead in each other's arms, their bodies already cold.

"Gaspar!" I complain. "Don't you know a song about the Pantanal?" We both grab for the bottle. He gets it first, takes a long pull, and exhales. He thinks a moment, then clears his throat and begins singing:

João de Barro
(Mud John, the Ovenbird)

The ovenbird wanted to be happy like me.
One day this bird decided to take a mate.
He flew back and forth bringing mud from
The little pond to build his round house.

In the branch of the paineira tree
This feathered stone mason of the forest
Sang so loud and long trying to please the
One he loved so much.

Then one day when he went for more mud to
Finish his nest he saw his mate with another.
Finding that out filled his heart full of pain.
He closed the door of his house to her forever.

This same thing happened to me and my love
And God made me calm in this hour of pain.
My ungrateful love I too put her out of my
House and where is she now? I do not know.

"Great . . . a broken-hearted bird song!" I say, slugging down some more firewater and bringing on a wave of shivers.

This leads to stories about the Pantanal. Such an imposing land with so much wildlife has to generate some pretty fabulous legends.

Dona Maria responds to our caiman adventure and tells us that a caiman's teeth are thought to have magical powers. The wealthy cast them in gold and use them as amulets to protect their children from harm and their teeth from abcess.

There's another *jacaré* story, she says, that details how the world is supported by a giant caiman. When the great beast grows tired of holding the world in one position, it shifts and with that movement creates earthquakes.

We pass the bottle around again; then I tell them about big-foot, the legendary abominable snowman that some people think lives in the forests of America's Pacific Northwest. "Don't you have animal stories like that?" I ask. "You know"—I struggle to find the right Portuguese word—"*panico . . . alarme . . .* creepy stories?"

"We have something like that," Maria answers, looking to Firmo as though she's revealing a family secret. "*Minhocão* [min-yo-cow]," she breathes. "All the Pantaneiros know *minhocão*. It's very old." She snaps her fingers for emphasis and adds, "But it's not a story."

Gaspar lights another Hollywood cigarette and picks up the story. "It's a huge creature—some say it's half fish and half serpent—that lives in the *rios* Cuiabá and Paraguay. Big. More than thirty meters long . . . black . . . and has horrible hair. *Minhocão* lives along the banks of the river in caves that it digs."

"Oh, go on!" I gush at the size of this fisherman's tale. A cool wind comes out of southwest, from the Andes, adding some real shivers to the tale.

"When *minhocão* swims at the bottom of the river, it creates a terrible turbulence—huge whirlpools in the water. They're so strong they're able to pull down a motorboat going full speed," Gaspar says without a hint of feeling.

"Ooh, it's true," Dona Maria pipes up. "I know a man who shot a jungle pig not long ago. After butchering it he lay the head on the river bank while he went off to the forest. Soon he heard a strange sucking noise and rushed back in time to see *minhocão* rise out of the water to take the pig's head. Down in the river it went, creating a huge whirlpool. A couple of minutes went by, then it tossed the head back up on the bank—cleaned to the bone!" Gaspar nods his head in confirmation.

Sated with stories and *cachaça,* we decide it's time for bed and turn in for the night. Firmo's the last in and asks "Are you going to sleep out tonight?" When I say yes, he shuts the door, leaving me alone in the hammock watching the flickering candle.

I don't know what to make of the *minhocão* story. If it's true, what could that creature be? An enormous anaconda? A gargantuan *jaú (Paulicea luetkeni)*, a catfish weighing more than 115 kilos that inhabits the Paraguay River? Or maybe a school of above-average piranhas? Then again, Maria, Firmo, and Gaspar could be elbowing each other with laughter, thoroughly enjoying their get-the-gringo story.

Before settling in for the night, I tiptoe around back to the kitchen and dig out a cup of cooked rice from a pot. Then I nudge the dog awake, hoping that it will make the fish bones easier to digest. Out on the veranda again, I climb into the hammock and rock gently in the fresh breeze. It's a lot nicer than the stuffy bunkroom that I share with Gaspar and our now ripe clothes.

Resting in the hammock is one thing; trying to sleep in its confining net is quite another—especially since I'm used to sleeping on my stomach. In the next several hours I try dozens of positions, wriggling like a trapped fish caught in the mesh. Finally I find a good one—propping the left lip of the hammock out with my bent knee, allowing me to doze off for a while. Then a distant bellow from a cow wafts in. A frightened capybara barks next and splashes into a water hole. A multitude of clicks, buzzes, hums, and feathery flutters leaves me with one eye open into the wee hours.

Trouble in Poconé

A little before dawn I begin assembling gear for the day's shoot when Firmo surprises me. He says he's heading for Poconé because the VW needs a new clutch. He'll be back in a couple of days.

When I return from my shoot seven hours later, Gaspar's on the radio with Cuiabá. The radio operator says that Firmo has had a heart attack outside Poconé. Apparently his car stalled on the road and he became exasperated trying to get it going again. Jacking up the car had jacked up his blood pressure and brought on chest pains. He's being brought to the hospital there, and the chief of the forestry service will be sending a vehicle for Dona Maria. Gaspar turns to me, patting the area over his left chest and whispering, "Firmo's had them before but didn't tell his wife. He's probably dying."

At first, the news doesn't seem to register with Dona Maria. She simply mumbles a few words to herself, gets out a black leather valise, and scoops up all the medications around the house. Then it dawns on her that the cat, dog, and chickens won't have someone to tend them. She sits down, bewildered, picks up a dirty towel, and cries.

Gaspar consoles her, adding that Firmo's in good hands, and I offer to watch the animals. Silently she begins getting ready to leave, putting the kitchen in order and deciding with great difficulty what clothes to take along. I guess part of the problem is not knowing exactly how Firmo is doing and wondering if or when she will return.

The time doesn't pass well at all. Waiting around for the driver and for news of Firmo's condition is killing her and making us crazy watching her growing anguish. So I talk it over with Gaspar and decide to call off the driver and let him take her to Poconé. He'll return in a few days.

Dona Maria has cooked and cleaned all the time I've been around and hasn't once let out a peep about my presence. I give her a twenty-dollar bill—something not seen often out here—thank her for her help, and wish her well with a hug. She waves good-bye from the truck, and within a few minutes all I can see is their dust trail along the Transpantaneira.

Bees from Hell

In the afternoon, dressed for the heat in jogging shorts and gym shoes, I take some photo gear and hike several kilometers south on the road to where another bridge and water hole are receiving many birds. This pond isn't out in the open fields like the others. There are woods on both sides of the bridge. Luxuriant growths of duckweed and water lettuce form a thick, floating mat that supports several good-size caimans.

Capybaras—those cumbersome giant rodents—are feeding on the water plants. The heat is oppressive to them too. One wades into a muddy part of the pool, raises its head in sheer delight, and wiggles its portly body deep into the mud. This adult is followed by four very young ones that appear to be entirely different animals. Missing are the adult's thick muzzle, heavy abdomen, and ungainly hindquarters. The little one's body proportions are more balanced, giving them a rabbit's charm as they scamper about the green.

Whole families of capybaras, numbering more than a dozen individuals, are one of the most common sights early or late in the day as they troop from one water hole out across the dry plain in search of another. Adults can weigh more than fifty kilos, making capybaras the largest rodents in the world. With webbed hind feet, these awkward-looking creatures are surprisingly excellent swimmers, allowing access to favored water plants. Some farmers in Venezuela have raised capybaras for meat and fur. But Brazilians generally have a low regard for capybaras in terms of money-making potential.

At the corner of the pool, a caracara and a black-headed vulture are fighting over a large, dead piranha. There's a good deal of flapping going on. Apparently, the caracara is making claim to the fish by placing one foot on it, then tossing its head back and issuing a rasping victory call, which the vulture doesn't accept. The vulture flaps its wings, rising more than a meter off the ground and stirring up dust, and lands practically on top of the caracara. Neither flees, so they begin poking at each other with their beaks.

This is a good scene to photograph, I think, and I fire off ten or fifteen frames, then run out of film. As I bend down to exchange rolls I notice a small, black bee land on my sock. It's relatively harmless looking compared to all the bugs that continually drone around our heads and splutter when they hit the hot candle wax at night. And it's furry too.

I jiggle my foot and kick at the air to scare it away, but it won't budge. Instead, the little thing bends its hinged body and stings me right through my thick athletic sock. "Eeeeeyaa-aaahhhh!" I bellow out, sending the birds fleeing for the safety of tall trees.

Suddenly, a furious zoology lesson is under way. Somehow I've blundered past a bee hive's territorial threshold, with one of the swarm's sentinels spotting me as a threat to social harmony. Without a millisecond's consideration for my enormous size, it's engaged me—the enemy—in a life-or-death battle, using its witch's brew of chemical warfare. The insect has unsheathed its raspy, spearlike stinger, punctured my flesh, and engaged more than twenty muscles to pump the toxic venom deep into the wound. The attack was a complete surprise. I hadn't a clue it was coming, not so much as a buzz. This was my body's Pearl Harbor.

I hit back, my bare hand mashing the bug in my sock. Now I'm feeling the first scalding pain. More guards join the attack. One flies in and stabs my right shoulder. "Arrrrrggghhhh!" I yell, lurching back on impact. Others freely sting naked parts of my body at will, forcing me into the wild gyrations of the dumb-jerk-under-killer-bee-attack dance. "Whaaaaaaa!" I scream in sheer panic and begin running, swatting, trying not to drop my camera. Part of the swarm emerges from underneath the bridge and begins pursuing me down the Transpantaneira.

I fly down the road, running for dear life, eyes wide with fear and arms pumping wildly. Quarts of adrenalin pour into my blood, kicking in a biological afterburner that lets me cover several kilometers at lightning speed. Halfway back to the *posto* I stop, daring to glance over my shoulder to see if they're still coming.

Gone. Bloody hell. I'm pouring sweat, my heart tearing loose from its moorings, and I can't catch my breath. I've lost my voice from wailing. Four of the buggers are smashed in my socks. I peel back one sock and see the stinger and bulbous poison sac stuck in my skin. The little bulb of poison seems to have a life of its own, twitching in muscular spasms (and probably forcing more venom in). I yank it out and limp back.

The *posto* is dark and abandoned except for the yellow hound dog and pesky cat. I sit down and assess the damage. There are at least nine rapidly swelling welts on my ankles, thighs, arms, back, neck, and forehead. I manage to keep my senses long enough to scrape out some of the stingers and lie on ice before the shock of the attack sinks in.

I use all the ice from the fridge trying to reduce the swelling. The ice seems to sizzle away in minutes, leaving me in a wet bed. I use an olive jar, hot-sauce bottle, condensed-milk tin, and beer cans—anything that's cool—to relieve the pain.

I'm afraid that I'm sliding deeper into shock and struggle to keep alert. I raid the fridge again, drinking all the cold water, old coffee, and a bottle of thick, sweet maracuja juice. I crawl into bed and put up my legs. Then I toss on blankets and feel huge, labored heartbeats rock my body back and forth.

The blistering pain throbs, producing a fierce, localized heat. After several hours the bites swell to puffy lumps as big as half oranges. The cool dusk isn't much help either. A fever sets in, and I shake, alternatively sweating and shivering. Staring into the dark, I replay the attack over and over in my mind. What an unsuspecting schnook I was. I had stood there, virtually naked, curiously watching the first little furry bee crawl around on my sock. It was so harmless looking, less threatening than a horsefly. Then it stuck me with a stinger the size of a turkey baster.

Visualizing myself fleeing down the road with a swarm of bees in angry pursuit seems like a strip from the Sunday funnies if it hadn't been so painful. Were they the much feared African killer bees? What did I do to provoke those little demon biters from hell?

After nodding off for an hour or two I'm awakened by the noise of a VW pulling up at the *posto*. A heavyset man walks into the dark cabin and asks in Portuguese with a thick German accent if anyone's home.

Werner is his name. He's a veterinarian on vacation from Santa Catarina in southern Brazil, and he's helping another vet make the rounds of *fazendas* treating sick animals. I tell him about the attack. "Got anything for me?" I beg.

"*Nein,*" he says. "There's nothing I can do for you. The stings must take their course. You are lucky that you are not allergic." The bee venom contains foreign proteins, peptides, enzymes, and amines to which some sensitive people react violently, at times causing a fatal allergic response. "You could have gone into anaphalactic shock," he adds. "Out here its the end. Kaput!" He sucks in air sharply, making a disturbing noise. This is luck?

Werner examines one of the mashed insects in my sock. "Europa honeybee [*Apis mellifera europa*]," he says. "Not killers?" I complain. He explains these are worse. African killer bees may have interbred with them, combining the honeybees' very protective nature with the aggressiveness of the killers; if disturbed by noise or motion, the whole swarm, numbering in the thousands, attacks. Each year three to four hundred people die from bee bites in Brazil, more than from any poisonous animal, including snakes. In 1971 one researcher found that the Pantanal contained an average of 107.5 bee nests per square kilometer. I just happened to be standing over one of them.

"If one of them is killed," Werner explains, "an alarm odor is liberated [a pheromone, isopentyl acetate 2-heptanone] that provokes the entire swarm. The unlucky animal that has raised their ire is incessantly attacked. Cows, capybaras, people, even jaguars have been stung to death. You had only nine."

That's plenty for me. Four days pass before the swelling goes down. The pain eases and is replaced by a tormenting itch that makes mosquito bites seem like minor tickles. Six more days pass before I'm completely mobile again. I learn later that the staff at the forestry headquarters in Cuiabá had heard about my experience and had a good laugh. That bridge was famous for its bees.

Three days later the swelling goes down enough for me to undertake a shakedown jog south on the Transpantaneira. Firmo's hound dog sees me leave and tags along. With the sun heading down, I think he'll be good company. As I try to tune in to the dusk, the dog reveals its favorite pastime: scaring the daylights out of the wildlife.

Down the road I see two house-cat-size animals climb the embankment and stand in the road for a moment. They're black and really do resemble house cats with bobbed tails. The dog bolts for them despite my yelling. All three tumble down into the field barking and screaming. Then suddenly the cats realize they outnumber the dog and turn the tables on it. The dog yowls, taking refuge by jumping into a pond further down the road.

I reach the pond as the cats disappear into a patch of forest, leaving us panting by a bridge. Damn! I'm standing near the same spot where I was attacked by the bees. Before I can grab the dog and retreat, a low hum fills the air. Ten meters in front of us the entire swarm appears. I'm so frightened I just freeze there, not budging a muscle as they buzz by. Gaspar tells me later that staying still probably saved my life.

Tracking the Great Waders

Each morning I have a chance to range further from the *posto* tracking the great wading birds on their fishing trips. But standing marsh and gallery forest prevent my following them back to their hidden breeding colony deep in the forest. I really want to study one of those colonies, but I'll wait for Gaspar's return.

Why do they select a particular hole to fish? From seeing another bird make a catch? And why do they leave? They never really clean out a pond. I'm curious to find out.

Making my way across the field proves a curious experience. From the road these fields are an idyllic apparition—washed green with thick grasses and flat, no problem for trekking. However, when I get out there, the wilted grass is thin and widely spaced. The ground isn't earth. It's clay baked to concrete by the sun and pocked with ten-centimeter-deep hoofprints everywhere. I simply can't navigate without stumbling.

Then there are the makers of those holes: the cattle. Again, from the road, they create a pastoral scene—clusters of big, bleached grazers dotting the horizon.

I walk very cautiously past a small herd of the long-horned bovines. They're supposed to flee at my presence, I'm told. But these animals are practically wild and thoroughly unpredictable. At times they've been known to charge, unprovoked, at an unhorsed man, Pamplona style. And I'm not eager to play toreador, risking my blue bag of precious cameras. I holler a few "hyaahhs" while they stare intently at this two-legged critter trespassing through their salad bowl. When I turn away, one charges to the front of the herd, then halts, alert and with its head up. What does that mean?

I navigate that field safely and approach a drying pool completely choked with *aguapé*. Although it's been virtually abandoned by the great wading birds, fish are rising to the surface. Working the edge is an adult wattled jacana (*Jacana jacana*), a compact, brown-and-black gallinule. Locals call it *cafezinho* (little coffee) for its richly burnished color.

As I grow closer the bird becomes more voiciferous, hopping into the air several feet and spreading its brown-and-yellow wings to reveal beautiful, translucent feathers illuminated by the sunlight. I get closer still, and the little wader scoots across the water's surface effortlessly, lightly touching the broad leaves of floating plants. The bird's thin, extremely long toes and toenails, like snowshoes, spread its weight efficiently so that even the thinnest lily pad barely dips with each foot strike.

Trailing a meter behind the bird are three of the smallest chicks I've ever seen. They can't be more than a couple of days old. Each is less than six centimeters long and is having a hard time climbing across those undulating plants — like babies walking on waterbeds. They peck weakly at the muck, keeping an eye on mother. I look around and make sure there are no predatory birds in the area, then approach.

When I'm within about seven meters the mother bursts into frantic behavior: jumping up and down, splaying her wings, and shrieking at the top of her tiny lungs. Her ruse works. I turn back to see the chicks, but they're gone.

The little sneaks are hiding. When I'm within about two meters I search the area where I last saw them. But they've vanished. A meter away. Finally I find one of the little stinkers beneath a round leaf. Absolutely still. Not even the body moves from breathing. The chick's down has orange and black stripes that paint it perfectly into the foliage.

Even closer. My big head looms nearer to its orange head, and I see a tiny, black eye that suddenly shuts tight as if I'm something from its worst dream. I hunt some more and find another. This chick has wiggled itself halfway up to its back in mud. All the while the mother keeps up her screaming some distance away, endeavoring to lure me away. The chicks don't so much as shiver while I'm near. Although I look around very carefully, the third little bird has disappeared completely.

Realizing their stress, I back off ten meters and sit down. The mother lands on the far side of the pool. Instead of making a beeline to her chicks, she nonchalantly works her way around, bobbing as if eating, making sure I don't move. It's a grand deception, and I'm thoroughly enjoying her performance. Now no longer screaming or flapping her wings, she gradually works her way to their hiding spot and pokes around.

She then murmurs a soft "all clear" tone. Within seconds two of the chicks pop up from the plants and begin following her. The other one is a mudball, two legs, and a beak. Encumbered by the mud, it stumbles along, meters behind. This makes it an easy target for a caracara. The mother turns back to the struggling chick and gives it a peck of encouragement. Then they reform their little avian safari with mudball at the end and disappear among the taller plants for an evening's shelter.

The air is cooling rapidly as the sun dips into the smoky atmosphere. A couple of large *jacarés* haul themselves out of the muddy pool and slowly make their way through the grass toward the line of white birds a thousand feet away.

It's an exhausting exercise. They don't crawl belly down. Instead, they hoist up on all fours and take a dozen or so steps until they can't haul their weight anymore, then plop down to rest. Ten more are up ahead, staggered in a dark, dotted line across the field. Several are dusted red, sporting odd hats of twigs and dry grass from their overland route.

Gaspar said that during the dry season *jacarés* can burrow in the mud and survive for several weeks before searching for water. Those overland treks to find new water holes can take days without food or water. This time those birds are a welcome sign: food and water ahead.

That day I daydream that I've made a wonderfully impossible time-lapse film covering the entire Pantanal. It's shot from a hot-air balloon in a wacky, hyper style reminiscent of Richard Lester's Beatles' film *A Hard Day's Night*. I float above the Pantanal for months, covering flood and drought periods. I shoot sky-crowding thunderheads, lightning shows, torrential rains, flooding, and the land filling up like a shallow bathtub. One day hundreds of white birds feed at a pond, then jump to another and another. A crazy photographer zigzags to each site shooting them. Click.

Then the skies clear and the sun is baking the land dry. Click. Animals trudging off. The flapping and crawling of wading birds, capybaras, and *jacarés* huddling in water holes. Click. The white train of cattle speeding across pastures, stopping, speeding, stopping. Click.

Fish trapped. Water receding. Lush water plants losing color, withering flat. A weak cow falls over. Shriveling. Black vultures flocking in to pick on the dead. Click. The hide shrinking like a bad suit, white bones poking through. Click. Fields turning clay brown. Cracking. Zooming in to a dead, white crab. Click.

five

Expedition to a Controversial National Park

The Pantanal National Park is a national park of *nada*.
— *Mato Grosso do Sul official*

I know what's there. Jaguar, antbear, river otter,
fish . . . . They don't know what they've got.
Zelito Dorileo, Pantanal rancher

Gaspar calls me one morning on the radio from Cuiabá with news that Firmo has survived his heart attack and is resting in his home in Poconé. He also says Paulo is eager to talk to me about making good his offer to go to the national park a hundred miles southwest of the *posto*. He'll get the vehicles if I pay for food and gas. And I throw in a bottle of Scotch. Deal.

On Friday morning Paulo and Gaspar pull up to the *posto* in a big, offroad vehicle pulling an aluminum runabout. Paulo has more news for me. Lúcia, my fiancée, is in Brasília and will meet us in Poconé when we return. Before dawn the next morning we're on the Transpantaneira heading south to Porto Joffre, where the road ends at the Cuiabá River.

To get to Porto Joffre we navigate another eighteen weak bridges and endure two hours of dusty, rutted road before it cuts through the river's narrow gallery forest and enters a clearing. There, several ranch-style buildings are set back from the road. The larger is a "sportsman's" lodge called the Hotel Santa Rosa, where wealthy Paulistas and gringos used to stay to hunt jaguar and marsh deer in the 1960s. But today it's just there to snag the odd well-heeled tourist. The others comprise a private home, guard shack, and gas station close to the river. While Gaspar and Paulo gas up, I walk along the riverfront to figure out if I really want to go to a national park that is in the heart of *coreiro* (skin hunter) country. Caracaras perch on a nearby bush. Pickup trucks park next to a line of cabin tents. It's hard to believe that this road falling into the river is dignified with the name "Porto." Ports have steamboats, bustling wharves, and stevedores clamoring over vessels. This *porto* is a sleepy backwater where fishermen, adventurers, skin hunters, and naive tourists board craft to points unknown deep in the Pantanal.

Seventy years ago the Cuiabá River represented the major link between the Pantanal's isolated cattle ranches and the civilized world. River steamers took out the cattle and brought in hardware and finished goods. To administer this booming trade the Ministry of Agriculture had established a district office out here. It serviced surrounding ranches, especially Fazenda Joffre, which owns the waterfront.

In the 1930s brave men with wonderful names, such as Lieutenant Casemiro Montenegro and Lieutenant Nelson Wanderly, hopped into fabric-covered biplanes in Porto Alegre and São Paulo and flew into this vast sea of green without the aid of radio beacons or navigable land features. I recall a visit to Brazil's surprisingly large air and space museum, located outside Rio de Janeiro. There many historic photographs document those early days of air service. The first air-mail pilots were a dashing crew indeed, sporting leather helmets and goggles, flight jackets, those jaunty, long, white scarves, pistols, riding breeches, and tall boots. They laughed at the dangers of getting lost or running out of gas over Mato Grosso.

They did so at about the same time that French pilots with a similar esprit de corps blazed air-mail routes over the immense North African desert. Antoine de Saint-Exupéry was the pilot-writer who so beautifully captured that spirit of flying in his famous book *Wind, Sand and Stars*. Saint-Exupéry also helped commercial airlines begin in South America.

Pontoon-rigged, open-cockpit planes such as Waccos and Curtisses, landed in the Cuiabá River at Porto Joffre, linking

these hinterlands to the populous coastal cities. Porto Joffre
has changed little. In fact, I think it's declined since then.

In 1983 numerous exposés appeared in mainstream
newspapers such as *Estado do São Paulo* and in *Veja* magazine,
showing tons of rotting caimans stripped of their skins in the
Pantanal. Eventually the outcry forced the federal government
to do something. Then-President João Figueiredo ordered the
military in to stop the slaughter.

When the army arrived in Porto Joffre, the papers played up
the effort, making it sound pretty successful. But here in the
bewildering, featureless terrain, the heavily armed patrols were
literally lost. It was something akin to sending Chicago cops to
Louisiana bayous to control moonshine. From their base at
Porto Joffre, soldiers would board runabouts with automatic
weapons and patrol the waterways in a futile effort to find the
hunters.

Gaspar jars me out of my thoughts to load the seven-meter-
long aluminum boat. It's equipped with a thirty-five-horse-
power Yamaha outboard and a smaller spare. I watch with
alarm at the amount of equipment being loaded on board such
a narrow, shallow-draft boat. To the outboards are added two
gasoline drums (Gaspar says gas is more important than food).

I've popped for plenty of food too: six cartons stuffed with
ten kilos of rice, a bag of oranges, three kilos of flour, a bag of
limes, onions, carrots, three dozen eggs, three tins of corned
beef, a dozen boxes of saltines, three dozen boxes of cookies,
eight baked cakes, one kilo of sugar, two kilos of coffee, four
thawing chickens, two kilos of black beans, pasta, three tins of
sardines, one cabbage, several heads of garlic, two cans of heart
of palm, three cans of condensed milk, a kilo of chocolate
candy, another of hard candy, packaged soups, ten candles,
flashlight batteries, a case each of toilet paper, paper towels,
mineral water, bottles of passion fruit, maracuja, and pineapple
juices, two bottles of *cachaça,* one bottle of Scotch, five cartons
of Hollywood cigarettes, and matches.

The rest of the gear includes paddles, hammocks, two heavy-
duty car batteries, a cooking-gas cylinder, pistols and rifles,
machetes, bags of clothes, and five passengers—Paulo, his personal secretary, Madeline, who will cook; Gaspar, Beijamim,
Gaspar's national park assistant, and a slightly spooked gringo.

When we are ready to shove off, I look at the mere thirteen centimeters of freeboard and ask Gaspar if this is a problem. "Nu-uh," he says.

I'm excited by this trip to the heart of the Pantanal, but I've also listened a lot to Gaspar. He points downriver. Weeks ago a Pantaneiro he knew was guiding fishermen from São Paulo when a wasp bit him. He stood up to defend himself, and a feeble swat sent him tumbling into the river. He screamed he couldn't swim as the current pulled him away from the boat. One of the fishermen jumped in. He reached the guide as their struggling attracted piranhas. But before the other fisherman in the boat could reach them, they slipped beneath the roiling, pink water. I feel sick to my stomach. Gaspar adds, however, that locals regard piranhas as a fact of life.

Pantaneiros, he notes, are more terrified of another river denizen. He grabs a stick and scratches a large oval with a long, thin tail in the wet sand. "*Raia*," he says. These are fresh-water stingray (*Potamotrygon brachyurus*). They grow up to half a meter in diameter and weigh nearly twenty-two kilos. Gaspar points near the base of the tail. The ray has a cigarette-size spine that makes them feared.

Raia use their oval "wings" to swim over sandflats, stirring up worms, snails, and small fish. Unfortunately, many fisher-men and bathers work these shallows, too, making for close encounters of the painful kind. When stepped on, the ray whips its tail, with the barb puncturing the victim's skin and injecting a dose of venom that probably won't kill you, Gaspar theo-rizes, but will cause you to hobble around for a month.

After hearing this, I board the craft nervously, staring into the murk and straining to see my potential attackers. Any un-expected movement in the boat makes me bark, "Step center, will ya!" or "Use both hands and stay low, damn it!" as I grimace and grip the gunwales.

At 7:30 A.M. we push the boat into the current and start the engine. My nervous sweat dries quickly from the blast of hot wind as Gaspar opens the throttle. The muddy river ripples from a head wind blowing against the current, creating a bottom-buzzing ride, as if zooming down an endless wash-board.

Small islands of floating vegetation—mostly water hyacinth

and driftwood—carried along on the chocolate current indicate the river is flowing west at a good clip. Gaspar, in mirrored sunglasses and straw Stetson (which never seems in jeopardy of blowing away), cranes his neck to port and starboard looking for other flotsam. Somehow he manages to light a cigarette and puff merrily away in the face of a twenty-knot wind.

Between the whistle of the wind and the whine of the outboard a noise barrier descends, cutting us off from each other. Except for pointing to a caiman wriggling down the bank or a capybara taking cover in the forest, we're limited to smiles, mouthing words, and pantomime.

The day is sunny, and soon it will be blisteringly hot. I am captive now of my decision, and I decide to relax and go with the flow. I hunker down between a couple of duffle bags and settle in for the ride. Unpacking my old aviation map of the region, I spread it on the bottom of the boat and try to estimate the distance to the park. We're on the São Lourenço River (the downriver name of the Cuiabá), a thin, blue line wiggling southwest from Porto Joffre to Porto Caracara near Bolivia. The river is also the boundary between Mato Grosso and Mato Grosso do Sul.

On the map the distance between those two ports measures about ten centimeters, give or take a few wiggles. That translates to about 130 kilometers. If we average forty kilometers per hour, we'll be there for lunch. Not bad, I think, at least on paper. Looking up, though, it is all intimidating wilderness.

At 17°20′ south latitude, 56°47′ west longitude, the river meanders four hundred kilometers from its source in the Serra Azul (Blue Ridge Mountains) on the western slope of a plateau. It's the major tributary of the Paraguay River system, receiving the discharge of no fewer than ten lesser rivers and seasonal streams, including the Manso, Casca, Coxipo do Ouro, Riberio Cocau, Piraim, Bento Gomes, Novo, Claro, São Laurenço, and Piquiri rivers.

In the Pantanal, those rivers are considered thoroughfares rather than feeding places for many fish. There are few backwaters, shallows, or islands providing habitat and graze for these plant eaters. Some fish, like *pacú,* actually don't feed in the rivers. Rather, they await the flood season, when rain and runoff fill the rivers until they overspill their banks and inundate the surrounding lowlands.

At that time the fish invade the floodlands in search of their favored food—fruit and seeds. Through some as yet to be described clues, they work their way through the inundated fields to bushes ripe with small, meaty globes of fruit. Wind and the drying effect of the sun release the fruit, which plops into the water. The fish gorge themselves, building up substantial fat deposits.

Through a matrix of subtle environmental indicators— perhaps length of sunlight, depth of water, and increasing water temperature—the fish sense the receding waters, and most migrate back into the streams to swim the waterways and head to spawning grounds.

I close my eyes, tilting back my head and catching the strong sun, and imagine underwater fish traffic resembling that of Los Angeles freeways. Then, suddenly, the gunwales dip dangerously and swing back again. Like a small plane caught in a severe crosswind, our overloaded craft has rocked violently. Everyone sits bolt upright with eyes fixed on Gaspar as he uses both arms, strugging to hold our course.

I lift my head as high as I dare to get a better angle on the water. At first I don't see anything unusual, until we gain distance. Apparently we're passing through the rim of a great, swirling current. It's a whirlpool more than a hundred meters in diameter.

I remember Lúcia's tale of her older brother's drowning at nineteen. He loved the water. He and some friends were partying in a river not far from Brasília when he accidently swam into one of those spiraling currents and was quickly pulled under. Her story, told in faraway Chicago, lacked reality for me at the time. But here, now, I was a true believer.

Not long after we cut through the vortex the outboard sputters and dies. Gaspar yanks the starter cord over and over, adjusting the mixture, squirting in more gas, without luck. In a sweat, he pulls off the housing as we drift downstream, jostling hoses and blowing them out. Nothing works; he and Beijamim very carefully unship the motor and set about installing the spare fifteen-horse outboard.

77

It's 9:53 A.M. We've spent more than two and a half hours in the boat. As Gaspar and Beijamim work, I look more closely at the near shore. At first, spotty, yellow-green foliage seems a North American autumn. Red and yellow colors look like dying leaves. Through the binoculars, though, they're flowers as red as poinsettias, blossoms of *ipê* trees.

The jungle presses close to the water's edge with few beaches. There are *buriti* palm (*Mauritia vinifera*), tall *barriguda* trees with gray trunks (*Bombacaceae* species), balsamum trees (*Myroxylon* species), *paratudo (Tecoma aurea)*, woody vines (lianas), dense *tucune açu* bushes (*Bactris inundata*), and many kinds of grasses on the bank. They weave together straight up from the bank in an impenetrable tangle that I notice even capybaras have trouble hopping through.

The Curandeira

Twenty minutes later the other motor is in place. A couple tugs of the starter cord and we're under way again, although at a reduced speed that registers frustration on Paulo's face. This chugging along will take forever. Half an hour later Gaspar spots a way out.

Around a bend in the river two brown huts appear, barely discernible from the dry thicket surrounding them. The sound of our motor brings out the inhabitants: three kids, a young woman, a middle-aged, caramel-skinned man, and a wrinkled, truly ancient-looking black lady with canary-yellow hair. They welcome us with more curiosity than affection, looking us over with a great interest that immediately makes me feel peculiar. Paulo wanders off as Gaspar shakes their hands vigorously and begins telling them of our engine trouble.

The young woman carries out a tray of demitasse cups, a bowl of sugar, and a thermos. She offers us *cafezinhos* and listens intently to Gaspar.

After the coffee, Paulo urges me to photograph something he's discovered. Behind the main house in a recently cleared field sits a large spectacled owl (*Pulsatrix perspicillata*). Up, down, left, and right the bird's head and great eyes circle, mesmerized by its reflection in my lens. The closer I get, the greater the head movement, until at a meter away the owl leaps right for the lens. "Yikes!" I shout, startled by its mock attack.

Paulo laughs. "This is an unusual pet," he says. "Maybe the old woman is a *curandeira.*" A Brazilian witch doctor. So, while Gaspar and Beijamim haul up the troublesome main outboard and begin taking it apart, Paulo and I pursue the old woman.

Paulo explains that it isn't unusual to find folk healers in Mato Grosso's backlands. Because the nearest medical help is several hundred kilometers away, people rely on healers for aches and maladies.

The rural people throughout the Pantanal live in very simple habitations, making use of local materials with good effect to create a self-sufficient, if not isolated way of life. The pole-and-palm-leaf shacks and cleared jungle pasture prompt Paulo to call these people *invasores,* illegal squatters. He guesses they've come from Salvador, on Brazil's northeast coast, a region known for its folkways. It's been ravaged by drought for years, forcing thousands of Bahianos to seek work in the interior or in São Paulo or Rio.

These squatters can't be removed easily, Paulo says. There's a long-standing legal precedent concerning wild lands—"unimproved," according to the government. Even if such land is privately owned, landless people desperate for a chance can live on it—that is, if they "improve" the land, meaning torch, chop, and clear a tiny farm. Then it's theirs to keep.

The only legal way the owner can oust the squatters is to buy back his own land at an increased value. That's the legal way, which is seldom used. More typical is to hire *pistoleiros*—thugs—who hunt squatters, often shooting the head man. Paulo says everyone else is so terrified that they clear out. This horrible way to control the country's homelessness problem will probably continue until the government faces up to land reform, perhaps the most explosive issue in Brazil.

The old woman finally has relented to our requests and invites us inside her hut. It's a marvel of local materials excellent at fending off torrential rains and keeping the inhabitants remarkably cool under a tropical sun. The off-center roof and sides are made of dry palm fronds tied to a pole frame. Inside, a mud wall separates the cooking area from the larger, all-purpose living space. The far end is occupied by festive decorations and a religious shrine.

Hanging from the wall are religious artworks depicting various Christian saints. One is a large, gilt-framed painting of Nossa Senhora das Dores (Our Lady of Pain). The table holds a crowd of statuary centered around a wooden shrine. Inside are two glazed figures of Cosme and Damião, described by the woman as high-ranking saints in Macumba, Brazilian voodoo. To the right is an ivory-colored statue of Saint George in armor, waving a sword and astride a stallion. He's a saint central to Xango, another sect of Macumba found along the coast.

In this room the lady serves meals, sews and performs healings. She shares some typical nostrums. For stomachache and worms, take grated manioc (cassava root, *Manihot* species) soaked in water. For earache and infection, prepare the fat of the ray; then mix in honey and place in the ear. For impotence, cook a *caldo de piranha,* a special piranha soup, to return lost ardor. As a general tonic, make tea from the *ipê* tree. As she is describing more remedies, we hear our outboard come to life.

Later, back home, I'll show slides of the old woman's shrine to friends. The statues of Cosme and Damião will quickly confirm Macumba practice. Macumba is described as a mix of African and Catholic rituals dating back more than 350 years. It developed in Brazil when Bantu, Yoruba, and Dahoman natives were captured for slaves from Angola, Cape Verde, Guinea, Nigeria, the Congo, and Mozambique.

In his classic study of blacks in Brazil, *The Masters and the Slaves,* sociologist Gilberto Freyre notes how the Africans brought with them their own rich cultural traditions. Just as their dende oil, okra, hot pepper, and black beans enlivened bland Portuguese cooking, the use of African dance, music, and colorful dress embellished Roman Catholicism. Certain obscure saints and even the ritualistic sacrifice of chickens added potency to prayer, much to the consternation of early Jesuit priests ministering to the colonies.

Although there are forms of Brazilian voodoo used to hex victims, that woman practiced good voodoo, used extensively today to improve farms, fertility, and the health of the supplicant. Song and dance often accompany these ceremonies, making them mysterious and impressive occasions.

Back in our boat again, the hours pass unremarkably until, without warning, a little catfish leaps from the river onto Paulo's chest, nearly startling him out of the boat.

The fierce sun beating down on us is made deceptively tolerable by the wind in our faces. What I haven't realized, though, is that shiny aluminum boat has become a solar grill, and we're the meat. Eyelids, lips, nose tips, and tops of the hands have been thoroughly fried, despite copious applications of sunblock 15.

It isn't only my skin that's burned. Paulo and Madeline have seldom ventured from their air-conditioned offices and are rapidly developing a whopping case of tourist burn, worse than mine. Gaspar and Beijamim, already deeply tanned from working outdoors, are amused as I tear through my gear bag. I slide an oversize long-sleeve shirt on my head, leaving a couple of buttons open in the middle so my sunglasses and nose can stick out.

We stop once more beside a river streamer that's cruising upstream to Cáceres, a town at the northern end of the Paraguay River's navigable waters. The fifteen-meter wooden boat is something of a floating general store, selling and sometimes trading for the odd bit that locals might need. Rope, candles, canned goods, *cachaça,* beer, some hardware, diesel fuel, and *ice.* I buy ice cubes for everyone to slurp. As we're casting off, the captain offers us a beautiful big *dorado (Salminus maxillosus).* Seems last night it jumped on board. He figures that at 3.6 kilos it's a baby and should taste pretty good. Leaping *dorado!* Gaspar sees me brighten in anticipation and assures me there are bigger ones ahead.

Pantanal National Park

The sun is low on the horizon when we slide onto the bank at Pantanal National Park. And so are we. It's been ten hours since leaving Porto Joffre. We're quite a sight. We're sunburned, and cruising along at forty kilometers an hour for such a long time has deposited an interesting variety of flying insects in our hair.

Paulo is curious to inspect the recently completed outpost.

There are two wooden lodges with toilets, showers, gas fridge, bunks, electrical generator, and beds.

An old caretaker guards the facilities while Gaspar and Beijamim are away. When he hears us coming he grabs his rusty rifle and puts on an old police cap to greet us. He says the outpost has been used by a patrol. The new bunkhouse is littered with cigarette butts, and some names have been scratched in the wood by those errant Kilroys.

No matter, I lie down in my clothes and sleep deeply until morning. There isn't a raucous bird reveille as there was at the *posto.* Only the roosters. And one hungry pet jabiru that has the disturbing habit of clacking its bill loudly until the caretaker tosses it a fish.

The outpost is a few kilometers southeast from Lake Gaiva, an enormous lagoon hemmed in by tall reeds and framed by a low range of hills to the west. It resembles a scaled-down Lake Titicaca.

After morning coffee, Gaspar, Paulo, and I take a boat ride to see the national park. Leaving the lake, we join the main stream of the Paraguay River, the major north-south watercourse in the Pantanal. It extends 2100 kilometers from its source in the northern highlands to Corrientes, Argentina. There the Paraná and Paraguay rivers form a great confluence in the marshlands of the Argentine Mesopotamia. At approximately 4000 kilometers long, the Paraná-Paraguay river system is second only to the great Amazon on this continent.

The Paraná-Paraguay river system drains the entire heartland of South America, including Brazil's central highlands and the Gran Chaco, located in Bolivia, Paraguay, and Argentina. Its enormous discharge of water flows slowly southeast past Buenos Aires into the South Atlantic Ocean.

The border between Brazil and Bolivia cuts right down the center of Lake Gaiva. It's part of an ancient frontier established in 1494 by Pope Alexander VI when he divided the non-Christian world with the Treaty of Tordesillas. In this treaty, claims between the Spanish and Portuguese were supposedly settled forever. It cut the South American continent down the middle some 370 leagues west of the Cape Verde Islands. This was done in Rome when geographic information about the region was scanty. Had officers and bureaucrats actually seen what Portugal was being awarded, they probably would have welcomed a jog in the line.

Bolivia, nearly eight times smaller than Brazil, is resource poor, except in tin, silver, and coca leaf. It clings desperately to this open border, allowing Bolivians to steal across seeking their fortune in the forests and cities of Brazil.

But the border connects two very troubled countries. In a kind of geopolitical osmosis, products and people pass from the area of greater concentration across to the lesser. And, surprisingly, Brazil depends on the Bolivian market as an outlet for forest and agricultural products, stolen cars, machinery, and smuggled gold. Most of those materials enter Bolivia near Corumbá.

Without roads nearby, this frontier is a perfect environment in which the *contrabandistas* operate. "They have fast boats, automatic weapons, radios, and airplanes," Gaspar says. He then points to all of the little O symbols on my aviation map. They are airstrips—more than a hundred just in the northwest sector of the Pantanal, making interdiction virtually impossible.

The Pantanal National Park was converted from the smaller, former Caracara Biological Reserve in September 1981. Officially it contains nearly 200,000 hectares. The park was created by Dr. Maria Tereza Jorge Pádua, then the national parks director and now head of Funatura, a new private conservation group in Brasília. Incredibly, this park and the much smaller (25,000 acres), state-owned Taiama Ecological Station in the north are the only "officially" protected areas in the entire Brazilian sector of the Pantanal. With 90 million hectares of Brazil designated for federal protection, it's an ambitious effort. With only eight hundred to a thousand men, it's a *piada*—joke—Gaspar says.

In 1975 biologists developed an initial plan for this flooded national park land lying less than a hundred meters above sea level: use it as a reservoir that would become critical habitat for wildlife during low-water cycles. High-water cycles usually last ten years. The idea was that animals would gradually concentrate here, something like what they do along the Transpantaneira during the dry season. Yet when the ten-year high-water cycle ended in the mid-1980s, the rains did not taper off as predicted.

One of the stories circulating about this controversial national park was told to me by several high-ranking officials in the region. They believe the landowner was unable to sell his land privately because it was always flooded. He had lost twenty thousand head of cattle since buying the property and was unable to sell it at his price.

Pantanal land usually passes down through the ranch-owning families; as a result, there are few opportunities for outsiders to buy in. When this landowner couldn't get an offer, he unloaded it on the government. And they gladly accepted.

Although this national park doesn't protect key watersheds nor major concentrations of endangered species, there was an advantage for a federal presence. In theory, a new national park would bring enforcement to an area racked by illegal hunting and drug trafficking. In reality, what difference would a few men and two motorboats make?

The park's scenery is pleasant enough, with luxuriant vegetation along the river banks, the wide expanse of the lake, and the isolated hills on the Bolivian frontier. Yet we see few birds and virtually no mammals. To designate this place a national park where visitors can go to know the "Pantanal" seems a mistake, especially after driving the Transpantaneira. Who would want to take such a dreadful, perilous journey here? In fairness, Gaspar defends the park, saying there's the right mix of habitats to support much animal life. The animals are here, he contends; you just have to out go there and find them.

Last of the Guató

While Paulo goes with Beijamim to another area, Gaspar and I take the next leg of our national park journey across the lagoon. We cruise through mirror-still waters without seeing one animal. Gaspar shrugs off my questions about the wildlife. Yet he still packs a pistol.

Closing in on the far shore, I can see a lip of land formed by the eastern slope of the hills of the Serra Amolar. The terrain is covered with thick forest down to the water. Gaspar slows, searching for a break in the dense vegetation. We beach the boat abeam of a swamped dugout canoe and follow a narrow trail through the grasses into a small hole in the wall of brush.

The forest is dim, without much dappling, making the going difficult. In the darkness mosquitoes are on us with a vengeance. After a few minutes we step into a clearing that reveals an ancient scene.

A pillar of smoke rises from a white-ash fire. The smoke licks at haunches of meat and a whole *pacú* hanging from a horizontal pole. To the left of the fire is a palm-leaf shelter with a spear, machete, long bow, and arrow leaning up against it. There are a few animal skins — caiman and anaconda, I think — hanging near the weapons.

A primitive wooden table, made by tying long poles together and resting them on sawhorses, sits before the fire with several hollow gourds on it. Cups and bowls, perhaps. Aside from a kerosene lamp, knife, and machete, there isn't a modern implement to be seen. On the ground are discarded bones and gourds. Gaspar picks up a bone — a capybara femur. Flies buzz us and the place smells from rotted food.

Gaspar says, "Don't move." We turn quickly to our left and are startled by a man watching us from the edge of the forest.

"*Oi*, José," says Gaspar in a new, authoritative tone I haven't heard before. The man comes forward. He's considerably shorter than Gaspar — maybe five-feet-four — stocky, with reddish skin etched with lines. He has high cheek bones, a thick mustache, and curly, black hair cut in a bowl shape. He wears a dark-green workman's shirt and dirty, old jeans and walks barefoot. He smiles occasionally in deference to having an armed forestry officer in his camp. And when he does, he reveals yellow, decay-eaten teeth.

José and his brother, Newton, who's fishing, are in their thirties but look older. They live here alone. They're native Guató, the last of their tribe living off the land. All the other Pantanal tribes — the Bororo, Caduveo, and Terena — have long since disappeared. They've been assimilated or have retreated to government reservations. From the look of their camp, the two brothers didn't seem far from extinction themselves.

Gaspar says not to worry; the sorry place only looks dead. The brothers, he notes, are *preguiçosos* — lazy. They scratch a subsistence life that brings to mind my father's ancient axiom: "Enough is sufficient."

It's an ironic bit of luck for me too. I had wanted to visit a native tribe in the Pantanal, but the thicket of bureaucratic regulations confronting foreigners was complicated and time-consuming.

Later, upon returning to the United States, I would try to gather as much information as I could about the Guató but would be amazed to find that there is virtually no thorough study of them. Either researchers have never felt moved to conduct fieldwork in these inundated lowlands or, when they did, the tribe had assimilated into the subculture of cowboys or had died away.

Although the Spanish explorer Alvar Nuñez Cabeza de Vaca made contact with them in the 1500s, the Guató have since been confused with the cannabalistic Guachi and warlike Guarani natives. One of the few scientists to actually attempt fieldwork among the Guató was anthropologist Max Schmidt in 1905. Even at that time he found less than fifty individuals living in this area, down from five hundred counted in 1848. During the late 1800s the Guató were caught between Brazil and Paraguay in the Paraguay wars and as a result suffered casualties from direct conflict as well as from European diseases.

The Guató had always made a living the way José and Newton now do: hunting, fishing, and gathering from the Pantanal's perpetual waters. Because their habitat was primarily water and the annual rains flooded them from their palm-frond houses, the Guató lived much of the year in dugout canoes. This observation led another researcher, Alfred Métraux, to suggest that this canoe-dominated lifestyle actually changed their bodies, resulting in powerful chest muscles and atrophied legs.

No one found evidence of ornamentation or religion, nor much cultural achievement beyond stone axes, unlike the comparatively sophisticated Bororos, the other northern Pantanal tribe to the east. The Guató did fashion many useful items, such as woven baskets, mats, and ropes. And they made a first-rate fly swatter. In fact, aside from boiling caiman tails and munching palm nuts, they seemed preoccupied with finding ways to relieve themselves from the dread marsh mosquito, thankfully one of the more than 1500 mosquito species found in Brazil that does not carry a disease. They created mosquito nets, swatters, and various kinds of smoke bombs made from slow-burning fibers to drive off those pests.

Although we're having a hard time seeing any living things aside from those flying jaws, the brothers do not. Gaspar notes the haunches of capybara being smoked and says, "Hey! This is a national park. You're not supposed to be hunting," pointing to the meat. Then he adds, "Where's the fat?" Rendered capybara fat is a delicacy used in cooking and a general tonic for what ails you.

José points to a gourd on the table full of the gray fat, which has congealed like bacon drippings. Gaspar pokes around in their kitchen midden and kicks out a *cachaça* bottle, fills it with the fat, and jams in a broken stick as a cork.

As we get ready to leave, José picks up his long bow and says he's going to meet his brother to shoot *pacú*. He bails out his swamped canoe, dumps in his gear, and shoves off. We follow around a bend to an area where reeds and squat shrubs rise from the water. There Newton poles into view.

José ties his canoe to a bush and steps into his brother's dugout, strings the bow, and notches a meter-and-a-half-long arrow. Then he edges onto the tiny deck and leans over, aiming into the water.

They glide in quiet water, pushing a slight bow wave that ripples the surface. Like an Eskimo poised with a harpoon at an ice hole, José keeps his vigil, the bow taut, the string pulled to his jaw, triceps straining. The waterlogged canoe has considerable momentum, moving within five meters of bushes with round fruits.

Despite the murkiness, a large head can be seen looming beneath the surface. At once José lets loose the arrow. There's a roiling of the water where the shaft sticks out, amplifying the fish's struggle. Newton quickly poles the boat forward as José kneels on the deck and picks up a heavy, wooden club. Holding the arrow shaft, he smacks down hard, splashing water and lifting the stunned oval fish on board. He holds up the large *pacú* and smiles, displaying his neglected teeth and ending the Gautó fishing lesson.

That evening, back at the national park outpost, we sit around a fire swatting clouds of mosquitoes and talk about the

Guató. Their isolated life has remained remarkably unchanged from that of their ancestors. Being lost in the national park is probably fortunate for them. Practically no one knows they exist. There's no Indian agency trying to "save" them on reservations, nor any zealous missionaries, as a friend says, "westernizing" their souls.

Settled in at the outpost, we sipped *cachaça,* which makes my sunburn heat up and quiets the other men. But soon it loosens Gaspar's thoughts, and they quickly spill out. Gaspar recounts the time he worked on the Cuiabá-Santarem road. "Those Guató brothers today live modern lives compared to what I saw on that road gang," he says. "Fifteen days before Orlando Villas Boas, the famous Brazilian anthropologist, arrived, we contacted the much feared Kreen-Akrore."

As Gaspar begins his story, far on the eastern horizon an enormous thunderhead approaches flashing forked lightning between its flat bottom and the waters of Lake Gaiva. That startlingly beautiful light is deceptively far away, maybe a hundred kilometers. The storm won't reach us tonight. Soon though, I muse, the rainstorms will be closer and more frequent, and before I know it, the place I'm sitting in will be three meters or more underwater.

Gaspar's story unfolds. The road crew had been told to expect Indians since the road cut through virgin forest. As a precaution, each day one worker would act as a scout and explore the area ahead.

One morning the lead man saw a colored shirt with animal patterns on it high up in a tree. When he climbed up to get it, Indians surrounded the tree. He slowly made his way down saying, "*Amigo . . . amigo . . . amigo.*" They gestured for him to throw down his gun. He pointed to their bows and arrows. Everyone put down their weapons; then they indicated to him that they were taking him on a long walk.

They walked and walked, through the forest and across rivers. All the construction worker could understand was that they had to walk over hills and more jungle. It took two days. When the chief indicated that they had arrived, they stepped onto the road right where he had found the shirt. The worker had been taken in a circle, and all the Indians had a knee-slapping laugh.

"They were shorter than me," says Gaspar, standing up to his five-foot-nine height, "but more muscled." He flexed his bicep. Gaspar is built like a halfback. We agree with an "Ooooh."

The chief's name was Ma Kree, and he was powerful. His shiny, black hair was bowl-cut with a bald spot, like a padre's. He had a palm-leaf design scarred on his chest. He, of course, knew no Portuguese, requiring everyone to communicate using pantomime.

They all went back to the construction camp, where the Kreen-Akrore began tossing things around until they found bananas hanging outside the food tent. Then all hell broke loose. They ransacked the food supplies, tearing open packages, tasting items, spitting them out, and throwing food on the ground. They especially disliked sugar, tomatoes, and farinha.

Gaspar said the Kreen-Akrore knew their jungle well and were superb hunters. The chief lay down on the ground and shot an arrow in the air, waited a few seconds, then rolled away as the shaft whistled down exactly where his head had been.

Ever the diplomat, Gaspar notices my envious gaze and adds, "You know, Vitor, people say there are many such Indians who have not yet seen a white man."

Those Golden Fish

Late the next day, Paulo, Gaspar, and I board the boat to try a fishing hotspot that's known to produce big *dorado,* the fighting fish I've been dreaming to catch. Those prized predators are considered by the few sportsmen who know them as *the* freshwater game fish of South America. They have been sought for more than four hundred years, ever since explorer Cabeza de Vaca discovered them in a Pantanal stream.

According to the International Game Fish Association, the all-tackle world-record *dorado* weighed 23.4 kilos and was caught in Argentina on September 27, 1984. However, Dr. Carlos Leite, a friend and well-traveled fisherman, says bulls weighing more than 30 kilos have been known. Before I left Brasília, Dr. Carlos gave me some tips on going after *dorado.*

He pulled from his closet surf rods and a Red Eye Wiggler, a twelve-centimeter chrome spoon with ruby-red eyes used to catch 300-kilo marlin.

When I showed him my backpacking rod, which fit into my telephoto lens case, and six-centimeter spoons, he said, "I don't think you want to catch *dorado.*" I had bigger rods—like an old, three-meter salmon rod back home—but this one was special. I had taken it with me whenever an assignment took me near good water: the Chilkat River or Outer Banks. When the day's work was over, I would steal away before sundown and wet a line. I didn't care if I caught anything. A little bit of quiet fishing put me in a sweet melancholy.

Besides, the rod was my late father's. When I rigged it, it brought to mind our rare outings to Green Lake, Wisconsin, in the 1950s. Dad, my brother, and I in a rowboat fishing for walleyes; then over to the Wonder Bar, a supper club, for huge T-bone steaks.

The *dorado* we're after are not to be confused with *Coryphaena hippurus,* the well-known ocean runners with the same common name. These golden fish fill an ecological niche similar to North American muskellunge: top fish predator. While *dorado* live in many of Brazil's streams, the big ones range throughout the Paraguay River system, at times leaping small cataracts on spawning runs. In those teeming waters they are adept at taking a wide range of prey: frogs, snakes, small mammals, water birds, and any of the several hundred species of fish found there.

Cuiabá's riverfront fish market had provided a chance to study *dorado* up close. They resemble stout, yellow salmon (a distant relative) with similarly shaped bodies but with strikingly different colors. Dark green shades to yellow along the belly, highlighted by orange-scarlet pectoral fins. A pale blue line runs laterally through the large eyes, cheeks, and powerful tail.

We motor downstream for half an hour, then follow a winding, weedy channel that opens into Lake Gaiva. For nine kilometers we slice through quiet waters to the other side. There two boats are anchored where a small outfall creates rapids as the lake drains into the Paraguay. They're the only other people we see all day.

"Any luck?" I shout. A man raises his left hand, shaking an

index finger. Must mean a *dorado;* piranha don't count. Not far from them we tie up to a sunken tree trunk and rig our gear.

"Vitor," Gaspar says, pointing off the stern to a shoal of bait fish called *lambaris.* Whap! Instantly one is halved. The oval fish is still alive, wiggling a pectoral fin, circling on its side. The others scatter among the reeds. In a blink it's gone. "Little *dorado,*" Gaspar mumbles, fixing his line.

From what I've learned about *dorado,* this seems a perfect place, with fast water and submerged rocks and logs. The outflow riffles along at five knots, bending long, green reeds downstream. The dying sun on the bay's still waters is framed by the distant Serra San Fernando. A classic South American wilderness scene.

I cast a spinner downstream, let it drift a moment, then reel in promptly, snagging reeds. The next lure brings up a large piranha, which Gaspar deftly handles in the busy boat. He cuts a palm-size chunk of flesh for Paulo's surf-casting rod and does the same for his laundry-line rig. It sports a hook whose J shape is big enough to hold a strip steak.

One of the treble hooks on my lure has been snapped off by the piranha. It was made from forged steel that had enormous tensile strength. As we fish, a procession of crazy-colored lures, including my mainstay Daredevle, are being gobbled as if fishy truffles. They are coming back wounded, displaying tooth impressions in the metal-hard plastic. I hold the sorry remains up, and Gaspar nods affirmatively, "Dorado . . . a junior."

Then I switch to a small Rapala Wobbler, a Finnish lure made from balsa that resembles a minnow. On retrieve the lure has a motion mimicking a swimming fish. I reel in the second cast swiftly against the current, bringing the lure closer to the surface. About sixteen meters behind the boat a dark dorsal fin cuts the water like the periscope of a submarine.

The fish catches the lure in a liquid explosion, tossing water in every direction. As the hook sets, the rod bends into an ill-advised C as the animal below uses its full weight and the current for defense. The line stretches taut, sending out an alarming, high-pitched *ahyeeng* that must sound like a creature in distress, because in the growing dusk several large bats swoop out of nowhere and buzz the singing line.

I have three-and-a-half-kilo test line on the reel—enough,

I think, to handle a good-size fish. Many anglers enjoy the challenge of catching big fish on light gear, and maybe I can, too, if I don't horse it in. But this thing is stripping line with abandon. If I don't halt its progress, it will simply pop the knot on the spool and be gone, trailing a couple hundred meters of monofilament behind it.

I have no choice. I tighten up on the drag, making the line harder to pull, while working the rod gingerly. The fish acts like a submarine, diving and maintaining considerable distance from me, demonstrating great brute force—so much strength that I'm wondering if it really is a fish.

Maybe it isn't. Fishermen in the region often hook into hungry caimans. Like unwanted sharks they smash up the tackle. The only way out is to cut the line.

"You sure this isn't a *jacaré?*" I grunt to Gaspar, who's jigging in his laundry line. "It's a nice *dorado,*" he says. "Maybe a daddy."

Slowly I gain back some line. Then, mysteriously, the line goes slack. Had his Middle Devonian cunning made good an escape?

I crank furiously. Then the yellow submarine blows its tanks, launching itself in a tail-walking leap, sheathed in a fountain of whitewater, and splash-lands in a tortured U three meters from us, full of fight. Gaspar comes forward and leans over the side. I watch, paralyzed, as he grabs the line and begins pulling it in hand over hand.

"Get the net!" I plead. "There is no net," comes the answer. We don't even have a Mato Grosso lawyer (a club). Gaspar brings the fish to the surface about a meter from us. The enormous head of the *dorado* rises out of the water with the silver lure caught on the left jaw.

The fish flares its blood-red gills, simultaneously chomping down its powerful jaws, and thrashes its head against the water, sending a great geyser over us. When I wipe the spray from my eyes Gaspar is holding a limp line in one hand. The front half of the lure is impaled in his straw Stetson. The lure's been snapped in two, cutting loose the taut line like a slingshot.

I sit there in a daze, not even noticing three mosquitoes sucking away on my forehead.

Paulo, too, catches nothing big this day and is thoroughly frustrated when we return to the lodge. "I'm ready to go back!" he complains lifting his shoulders and holding out his arms, a disappointed, *pfffft* noise escaping his lips.

I'm not relieved to depart. There's that awful, ass-breaking boat ride to face.

six

North from the Posto

In the early part of the twentieth century
explorers reported flocks of hundreds of hyacinth
macaws . . . where today the species is totally extirpated.
— *Charles Munn, Jorgen Thomsen, and Carlos Yamashita,*
Audubon Wildlife Report, 1989–1990

Our Pantanal National Park adventure has been a perilous
and draining journey. On the drive back to the *posto* we are
lost in our own thoughts.

While we were away the rainy season has begun turning the
Transpantaneira darker, with standing brown water in deep
potholes. Several capybaras have taken up residence in a large
one, wallowing in the mud and refusing to budge until the
Bandeirante is brought within about a meter. Seems the road
is now an island refuge.

By midday we cross the bee-bite bridge — speedily. Within
minutes I can see the *posto* and a tall feminine figure and a cowboy standing in front. The woman certainly isn't Dona Maria.

I know that alluring profile; it's Lúcia. "Surprised, hey,
Bito?" she says, greeting me with a big kiss when we park the
Bandeirante. Although business has brought her to Brazil, she
can't resist seeing the Pantanal during the rainy season. And I'm
glad she's here. It's a time when the bleached vegetation and
parched land are transformed into a lush primeval garden. The
presence of standing water relieves the dry season stress on
animals, allowing dangerous concentrations of them to disperse

94

in the now very green environment. It's a very attractive place to be.

But not for Paulo and his secretary. They can't wait another minute and announce they're returning to Cuiabá immediately.

Lúcia caught a ride in with Tutu, one of the Falcão brothers. He has been recruited by the environmental agency in Cuiabá to guard the *posto* until Firmo returns; otherwise it would be ransacked.

While Lúcia is settling in, Gaspar heads into the kitchen to scrounge something for lunch. And when I hear him starting to fry some meat, my guts revolt. "Oh, no, you don't!" I roar, taking the skillet away from him. "We're eating decent food today." I push him out the door.

Lúcia gathers some local ingredients as Tutu and Gaspar join me on an impromptu fishing trip. We drive south, where the now flooding fields gradually merge into lush, permanent wetland. Gaspar and Tutu shake their heads no when I suggest we stop at a large pool. "Only piranhas here," they say.

Nine bridges down, the water is dramatically different, free from turbid chalkiness. With the rainy season under way, there is sufficient water to produce a flow of good volume, bending long grasses and pushing the water hyacinth aside. When I stand on the low bridge and look down, I can see the sun's rays penetrating the water's tea-stained depths, illuminating a sandy bottom. A fish darts from the bridge's shadow, snatches a food particle floating by, and scoots back. Larger ones swim in a small school, sculling in place as the water flows by them until they see my motion and ride the current away.

"Those piranha?" I ask. "No," says Tutu, "they're *piraputanga*"— *Brycon orbignyanus,* one-to-two-kilo river fish. They're hard fighting, beautiful, with gold-orange tail and fins. Their delicate, white flesh is delicious if you can dissect away hundreds of sharp, nearly invisible bones.

As I run a line through my fishing rod, Gaspar and Tutu search the river-bank bushes. Tutu doffs his straw Stetson and begins plopping in grape-size fruits from the bushes. Pretty soon they have a hatful and join me at the center of the bridge.

Gaspar pulls from a cloth sack two short boards. Wound around them is line nearly the gauge that holds laundry. They both skewer a fruit to their hooks and swing the lines overhead, lasso-style, releasing them perfectly into the tongue of current. I shake my head in disbelief, muttering, "Fruit?"

I pick out a Mepps spinner and clip it to the line. Gaspar sees this and gives me a "you're not serious" look. I hold it up, tinkling the hook against the spinner, making a noise like a dinner bell. "This is gringo magic," I declare. We decide to have a contest for the biggest fish—their fruit against my lures.

I cast the lure on the edge of a weed bed about twenty-five meters out. The spinner kisses the water, followed by the line collapsing in a gentle arc on the surface. As I reel in, I feel the light resistance of the spinner working against the current. At first nothing happens. Exercising a slow retrieve, I can see several dark forms follow it, then disappear. When I start to raise the lure from the water one strikes.

Out of nowhere a bigger fish grabs the lure, flashing a metallic-flecked belly, taking it and my rod tip down. More of them huddle in a school nearby. The fish sees this and tries to toss the lure and get away from them.

I pull the fish wriggling from the water as the others rise up and clip off its tail. As it flops on the bridge, Gaspar says, "Piranha." It's a whopper, maybe about a kilo. I offer the pliers to him, but he digs out the hook, breaking it off at the shank and tossing the fish onto the bridge. For these men there isn't much sport to good fishing. Hook the fish and yank it in. About the only contest is to haul in the fish before it's been devoured by other piranhas.

"You're going to eat piranha?" I ask. "It's good," says Gaspar, smiling at my squeamish question.

I catch several more piranhas, then switch lures to a floating fly made from a bit of cork wrapped with a tiny plume with an eye painted on. I drift this downstream with no luck, until I retrieve it. As I'm lifting the fly from the stream a golden fish leaps, hooking itself onto the fly and taking off with the line.

"Wo!" I say, entranced by this grand display. It jumps high again, shaking its head in the air and making a shower of silvery water. The fish fights with the power of a lunker bass. But this one's elegant and weighs about a kilo.

I quickly raise the fish from the water and put it on the bridge. *"Piraputanga,"* Gaspar notes. The fish has distinct, carp-size scales of burnished gold. The fins and tail are rhubarb-red.

The mouth has rows of needle-sharp teeth. It's a beautiful, fighting game fish that's virtually unknown outside the Pantanal. And good eating, too, adds Gaspar.

Tutu sees my luck with the artificial baits and asks to try one of the flies. He drifts one downstream fifteen to twenty meters when another *piraputanga* strikes. Even with his heavy line, the golden fish skips the surface as he pulls it in by hand.

In less than an hour there are ten piranha and three *piraputanga* piled on the bridge. "Lunch time," I announce.

Back at the *posto,* Lúcia has cracked open a fresh coconut, saved the milk, and begun shredding the meat. She has gone out back and plucked about a dozen green, hot peppers and fresh limes. Onions and garlic sautéeing in a big pot fill the air with aromas that make me salivate.

"I know what you're making," I sing out smiling, scanning the dandy ingredients. *"Muqueca"* (pronounced moo-kek-uh).

Muqueca is the bouillabaisse of Brazil—fresh seafood cooked in a unique swirl of African and South American spices and ingredients. It's the traditional cuisine of Bahia, the famous sultry northeast coast of the country. Lúcia's version is splendiferous. In Chicago, we would go to Isaacson and Stein fish market, where the better chefs come personally to sniff the latest offerings. We would buy more than half a dozen kinds of seafood—grouper, swordfish, shrimp, squid, clams, mussels, whatever looked good—then head home to cook up a grand feast.

It's a bold gesture to appease our rebelling stomachs. In no time Lúcia turns us into galley slaves, cleaning the fish, cutting the veggies, and setting the table. I'm cutting more onions and garlic, tearing up in anticipation. Tutu and Gaspar clean the fish at the edge of the pond out back with a growing audience of two caracaras, chickens hiding in the shade, and one caiman lying motionless watching the men toss guts into the water five meters away.

The big, iron pot is soon bubbling with a heady stew of coconut milk, onions, pepper, garlic, and a dash of palm oil. Then Tutu carries over a bowl of cleaned fish and slides them in. In a few minutes I'm slurping the cook's spoon and am caught. "Out, damn it," demands the chef. "Hey, I gotta taste . . . to see if the spice is right." "Liar, you wanna eat out of the pot." She knows me too well.

I sit outside with the other men, in silence, like expectant fathers awaiting news from the delivery room.

Luce finally carries out the bubbling cauldron. She lifts the top, letting loose a heady cloud of steam. When it clears, there is this divine broth. The red fins of the *piraputangas* have practically dissolved, leaving behind a rich, red liquid streaking the surface. Poking through the steaming surface are the intimidating fish heads and toothy jaws of the piranhas, gaping one last time.

We fill our bowls and pile on a dollop of rice, then a squeeze of lime juice. Instinctively, I poke a piranha's head with my spoon; then I dig in. Their pearl-white flesh falls away from the bones and tastes surprisingly like whitefish, only with thicker bones. Not a word is spoken. Slurping and juice-zooping sounds fill the air. Tutu picks up a piranha and sucks its bones clean. I add a drop or two of the aged hot sauce and croon, "Oh, I'm in love." And I give Luce a great big fishy kiss of gratitude.

The other men finish their bowls and fill them again. Gaspar takes an impressive third helping. A Pantanal *muqueca* has tamed the beast in all of us, just as an alligator is soothed by a rub on its belly.

I crawl into a hammock and sleep deeply through the afternoon heat. It's a time when there's little human noise or activity. The chickens, ever braver for our inaction, take charge of the veranda, pecking at our lunch time detritus. Two manage to get up on top of the table.

Their cackling and scratchings become a comfortable background sound to my own musings. Twice each day we have been having great adventures. It's been deeply satisfying. But suddenly the chickens are silent. And that silence is loud enough for me to open an eye. They have stopped their table grazing and are huddled with the largest hen along the front wall of the house. There is a motion in the bushes.

A scaly, green head pokes through the foliage, and a red tongue flicks in and out, testing the air. Finally, an anaconda. The large head emerges, then two legs. No, it's a caiman. Then the entire body. It's more than a meter long. Something doesn't look right. The body is like a huge iguana lizard without the serrated crown, and the head is flat—a strange mix of snake and caiman features. And it's coming closer. Now the chickens scatter, their legs shifting into high speed; they skid wildly on the varnished cement.

I tumble out of the hammock and run (mostly for my camera) and try to whistle up Gaspar, who's sawing wood pretty good. When I return, the lizard-thing is three meters from a young chick. "*Vibora*," says a groggy Gaspar as we give chase, pulling up our pants. It's frighteningly fast, scurrying through the brush, across the road, and down the embankment into the safety of a roadside pond. "No," Gaspar corrects himself, "it's a *teju*." *Tupinambis teguixin.* Some people call them caiman-lizards; they have the head of a huge iguana and the body of a croc.

Fião and Tutu's Place

We're going back to the Falcão brothers' ranch to photograph some of the animals, hopefully see those haunting singers, the howler monkeys, and maybe catch a glimpse of those blue parrots. We get up at 5:15 A.M. for a blazing orange, then gray-and-scarlet sunrise. Groggily we shake out our boots and wake the durable Gaspar.

Many weeks have passed since we visited. Now, on our way, the second hour-long sun shower has made the road a mess. Out across the fields water is beginning to glisten among the dry grasses. A cluster of tall, gray termite mounds form a natural Stonehenge; two have sentinel black buzzards perched on top. It's hard to believe that in less than a hundred days the rains are going to swell the rivers and transform this parched grassland into an enormous lake. There's good proof: a tree has a black wet stain four meters high on its trunk.

A man we see along the road says the waters up north have risen dramatically, submerging one of the bridges. Gaspar wiggles the palm of his hand, doubting the statement. "The bridge isn't washed out; it's probably flooded," he says. The Bandeirante should be able to ford it; we have four all-terrain tires (bald in the center with not so much as a fingerprint's depth of tread). Gaspar points confidently to their side walls, still bumpy with snow-tire impressions, as evidence of their usefulness.

A semi-trailer full of cattle being taken to market has become mired in the hub-deep muck. We stop to join the drivers and cowboys scratching their heads about how to extract the mooing twenty-meter-long vehicle. With the cattle complaining and the engine impotently whining, it's like a modern-day beast marooned in a South American tar pit.

Horses or water buffalo could be hitched up, but the nearest herd is adjacent to that last gas station at least a hundred kilometers north. The closest tractor, says Gaspar, is at Tutu's ranch, where we're going. But the truck really needs a bulldozer, and the only ranch in the vicinity that has such heavy equipment is Fazenda São João, that controversial ranch that we passed along the Transpantaneira. Gaspar adds cryptically, "You should see what they've got there."

Gaspar slips the Bandeirante into four-wheel drive and we slide sideways, then angle fifteen degrees down so that the view out my window is wall-to-wall muck. It takes us another two hours to get to the ranch. We have to park the truck near the road and wade in. A charcoal-plumed snail kite perches on a low, green bush with yellow blossoms and gives our troop a raptor's Bronx cheer—"Keeeessssss"—for invading its territory.

The "driveway" is a two-kilometer river of mud splitting a green field. We squirt and slog through. When I bog down, I use the barbed-wire fence running along one side of the drive for support. Gaspar says he can always tell the wealthy ranchers because "their long driveways are high and dry."

Fião is sitting on the front porch. It's striking how much Tutu and Fião look like twins: the same twinkling eyes, walnut skin, missing teeth, sinewy bodies, and three-day beards. Only Fião's gray hair sets them apart.

Fião's in his everyday farm wear: faded dungarees rolled to the calf, open knit shirt, sweat-stained straw hat, and favorite footgear—old shower thongs. His feet are brown from the sun, caked, and cracked. And I start to feel sorry for him until I realize we're talking to the landed gentry of the Pantanal—working ranchers, cash tight and land rich.

Fião insists theirs is not a true ranch, only a *sítio* (pronounced see-too) comprising some 4000 hectares (8800 acres); real ranches begin at 50,000 hectares. There are fifty "real" ranches in the area. One of those, Fazenda Santa Izabel, is owned by

Zelito Dorileo, a distant cousin of the Falcão brothers. A rich distant cousin. Sometimes he's referred to as the baron of Poconé, the village his ancestors helped found. In fact, they say, nearly all of the ranch owners are in some way related to each other.

Still, the Falcão brothers own a lovely patch of land with running water, sitting water, seasonal lakes (pastureland when dry), and standing patches of forest. There are cows, horses, chickens, turkeys, coconut and citrus trees, and an awful lot of wildlife.

A couple of old tractors are strategically parked on the highest little hillocks in an attempt to keep them dry. The main house is a simple stucco cottage painted blue with a red-tile roof. We sit on the veranda sipping from green coconuts. It's hard to realize from looking at him, but Fião is pretty well off by Brazilian standards. A couple of hired hands do the drudgery, laundry, and cattle driving.

We're invited to share the family's midday meal. Rice, manioc, cooked meat, roasted chicken, filtered water, and later coffee. While we eat and talk I notice they have sharp country accents that pepper the chat with rolling *r*'s as in Castilian Spanish (from being close to Bolivia? or maybe from years around Spanish-speaking ranch hands?).

The view from one open window of the cottage is entirely occupied by their prized brown bull, which, Fião assures us, will not be slaughtered. It's a pet. Through the other window is an open, wet field with two jabiru storks and a lone, whistling heron (*Syrigma sibilatrix*), much smaller than the storks and colored like a Japanese woodblock print. It has a buff-colored neck, coral beak, coral cheek, a patch of blue around the eye, black cap and plume, white throat, and gray back. With finely sculpted body proportions, it's a truly elegant bird. It takes measured strides, poised to strike into the shallows for small fish and frogs.

But this is a cattle ranch, pets or no. There are some 540 head of cattle on this land that their father settled. Some are used for milk and meat; others are bartered for goods or a bit of cash. Fião doesn't mince words about it. A bull is put down where its stands (or wades) and is bled to death by cutting its jugular. The hide, legs, and salvageable beef are piled into a canoe and taken home. Entrails are given to the dogs. The meat is sun-dried.

"To keep the ranch hands here", says Fião, "we have to provide food. If we don't have meat they'll leave. At Zelito's, in the dry season, they kill one in the morning and another in the afternoon." Times are changing, though.

Fião bemoans the fact that big family ranches are coming under new pressures. After two and a half centuries of the same lifestyle, the *donos'* heirs are not good cattlemen, nor efficient managers. Instead, they're interested in making quick money. Some have tried moneymaking schemes by attempting intense agriculture in the poor soil or selling off land in smaller plots. It means trouble for everyone. In this impoverished land, cows need about ten acres each to survive. Smaller, fenced parcels curtail wildlife migration, especially during the wet season. It could be a disaster.

To save the Pantanal's open lands and wildlife, it's necessary to support what a university professor in Cuiabá called those enormous "feudalistic" ranches, an awkward step for a government wanting to encourage democracy and land reform.

The Falcão brothers have supplemented their cattle raising with horse breeding. In the past they've had good luck, but now they have only three horses. "Most of the horses had anemia. The vet didn't know how they got it, but he said they had to be destroyed," Tutu recalls unhappily. "The survivors became infertile." They think the disease may have come from foreign horses purchased at auction in one of the stock expositions in Cuiabá.

The Pantanal horse is something like Chincoteague ponies on the U.S. Delmarva Peninsula. Brought over by Spanish explorers nearly 350 years ago, Andalusian, English, Arab, and Berber bloodlines interbred for several centuries here. After such a period of isolated breeding, they've become regarded as their own breed, called Pantaneiro, with slight variations throughout the region. They've become recognized for their thick necks and small dimensions, and some breeders swear their hooves have broadened considerably over decades of adapting to marsh conditions.

Staring at one horse while Lúcia rides another, it's clear these creatures aren't the prettiest animals afoot. Rather, the

Pantaneiros are prized for a tough disposition and the ability to thrive off meager forage and endure a brutal climate. They're real survivors.

On the veranda again, I tell the brothers about the mired truck needing a tow. They don't like the news. It means they'll be asked to help. "Not long ago," Fião says, "a refrigerated truck heavy with fish broke one of the bridges. They said they were 'tourists,' yet the government says we can't use fish nets or a bow and arrow for hunting—all prohibited. And the 'tourists' come here and shoot the *jacaré, ema* [ostrich relative], snakes. If I kill something to eat, they put me in jail."

What about the new kind of tourism, focused on the animals? "Gringos don't take the birds . . . or kill so much," observes Fião, "but they like to shit in the *estrada*. If I had my way I would break every bridge; then the government would have to be here. When the tourist buses ruin the Transpantaneira, we have to pay or fix it ourselves. They pay nothing." Half joking, I suggest, "Why don't you and the other ranchers put up a toll booth?" He laughs, then raises his eyebrows in contemplation.

A Night Adventure

In the late afternoon, Tutu has come from the *posto* to take Lúcia, Gaspar, and myself on a small expedition down the long "driveway" leading to a nearby ranch. There, along this forested road, we will try to call the jaguar.

We set out in the Bandeirante, moving slowly, yet the spirit of anticipation rises quickly as shadows cast across the road and I wonder what's lurking out there. Tutu taps Gaspar on the shoulder and we pull over at the entrance to a dense grove of short palm trees. "In there," he says, "a week ago there was an *onça* [jaguar]."

Inside the grove, it's not as claustrophobic as I thought. It is, however, dank; many tightly curled vines hang down from the trees. Gaspar points to the hollowed-out crotch of a tree. A pair of large, white eggs rest directly on the ground. A vulture nest.

The palms are *bacuri* (*Atalea phalerata*), which seldom grow higher than about seven meters. The trunks are thick and deeply scarred from the growth process where the stalks of the leaves have fallen away. The crown is a tussle of palm fronds hanging listlessly. A tight cluster of green, egg-size coconuts hangs from the cluster. They're covered with a tough, waxy husk beneath which is a woody structure that I cannot cut through with a hunting knife. Yet scattered at the base of some of these trees are blackened piles of old palm nuts, many cleanly cut in two as if by metal snips. In fact, the floor surrounding these trees is a mess. What did that?

Lúcia kicks over one of those detritus piles and pulls out a dirty, cobalt-blue feather. "*Arara azul*," says Tutu. Blue parrots! The endangered hyacinth macaw (*Anodorhynchus hyacinthinus*), largest parrot in the world. Tutu nonchalantly mentions that these palm nuts are their favorite food. I've been wanting to document these great birds since I heard that the Pantanal is one of their last haunts. And now we've stumbled onto one of their prime feeding sites.

The guys don't seem to understand my excitement. For Tutu and Gaspar, the Amazon parrots around the house and the hyacinths are simply another part of their farm world. But for a guy from the cold north, opportunities to experience these colorful, exotic birds are limited to seeing them in pet stores, zoos, and travel commercials. To watch such animals in the wild is the thrill of a lifetime, and it makes me grin from ear to ear. Before dawn, I assure them, I'll be hidden among the palms praying this is their breakfast nook.

In the meantime, we walk down the road with the setting sun lighting up a cloud that resembles an unusually long horse in stride; then it fades away.

Tutu grabs a large coffee can from the truck. It has no top or bottom, and a skin is drawn tight like a drum on one end. Dangling from the skin is a thong, which he begins to pull through his grasp. The motion produces a low growl, which at first sounds impossibly artificial.

Tutu pulls the thong in groups of twos and threes, then pauses. I'm trying to quiet my breathing to see if there's a response. I open my mouth and strain my ears so hard that my scalp pulls taut. Nothing.

Tutu sends out another series of growls. Pauses. My ears kick back. I cant my head. He calls in a stray dog and gets wisecracks from us.

The forest is dark now, with just the sandy road visible, and I can barely make out Gaspar by the orange glow of his cigarette. He whispers to me, "That's no jaguar call." He opens the truck and fumbles around for a pail. Then he goes to the front of the truck, squats down, sticks his head half inside the pail, and starts to make grunting sounds, just like he did on the bridge that night when he scared the hell out of the caimans.

He tries grunting again. And this time a hundred meters up the lane there's a chilling reply. It's an awful imitation of rapid-fire castanets, only using dry bones. The sound echoes through the quiet forest.

A thick-bodied animal perched on spindly legs emerges from the forest twitching a thin, short tail. A capybara? In the fading light we can see a large *porco do mato,* a jungle pig. Another steps onto the road and then another; eight in all. Each weighs about eighteen kilos. I start walking closer, but Gaspar yanks my shirt; they're dangerous and could turn on us.

Tutu, now on the jaguar caller, gives the thong a pull or two, and the lead boar answers with more nervous jaw gnash-ings. Gaspar demonstrates by baring his dentures and chomp-ing several times. It's the pack leader warning the group of the jaguar. They reverse directions, cross the road again, kicking gravel in their escape, and disappear into the forest.

Now my scalp is pulled tight against my skull. I've never heard a noise like that. Gaspar smacks his shoulder, demon-strating that the pigs are white-collared peccary (*Tayassu tajacu*). Walking back to the truck, Gaspar says they aren't as dangerous as their relatives, the white-lipped peccary (*Tayassu albirostris*). Those have been known to travel in packs of more than a hundred individuals. Hunters have been caught in life-threaten-ing situations.

Tutu tells of one incident in which a hunter, having spent his bullets on some of the peccary in a large pack, had to climb the nearest tree for safety. The pigs saw that the tree was thin and started chewing the trunk through. If they had gotten the hunter on the ground they would have devoured him alive. "You know how he escaped?" Tutu asks, smiling. He says the man pissed on one of the pigs, and the herd turned and killed it, allowing the hunter to slip away.

Good Morning: Blue Parrots

No way I am going to miss this encounter. I'm up at 4:30 A.M. and tiptoe from the veranda, leaving everyone still sleeping. I drive to the palm grove and set up my tripod behind one of the trees, tying some of the overhanging leaves to the legs as a makeshift hide. I spread a small tarp on the ground and settle down to wait as the first notes of birdsong break open the night.

There are doves, flycatchers, a chattering flock of monk parakeets, a pair of Amazon parrots, and two pairs of woodpeckers syncopating for tree grubs. Many more I can't identify. No macaws, though, and I pray Mr. Jaguar is dining elsewhere.

I settle down to wait. You can get just so close on the move, then you have to track the birds to a roost or feeding site and hide. Some photographers use robot cameras, triggering them by timer or infrared beam.

I don't mind seat-of-the-pants shooting. At times the experience takes on the aura of Zen meditation. The last time I did that was back some years in central Wisconsin. I had talked a refuge manager into letting me stake out a road-killed deer in the middle of a marsh to see if we could lure in young bald eagles.

It was November. I sat in a shallow pit with my head sticking above ground, covered by grasses. I was in a down suit and had a thermos of tea with honey and a dollop of Irish whisky. The necessary concentration on watching made everything else disappear. The autumn sky and foliage set a grand stage.

Then one juvenile landed on the deer; later two more joined in, with ravens at the perimeter awaiting their turn. The bald eagles fought, then fed, and fought again in a raptor "Punch and Judy" show. A skunk waddled in and nibbled for intermission. Then two eagles returned on a powerful northerly wind that blew their feathers out of place, revealing the patches of milky down underneath.

It was my own private wildlife show less than fifteen meters away. Those great eagles fought from dawn until late afternoon. While the feeding behavior continued, I lost a sense of time. Being privy to the spectacle—seeing a rare bit of animal life—left me feeling exhausted and deeply satisfied with memories (and pictures) I could call upon for years to come.

Now, in the dim palm grove, the light is beginning to come up, touching the topmost leaves. No big birds have flown in, yet I become aware of a new sound. I lean a bit to my left, scanning another part of the grove.

A long, blue tail dangles down between the dark palm leaves, and my heart quickens. One of the hyacinth macaws is already here, munching away on those palm nuts and making a noise akin to thumping little melons. How did it get in there so silently? Could it have been here all night?

The bird works its way up the nut cluster and reveals the rest of its body. Even in weak light it has an iridescent color— blue with hints of deep purple on the tail, cobalt on the breast, and turquoise on the head. But such an ungainly head—one that seems much too big for its body. Or maybe the head size is unbalanced by that monkey-wrench-size beak, which looks more like a curved, black lobster claw.

It's eyes are jet black and huge—at least two, maybe three times bigger than the beady Amazon's. The canary-yellow orbital rings around them seem to add to their dimensions. And bussed on each cheek is a similarly yellow crescent moon. The bird is an accomplished gymnast. It holds on to the nut clusters with one short leg while grasping a nut with the other. Working through the husk isn't easy going either. I can hear the macaw's labored puffing as it rests for a spell, its yellow-striped black tongue moving up and down from the effort.

The hyacinth easily tears off the cap and tough green husk. Then it opens the woody structure by rimming the nut and shearing it neatly in half, as if cut by a powerful tin scissors. It rests again, tilting the open end toward me. The new angle reveals not a single meat, but four tubular chambers of a creamy white substance. The bird emits a chortle, pleased indeed at having reached that prized food.

"Aaarrk." A call shoots across the grove from another unseen macaw in the forest. "Raarrk," this one replies, then goes back to breakfast, jamming its long tongue deep into a seed chamber and licking out the material.

With such a clownlike appearance it's difficult to believe that such a creature is the king of parrots. Of 340 species found worldwide and 18 long-tailed macaws in the New World, the hyacinth macaw is the biggest, measuring more than a meter long and weighing over one and a half kilos. Not exactly the size of buzzard. But then again, how many collectors want to pay U.S. $10,000 for vulture?

The hyacinths are the largest and major surviving species in the only group of all-blue macaws (*Anodorhynchus*). The similar-looking, but smaller, Glaucous macaw is generally regarded as extinct. Lear's macaw, also a lookalike, is on the brink of extinction. The gray-blue Spix macaw, a different genus, may have been recently extirpated, with perhaps fifty left in captivity.

It's also hard to believe that not long ago they were eaten by Indians and plucked of their striking feathers for ornaments. And now they are heavily sought by pet traders. In the Pantanal, loss of suitable nest trees and the pet trade are the main reasons for their decline.

Three more macaws materialize from the shadows, crunching nuts and preening their feathers. One pair stops feeding and locks beaks in a macaw embrace; then they fly off uttering an even louder scream, which is answered far off.

My lower back and knees are aching after sitting motionless for more than four hours. I walk over to the tree where the birds have been working to examine the half-eaten nuts. In the process I bump a narrow plant; it looks like a rubber-tree plant: rich green, waxy stem, broad light-red leaves. Beneath one of the leaves there are little swollen lips around a hole. As I brush the plant, red ants come spilling out, climbing up and down the stalk and obviously agitated, looking for the source of the disturbance.

The ants have a symbiotic relationship with the plant. They are provided with ample quarters inside the stalk, in return for which plant agitation or molestations are greeted with columns of marauding soldiers armed with sharp mandibles, quite capable of inflicting painful welts. I'm busy flicking off some of the buggers when I'm startled by a low, mean-sounding, guttural growl.

A hyacinth perches on a large palm leaf dropping its nut as I stumble out. "Aaaarrgggh" again. It's more like a noise from a snarling Doberman than a tropical bird. But there it is with good effect: those growls bring me up short. "Aaaarrgggh-aaaarrgggh-aaaarrrgggh" louder and louder. The bird flares its wings, making a cobalt cross for an instant, and then blasts into the air, taking its screams with it.

The grove is quiet now—empty it seems—but my ears are ringing from that hyacinth's screams. This was a tantalizing first glimpse of these giant, hard-to-find parrots. As I leave I feel lucky—as though I've discovered an emerald.

Back at the cottage, people are up having their morning coffee and watch me walk back with this glow on my face. "I found them—five hyacinths," I blurt out.

Tutu, I think, understands my satisfaction, even though he grew up with such animals around him. "About two years ago," he recalls, "twenty-two *araras* [hyacinths] flew over the area. There used to be a large tree where a family of them nested."

The Most Controversial Ranch in the Pantanal

I give Tutu and Fião my artificial flies as a small thanks; then we hit the road. An hour and a half down the Transpantaneira we pass the Texas-style gate to that much talked about ranch, São João, owned by Sr. Sebastião Camargo Correia, considered one of the five most influential men in Brazil. I ask Gaspar to pull up so I can inquire.

"Don't you know because you're with me, they'll never let you in," Gaspar offers defensively. "They never let anyone in here who doesn't get permission from the office in São Paulo."

Just the same, we hail the guard and tell him we left a note a couple of months back, wanting to see the ranch. "*Minuthino*," a little minute, the old guard replies. His home is the gatehouse beside the wind pump. He turns on the radio and requests authorization for us to enter the property.

And surprise. In very short time, the permission is granted and the gate swung open. The guard says we're to meet one of the ranch hands at the end of the driveway, near the main house. What I don't realize is that the road in is at least fifteen kilometers—and we have the place to ourselves.

Gaspar is obviously impressed with this driveway. Unlike Tutu's it's been built like the Transpantaneira itself. Trenches have been dug alongside the road and dirt piled above ground to elevate the drive from floods. The trenches have filled with water, but they're not as choked with plants as those alongside the main road. Still, there are a good number of caimans floating and sunning themselves; so there must be edibles in with them.

At first the road runs close to a patch of forest. The dirt is moist and easy to drive without getting bogged down. Other creatures appreciate it too. We scare up half a dozen jabirus that use the road as an airstrip to get aloft. A few kilometers further we enter a newly cleared section of land. Here the forest has been completely cut down to the soil. As in the surrounding high plain called the Chapada dos Guimarães, bulldozers scraped off the remaining scrub plants and stumps, piling them into immense windrows of dead vegetation one to two and a half meters high. They are several hundred meters long, stretching across the entire width of the field. As we drive along we count maybe a hundred. Gaspar says they'll be torched at night.

A flock of green monk parakeets flies over the prepared field. Instantly they change direction, taking on the color of their gray bellies and alighting en masse on a bush poking through some water.

So many land on a small limb that it bends down to the water. They don't fly off. Instead there's an impromptu water show. One parakeet tries imitating an osprey, beating its wings heavily to hover above the water, touching the surface, it flies off. Another hangs from the green limb, parrotlike, and eases down into a neat pike position to scoop a quick drink.

A series of cattle gates and fences leads us through to the main grazing lands and what seem to be feedlots. A pickup putting out a dusty rooster tail pulls up, and the young cowboy tells us to follow him. He drives breakneck, and we eat the dust through several kilometers and more cattle gates.

We pass a herd of black Asian water buffalo. Then come

many vehicle sheds, more than a dozen yellow bulldozers, and more heavy, mechanized, diesel farm and construction vehicles. When we reach the main ranch compound, a young manager named Afonso introduces himself as our host and guide while on the property. He's tall, good-looking, and appears studious in wire-rim glasses, white shirt, beige pants, and riding boots. Afonso tells us he hasn't done this before and seems prepared to show us practically anything we want to see on the ranch. He gets in and we're off.

I ask about all the earth-moving equipment. He says the *dono* brought it in for an experiment in the mid-1970s. For centuries the annual flood had been considered an obstacle that virtually wiped out the possibility of serious year-round farming and cattle raising on the Pantanal floodplain. The concept was simple enough: the bulldozers would be used to build an earthern dam surrounding the entire ranch.

The idea of holding back those seasonal floodwaters had been pondered by many individuals and groups—some international. In 1966, for example, a joint Brazilian-UNESCO team of scientists conducted a hydrology study of the Paraguay River and its tributaries. They wanted to see if it was feasible to construct a network of dams to control the widespread flooding and extend year-round navigation with an eye for "improving" the region's prospects. It was at a time that important wetlands worldwide were receiving similar "help."

Constructing more than three hundred kilometers of meter-high, earthen embankments around the ranch's 120,000 acres required a pharaonic effort in crew, a fleet of mechanized equipment, and cash. When the job was completed, the embankments worked even better than they had hoped.

More land was cleared, then planted with non-native grass. Then Afonso shakes his head in disappointment at what happened next as he points to yellow tank trucks with sprayers attached to the back. After keeping back the floodwaters for several seasons, the managers discovered the nutrient-poor soil wasn't being recharged. The cleared land had become less productive. They had to begin pumping in fertilizers at considerable expense. São João was the first ranch in the Pantanal that attempted to keep back the flooding in 250 years. Controlling the floodwaters affected other ranches too, by encouraging ticks and canudo weeds to flourish and keeping standing water from draining away sooner.

As we the tour the center of the ranch we see many farm buildings, ranch-hand quarters, management offices, equipment storage sheds, and vehicle depots. Afonso says, "I think you want to see the *museu,* no?" What museum? "Why, the home where your president stayed," he says. We drive over to a grand old building built in the style of a Spanish hacienda — whitewashed stucco, great arched columns, and a regal entry-way set off by tall, stately palms.

Afonso unlocks the doors. He wipes his feet first and doffs his cowboy hat before entering. Inside, he speaks in a low, reverent voice.

The old *casa* is elegant and immaculate, with polished tile floors and large, comfortable, leather sofas and armchairs. The dining room has a long, formal table that seats thirty or more.

Afonso thinks I know about this place, being a North American. In fact, hardly anyone knows about this place. It's a little-known private shrine devoted to preserving the memory of American President Theodore Roosevelt's visit here with Brazil's first-rank explorer, Colonel Rondon.

Back in 1913, Colonel Cândido Mariano da Silva Rondon was acclaimed as *the* explorer of Brazil's poorly known heart-lands. In 1907 Rondon had built the first telegraph lines through the unsurveyed reaches of Mato Grosso and neighboring territories. An adopted Indian himself, Rondon later worked to ease the plight of Brazil's extensive and varied native peoples by establishing the Indian Protective Service. Eventually his considerable service to his country was rewarded by naming a new state after him — Rondônia, a state that adjoins Mato Grosso. Today, many distant relatives of his family bear the name Rondon and can be found living on ranches in and around the Pantanal, especially west of Campo Grande.

In 1908, facing the end of his term as twenty-sixth president, Roosevelt was considering returning to Africa on safari. A close friend and Catholic priest, Father Zahm, had recently returned from crossing the Andes and descending the Amazon. He urged Roosevelt to make a voyage up the Paraguay River to explore Brazil's seldom-traveled interior.

Colleagues from the American Museum of Natural History

in New York (which his relatives helped found) encouraged Roosevelt's trip, giving the project an official reason: a major zoological expedition to that part of the world would add immeasurably to the museum's study collections. Plans were set into motion for a spring 1913 departure of the Expedição Scientifica Roosevelt-Rondon, as the Brazilian secretary of state had called it.

The fifty-five-year-old former president was accompanied by his son Kermit, George Cherrie and Leo Miller (bird and mammal curators from the museum), Father Zahm, and Anthony Fiala, an arctic explorer and expedition manager. Colonel Rondon would meet the party north of Asunción.

The plan was to cruise from Buenos Aires up the Paraguay River by steamboat as far as navigable, then switch to dugout canoe. After that they would strike inland to search out where the Paraguay and Amazon river basins divide. And, if possible, they would try to descend the Gy-Paraná River, an uncharted waterway, attempting to reach the Amazon.

Armed with his insatiable sense of adventure and scientific mission, as well as his favorite Springfield rifle and Colt revolver, Roosevelt was enjoying the Paraguay River trip. According to his notes, which would later become the widely read account of the trip *Through the Brazilian Wilderness,* Roosevelt was having a pretty good time afloat, shooting up the local wildlife, philosophizing with Rondon, and observing birds that locals gave odd names (jacanas, for example, were called "Jesus Christ birds" because they seemed to walk on water).

On December 28, 1913, the expedition was welcomed to this very same ranch beside the Cuiabá River by the owner, Sr. João da Costa Marques, an influential landowner. With some 60,000 head of cattle on the property, São João was even at that time one of the largest and most important ranches in this part of the country.

Roosevelt rode those tough, small horses out from the ranch into palmetto scrub country looking for big game: caimans, capybaras, marsh deer, and the much sought jaguars. Despite drenching rainsqualls and 100°F heat, the wonders of the Pantanal weren't lost on him: " . . . we had been passing through a hot, fertile, pleasant wilderness . . . I wish emphatically to record my view that these marshy plains, although hot, are also healthy . . . The country is excellently suited for settlement, and offers a remarkable field for cattle-growing. Moreover, it is a paradise for water-birds and for many other kinds of birds, and for many mammals."

We move slowly through the *casa*. The hallway to the bedrooms has a gallery of large, black-and-white photographs of Roosevelt on safari in Africa.

Afonso ushers us into the room where Roosevelt slept. He says everything is as the president left it. There we see a bed with blue-dyed covers, a night stand with candle, and a sitting chair draped in mosquito netting. The afternoon light is now streaming through the blue slats in the shutters, adding dramatically to the almost churchlike aura of this place.

After leaving the ranch, Roosevelt went on to explore the Duvida and Gy-Paraná rivers, completing thousands of wilderness miles before returning to New York harbor. The government of Brazil later honored him by sending home an official map of his expedition. The chart had been altered: Rio Duvida had been renamed Rio Roosevelt.

On one of my research trips to the American Museum of Natural History in New York, I was allowed to delve into one of their storage vaults looking for memorabilia from Roosevelt's trip. We saw some old, disintegrating, 35mm nitrate footage from the expedition. The Teddy Roosevelt Association in Oyster Bay, New York, had conserved that and other footage, producing a remarkable silent film of his trip. To see the flickering image of a retired, aging American president exploring and thrilling to the sights of a Latin American wilderness begs for a moment's pause. I wondered what president in the last sixty years would have made such a trip into any remote part of this hemisphere. Maybe Carter? Roosevelt was truly one of a kind.

Today, Afonso informs us, Sr. Sebastião, who lives and works near his engineering firm in São Paulo, seldom receives friends coming up the river. Instead he has built a modern jetport capable of handling planes as large as Boeing 727s. All the recent presidents of Brazil have visited the ranch, as well as chiefs of state from throughout Latin America.

Afonso says it's time to return to work and hands us a map showing the way out through the maze of pastures and cattle gates. We take the long way, passing close to the river where it takes a sharp elbow curve. Here the Cuiabá pushes through a narrows, creating a nice riffle where some interesting fish might lurk. From the steep banks, Lúcia, Gaspar, and I lose nearly all my remaining lures hooking and losing some of the biggest *dorado* I've seen.

Back on the Road

We've driven for more than three hours and need a break. Gaspar points to a bridge ahead; we'll have one more fishing contest, natural bait versus gringo magic. The stream lies nestled amidst a rich gallery forest, its waters quick moving and clear enough to see through the bending grasses to a sandy bottom two meters below.

Lúcia points out a good-size school of fish riding the current in the shadow of the bridge. We quickly rig up and toss out our lines. Lúcia catches a nice *piraputanga*.

I switch lures and cast further downstream. In the retrieve, fish follow the line in, only to disappear in the next instant when a big, brown animal cruises underwater beneath the bridge. "Otters!" I scream with joy. Another comes barreling by. These are rare giant river otters (*Pteromura brasiliensis*). They're enormous, at least two meters long and weighing more than eighteen kilos. They're curious, toying, and spinning around (yet seemingly aware of the hooks) with my shiny lure.

Despite the considerable current, one of the otters uses its powerful, meter-long, flat tail and makes a U-turn midstream. It swims against the current, past my lure, under the bridge, and disappears into the tea-stained water. I continue to cast, my hands shaking in excitement.

A few long minutes pass. No otters. They've gone. Gaspar saw only the tail end; Lúcia not a glimpse. The fish are back riding the current. I cast a few more times. The third cast I toss on the upstream side of the bridge. And bingo! A brown torpedo barrels back downstream! I quickly reel in, thinking I can lure him in. But another one swims under the bridge, sculling and waiting deep underwater for the shiny, metal object. When I'm about to pull my line from the water, the otter surfaces on its back like a sea otter. It stares up with its dark, eerily clouded pupils, sees my looming figure peering down, and utters a high-pitched shriek, "Yeeeeee." I'm shocked too and yell, "Eyaaaah." The otter turns upstream and swims away.

The otters surface about fifteen meters away: two wet heads cutting a sleek wake. Gaspar sees them too. They scream a cat-like call that echoes off the forest walls as they become dots on a golden stream. What a jolt of adrenalin! Months later I can close my eyes and see those images as fresh and exciting as the moment I first saw them.

In one of the dry sections of the road, we spot a small mud-hole, what's left of a large pond. The surrounding bottomland is already pavement dry and cracked open. We see dead sea-weed and one white crab, also dead.

At the lowest part, where the pond used to be, the mud is still damp. In fact, what first attracts my attention is the mud: it looks like it's boiling. Every now and then the brown surface erupts in a twitch, spattering the thick liquid near a little mound.

When I get closer, I see the bubbling is coming from the last throes of a fish. What surprises me is the little mound. It has eyes and falls over. I scoop it up and pour some mineral water over it, washing away the caked mud and revealing a bird.

Apparently it, too, had seen the struggling fish and went after it, only to be mired in the drying mud. I wrap the weakened bird in a wet rag, take it with us to the guard post at the beginning of the Transpantaneira, and leave it with the men there.

Along a forested stretch of road about forty kilometers south of Poconé, we come upon a Pantaneiro who has left the surrounding countryside to make better speed on his mount on the road. He's trailed by his pack of hunting dogs.

When we pull alongside him we're privy to a vision not normally seen in this region in many decades. The man is dressed more like a nineteenth-century woodsman. He's wearing an open, sackcloth shirt with balloon sleeves, a wide-brimmed cowboy hat, riding pants, and tall, worn, leather boots with Spanish-style spurs (with pointed wheels). Cradled in his arms is a long, lever-action Winchester rifle. A devilishly proud smile spans his grizzled face.

The hounds are excited, nipping and yelping at the horse's hindquarters. I can't see why until we pull abreast. Tied behind the saddle is the headless carcass of a jungle pig flopping with the rhythm of the fast trot. Coagulated blood drizzles from the now purple, gaping trunk and stains the entire right flank of the horse, driving the dogs crazy.

seven

Flight to Descalvado

From horizon to horizon the green mat of trees makes one
crave (and particularly when in an aircraft whose instruments
have largely been replaced by pictures of the saints) for some
relief, for an open patch, a clearing or a landing place other
than the carpet of branches at least sixty feet above the ground.
—*Anthony Smith, Mato Grosso*

A month of working the Transpantaneira Highway has re-
vealed a rich showcase of wildlife along that road. With those
water holes, I never know what surprises lie around a bend in
the road. If an animal can crawl, slither, or fly to those ponds
it will be provided with water, food, and protective habitat—
life-saving elements—throughout the long dry season. And, inadvertently, the ponds produce some of the most spectacular
animal gatherings I've seen in the region. By all accounts the
Transpantaneira has indeed become a de facto national park.

"Unnatural," biologists had said to me back in Cuiabá. No
matter how arresting those roadside attractions are, they rea-
soned, the water holes are artificial, creating dangerously high
concentrations of animals that can easily fall victim to disease.
The biologists argued that many of the animals seeking refuge
along the road would have most certainly perished during
stressful drought times if not for those pools. And animals
along the road give visitors the wrong impression of the Pantanal; it isn't like that in other places. To discover the true
Pantanal, they had insisted, one must travel far from the
Transpantaneira.

TOP: Tutu fishing for pacú
BOTTOM: Commercially important fish, Barão de Melgaço
OPPOSITE: Rainy season thunderhead

RIGHT: Mining aftermath
BELOW: Mercury used in
gold mining
BOTTOM: Assay office,
Poconé

LEFT: Confiscated skins
BOTTOM: Illegal wildlife
market, Duque de
Caxias

Distant Pantanal viewed from plateau, Chapada dos Gumarães

I rather like that "unnatural" road and its many critters. But eventually I have come to realize that I should see as much diversity of the region as time and resources allow. And so on our return to Poconé, I decide to put together an aerial photographic expedition—that is, if I can find a pilot with a high-wing aircraft who's willing to pull off the passenger door to allow unobstructed filming.

Finding a good pilot, especially one who knows this bewildering region, proves an agonizing problem. It's akin to locating a doctor in a new town. You ask around until you find one who hasn't killed too many clients. If I don't find one here, I'll have to go all the way back to Cuiabá, where the big city has plenty of air taxi companies. They'll happily fall over each other to gouge a gringo at U.S. $250 an hour or more. Zooming about the hinterlands (with which they are unfamiliar) could easily break my budget and leave us no closer to discovering the Pantanal's remote wildlife areas.

The pilots working out of Poconé service the area's far-flung ranches, thus by necessity have to know it well. But the choices are slim today. Agamemnon, an excellent pilot who flew me several years before, has called it quits. Locals say he worried about his good luck running out (he's never crashed), and like a cautious gambler ahead at the crap table, he cashed in his chips before lady luck did him in. I didn't know anyone else.

When we pull into Poconé's little airstrip on the east side of town, there's a nice, shiny Cessna parked on the grass. A mother and her twinkling-eyed daughter are passing away the morning in the shade next to the black Chevy Monza. We're in luck, I think.

Lúcia begins talking with them while I poke my nose into a couple of hangars to see if there are planes. Beside one of the hangars a destitute family has made camp. Their housing consists of a plastic drop cloth stretched over cut branches, making a midget-size teepee. A man in ragged clothes is roasting some kind of animal over a small fire. The blue smoke rises straight up into the clear sky. Both hangars do indeed have small planes, but an old attendant shoos me away, saying that the owners are away in São Paulo and won't return for weeks.

Lúcia explains that the lady is waiting for her mother, who

has taken deathly ill on a distant ranch. An aerotaxi has been called to bring her back here to the hospital. "Who's the pilot?" I inquire. "Jarí," says the lady.

Gaspar looks surprised. "You know him?" I ask. He nods yes. "Great! Is he a good pilot?" I ask, thinking our search has ended. "Depends on what you want him for," he shoots back. He knows Jarí, all right. At some distance from the lady, he tells me a story.

About four years ago Gaspar was investigating a tip that some skin hunters were working out of a big ranch not far from Poconé. Several raids proved fruitless: when he got there the ranch was clean. Someone was flying the skins and men out well ahead of him. Gaspar returned to this airstrip, examined all the planes, and found jaguar hairs, among other evidence, behind the back seat of Jarí's expensive red Cessna.

He brought Jarí to Cuiabá, where he was formally charged with aiding and abetting the *contrabandistas.* If proven, that charge could have meant confiscation of the plane, a fine, and perhaps a prison sentence. But Mato Grosso justice was skewed, and Jarí knew how to work the system. Within a matter of days he paid a small fine and was back at the airport. Gaspar said in a whisper of understatement, "I don't think he'd like me in his plane."

"Jarí should be back pretty soon," says the lady. "He left early. It's only an hour flight there. Then he'd have to walk a bit to the boat, then paddle across the river and pick mother up. That's another hour. And an hour back," she says, noting the time.

There are no radios at the airport to reach him, so we decide to wait. Out of curiosity I ask the lady, "Do you know who owns that Cessna parked over there?"

"Oh, yes, that's Sr. Ganchão's plane," she says without blinking. I ask if she's seen him, figuring here was a plane ready to go—if only we could locate the pilot. "Not yet," she says, "but I wouldn't want to go with him." I'm surprised by her candor and ask why not. "He's a bad pilot—doesn't take care of the plane much. None of us [in Poconé] fly with him anymore."

Our conversation falls off because we can hear the approach of a single-engine plane. The lady smiles in relief. It should be her mother. And I, too, am relieved. We won't have to hunt around anymore. In a few moments a red plane makes a slow half-circle above us, reduces engine speed, and lands.

When the plane taxies up to the hangar, we wait for the passengers to leave, then Lúcia walks up to Jarí and introduces us. He doesn't bat an eye when Gaspar steps forward; they even shake hands. There seems to be no ill will between them. Or maybe it's that we represent cash customers.

The plane is high-winged and Jarí is free for the rest of the day, but, he points out, the plane's passenger door cannot be removed. Nor does it have an opening window on the passenger's side. He turns to the other plane parked on the grass and says, "The owner of that one can pull the door, no problem." He's handing us over to someone the lady says is negligent. Maybe he wants to get back at Gaspar.

Flying with Sr. Ganchão

As we talk with Jarí, a man drives up in an old, beige, VW Beetle and releases the tie-down lines under the wing of the silver Cessna. He's tall, skinny, maybe in his late forties, and a little disheveled. His light-brown hair is uncombed and his shirt tail is out. The lady gives us an "I told you so" look.

Sr. Ganchão (Lúcia mentions later that his name means "big hook" in Portuguese) says he can fly us after lunch, and he will take off the door. He's flown the area for fifteen years and knows many places where wildlife congregate. The rate is U.S. $125 an hour—a tad more than the local yokels get, but not a Cuiabá soaking either. I don't have the nerve to ask straight out if he's been in a crash lately, or when was the last time he gave the plane a tune-up.

But he's a testament to his flying abilities (he's alive), and I have this feeling that he likes it that way. "Sounds pretty good to me," I say, smiling. Gaspar grimaces at the thought. I shake hands with the man and seal the deal.

After a nervous little lunch we head back to the airstrip, arriving the same moment as Sr. Ganchão. He walks around the plane for a preflight check. As we pull the cotter pins on the right door, I make small talk to ease any lingering doubts. I ask how old the plane is. "It's a 1964 Cessna 172," comes the reply. Terrific, we're going to fly the wilderness in an antique.

Sr. Ganchão sees that my eyebrows are knit together with worry and pats the shiny engine cowl. "That's the best plane in Poconé," he says. You mean the only one available, I think to myself. It doesn't do much to bolster my confidence.

The interior has yellowed plastic seat covers, and as Lúcia, Gaspar, and I climb in, I notice that the dashboard is practically empty. There are all these black spaces where basic equipment—such as a radio and artificial horizon—should be. I ask our pilot where the rest of the dashboard is, and he says the other instruments aren't necessary. I've seen more instruments in a shopping-mall video game.

I look to Lúcia, who's been awfully quiet in the back seat. Her green eyes are wide with fear, and I'm having second thoughts too. Sr. Ganchão senses a cash customer about to flee and pushes the throttle forward, taxiing down the grass. He genuflects quickly, then guns the engine.

With the tires still spinning, we gain altitude quickly over Poconé. A tornado of air roars inside the cabin whirling dirt and paper up and out the door. It's not only the miracle of flight but also the absolutely arresting landscape that makes me forget about the dangers. Even though my right shoulder feels the blast of the air stream, it's not as frightening as I thought. I'm totally mesmerized by the terrain falling away from us.

Below, the town square and the gleaming new church blur by, then city hall, and then schoolchildren walking home in the middle of the street. A little higher and we pass over a huge, red-earth area beside the city's greenery. "What's that?" I shout above the roaring wind, pointing to many bomb-crater-size pockmarks. "Gold miners," Ganchão bellows back.

At about two hundred meters altitude, the patch of ground being worked by the miners looks nearly as big as the town itself, with its mud roads, hills of tailings, yellow dump trucks, red waste-water ponds, and lifeless trees. The air over the town is rough, making filming difficult. "Ganchão, will you make another pass?" I yell. "No," he says. I think he doesn't understand me, so I jab his arm and make a half-circle with my hand. He shakes his head no again.

"Lu, what's the matter with him?" I ask. After a few moments of conversation with Ganchão, she yells back, "He says the last time he flew a television crew over the gold diggings, the miners had a reception committee waiting when he landed. They warned him if he wanted his plane to stay in one piece not to fly reporters over the site again." The only way we can get away with buzzing the gold mine again is to have the miners see this overflight as part of a longer trip. He promises that if we have light on our return we'll shoot some more.

From five hundred meters this enormous flood plain occupies the entire horizon. It's a tractless sea of green forest, brown rivers, and grassland. And well away from Poconé there appears to be remarkably little evidence of human occupation. This breathtaking, uninterrupted panorama gives the same easy feeling that I get staring at the ocean. It's the sort of feeling about which Wallace Stegner wrote: the Pantanal represents a "geography of hope"—one of those increasingly rare, unspoiled places left on earth that most people will probably never visit. But it is assuring to know that such a place exists.

That sweet sentiment lasts a precious few minutes until we turn south and pick up the Transpantaneira's red gash cutting through the land. It's arrow straight. Barbed-wire fences abruptly tack away from the road, going nowhere in particular, dividing absolute wilderness into enormous tracts, the only other reminder that this region—about the size of France—is all privately owned.

We're overflying the road, doing a notch under 165 kilometers per hour. In less than fifteen minutes I can make out points along the road that took us several hours to reach in the Bandeirante. I'm giddy with relief that we're not banging around down there in those ruts, like a truck we see slowly picking its way around the potholes.

The pilot points down to a thicket that we're approaching and hollers that he's seen marsh deer and jungle pigs there. But this is the heat of the day, and most big animals take refuge in the thickets until sundown. He begins a slow turn to the northwest: we're going to investigate a rumor that local people told me; somewhere near the Upper Paraguay river lies one of the largest bird rookeries on the continent.

Ever so slightly the terrain begins to change, from flatland, with lakes and drying ponds, to distinct, narrow rivers trimmed by dense gallery forest. Soon the forest stretches well beyond the water's edge. A muddy river meets a clear black one in a giant Y, a mixing of coffee and cream colors. It's a Pantanal version of the famous confluence where Rio Negro enters the Amazon nearly 1600 kilometers north.

A small ranch comes into view. There's a shack and a corral with some horses. Nearby a herd of cows—white dots against the dry grass—meanders single file along a well-worn path. Several large, white birds with black heads dot the pasture. "Jabirus," Gaspar points out.

A little outpost of humanity in the middle of nowhere, I think, with not a road or navigable watercourse for kilometers. And in the rainy season it's probably transformed into an island (if not totally inundated) by the flood waters of the Paraguay River. I scan the area and can't spot a single other house; no neighbors either. Do they care?

It means months of isolation, reminding me of Admiral Byrd's long stay alone through the antarctic winter. Do they have a radio? Or maybe they really want to live that way, mimicking South America's isolated animal life. Perhaps some curious evolution is taking place down here: a watery Eden producing peaceful creatures at one with their world? Or maybe they've succumbed to bucolic torpor.

In the distance, through an increasingly smoky haze, I can make out a hill rising in the northwest. Its rounded, reddish hump is the main topographic feature of an elevated ridge. Gaspar says its Serra do Boi Morto—Dead Bull Mountain—a colorful reference to the highest point in the region, which rises seven hundred meters above sea level and is supposed to resemble a bull on its side.

Below, I see a small V formation of big, white birds flying due west and cutting sharply across a river beneath the belly of the plane. Their big, powerful wings, lined in black primary feathers, pump easily. Tucked together, the long, sturdy legs trail behind. The large, gray head and beak are a giveaway. They're flintheads—American wood storks.

Gaspar recognizes where we are and pats the pilot on the shoulder, he tilts his palm back and forth, indicating we're to follow the snaking river below. Ganchão shakes his head okay and pushes the steering yoke forward. Down we go to 150 meters, tracking the thin, shiny black waterway. We trace sharp elbow bends with luxuriant forest along the water. Another flight of storks heads in from the north, with still more formations lined up behind them. Then more. This is a grand invasion on a Normandy scale.

Now the orderly V formations are lost in a crowd of white so dense there seems to be a pale cloud hovering above the forest canopy. We gain more altitude to see the whole flock, but even at 760 meters again, I can't see them all.

In the confusion of big birds, what I take as a single flock is composed, in fact, of hundreds of storks returning in the late afternoon to roost; beneath them are thousands more already in the trees. The "white cloud" is also made up of the trees themselves—trees that have been washed white from years of nesting, until the sheer mass of the birds, their nests, and their excrement have killed some of the trees in the rookery.

I'm dying to get closer. (Perhaps that's not the best choice of words, for at 120 meters altitude and 180 kilometers per hour, with hundreds of four-kilo birds in the air, hitting one in our little plane would carry the impact of an anti-aircraft gun.) I pipe up, "Is it possible to get closer—from the ground?"

Gaspar senses my enthusiasm and tells Ganchão to carry on further upriver, and soon the big, white birds thin out and disappear along with the thick forest next to the river. In a few moments we see a clearing, then a large cattle pasture. We descend rapidly, flying above a huge, silver-domed building, then a church, and a big, hacienda-style house right on the water.

Estância Descalvado

Ganchão heads the plane in a slow arc, extending the flaps and idling the engine. We head in perpendicular to the river, right over the sprawling ranch house, and settle on a slight upgrade. This is Estância Descalvado, says Gaspar.

It's one of the biggest cattle ranches on this part of the Pantanal, originally 12,000 square kilometers (about half the size of Belgium), and one of the most famous too. We're met by an old ranch hand who's practically the only one around. Is the place abandoned? No, he explains, the ranch owner lives far away, and it hasn't been operated as a commercial ranch in years. He mentions that the owner is seriously thinking about renovating the ranch house and making Descalvado into a luxury resort. At the moment there are only a few other men and their families here to care for the property.

I mention our interest in going downriver to photograph the stork rookery; he suggests that we talk to a young man down by the water who has a boat. He might be willing to guide us there if we pay for the gas.

That silver-domed structure we saw from the plane is an enormous, rusted-out slaughterhouse. The old man walks us over to it while reminiscing about the ranch's heyday. Inside the dark, cavernous building, patches of sunlight show through holes in the galvanized roof. They spotlight patches of dirt floor and huge, geared wheels rusted together that resemble a grand clockworks.

At the beginning of World War II the ranch was owned by the British. In these dreary confines, several hundred cows were butchered and processed each day into millions of cans for shipment overseas. The British called it "bully beef" adapted from France's *boulli bif* (boiled meat). Whatever it was called, the tinned meat was a forerunner of K rations and became a love-hate object in England throughout the war years. The Descalvado boomed like a tropical Chicago stockyard.

Organs, hides, horns, bone—just about the entire animal—were utilized. As for the unusables, they were chucked into the river in a great, gory plume. The old cowboy tells us that hundreds of black vultures sat in the low trees along the river waiting for pieces of escaped offal. I shake my head, easily conjuring up the slaughterhouse scene as we walk along the path that the cattle trod. The man explains further that the considerable water flow from the Paraguay never allowed the blood and guts to stagnate and choke the river—at least not here.

Great cargo barges stopped by to pick up the meat. They also carried other jungle commodities: palm nuts and oil, rubber, dried fish, and sugar cane. The shallow boats regularly plied the Paraguay River between Cáceres, a small town about eighty kilometers due north of Descalvado, and Corumbá, the Pantanal's southern gateway city. The trip required a week or more during the rainy season to complete the 250-kilometer journey. In the dry months, low water prevented any predictable commercial traffic along the Upper Paraguay waterway.

From Corumbá, the barges made their way another 1600 kilometers south to Buenos Aires via the Paraná River. There the canned goods were transferred to ocean-going vessels that entered the South Atlantic Ocean bound for London.

A few hundred meters from the slaughterhouse is the majestic-looking old ranch house by the water. It's in total disrepair. The bright pastel paint faded long ago. Sooty marks run from the tile roof down the walls, and blotches of mold discolor the graying pink.

Yet even in its present state of decay, we are mightily impressed at the scope and grandeur of the lines. Huge, arched portals create an airy eastern wall along the riverfront. That wall joins a large, overhanging roof, forming a spacious veranda serving as a comfortable back porch. Verandas were the hallmark of laidback country living and are still an important architectural element of tropical homes.

Inside there are elegant, high-ceilinged dining and sitting rooms, a library, guest quarters, and a kitchen large enough to feed a small army. And indeed, says the old man, when the ranch was in operation, several hundred ranch hands lived in a little village of whitewashed cement houses not far from the runway. The ranch was so self-sufficient then that it had a church and even its own post office with special postal code.

The lifestyle in the hinterlands was by no means primitive. While certain conveniences had to be deferred, there was always plenty to eat—those cattle— and the Paraguay River offered a diverse bounty. What wasn't caught or butchered, barges carried in: rice, beans, coffee, fruit, *cachaça,* and yard goods.

Wealthy families came from faraway coastal towns to visit the rancher, he says. And there used to be suspicious characters, too, who sought anonymity and safety in this backwater. After all, the ranch is less than eighty kilometers from the Bolivian border. Men running from the law found work here as laborers or cowboys to lose themselves—or to prove something.

After the war the ranch passed to the hands of a Texan, John

T. Ramsey, and then to its present owner, a Brazilian business-
man who lives in São Paulo. During the late 1940s and 1950s
the *dono* encouraged guests to hunt, safari-style, and hired
professional hunters to rid the ranches of cattle-eating jaguar.
And if guests shot up the place a bit—the odd tapir, capybara,
jabiru, or caiman—they would go home with a trophy and the
place was well rid of a pest. The old man said at its peak, this
place had more than 100,000 head of beef. And he claims that
one year (right after the war) jaguars were taking six thousand
of them annually.

The Rookery

The old man walks us down to the river, where we meet the
young fellow whose name is José. He's about seventeen, athletic,
with smooth, olive skin and darting, black eyes. He wears a
woven straw hat, something akin to a sombrero, that hangs by
a thin, brown cord down his back. The cord slides just under
an enormous Adam's apple, which doesn't move much because
José seldom speaks. He prefers to nod and stare with great in-
tensity right through me.

José agrees to guide us to the rookery in his five-meter-long
aluminum boat. At this point the Paraguay is more than a
hundred meters across and its muddy waters clip along at better than three knots. Nothing to fool around with, I mutter to
myself as I step into the boat, considering the healthy populations of piranhas, caimans, and other predatory critters lurking
below the roiling current.

With a couple of tugs of the starter line, the Yamaha outboard kicks alive with its reassuring drone and we plow
through the current upstream. As we motor away from the
ranch, the grand house still looks impressive. During those war
years Descalvado must have been quite a place. On steamy
days, that lovely veranda on the water probably was the best
place on the ranch to escape the heat. I could imagine people
rocking in shaded hammocks, catching a cooling breeze that
flowed with the Paraguay.

In about a half an hour hundreds of those big, white birds

are wheeling above us in the afternoon sky. We're nearing the rookery, but it isn't as close to the water as it seemed from the air. We'll have to beach the boat and strike inland through an imposing wall of forest.

As soon as José cuts the engine, other sounds fill the air: a raucous chorus of beaks clacking and gruntings that sound as if young pigs are in those trees. The light wind fills our nostrils with rotting fish, and when it changes direction, an eye-watering smell of sulphurous swamp muck takes its place.

Huge, green bottle flies, maybe half a dozen or so, do perfect little Indy 500s around our heads. Their roar is furious and enormously annoying; thankfully they don't land or bite, but the buggers won't fly away either. I swat at them spastically, which only makes them rev their little insect engines more.

A dense mat of marsh plants fools us into thinking we're moving onto stable ground. The first steps away from the beach prove otherwise: we ooze up to our shins in thick, cool mud crisscrossed with dead vines and roots. This forest debris makes an ideal cover for predators—snakes or caimans—passing the day's heat away. José warns us to step cautiously.

Luxuriant grasses and bark-covered hanging vines grow together in a thick weave that soon halts our trek. José and Gaspar unpack their machetes to hack a path through.

High above the forest canopy a number of wood storks join black vultures in a rising thermal, circling in a column of warm air hundreds of meters up that drifts slowly to the southwest, eventually disappearing into the smoky, blue sky.

As we get closer to the rookery it's clear there's no downtown in this bird city. The big birds are spread throughout an enormous area that we figure covers several square kilometers. And they aren't all American wood storks.

There are other white waders: great egrets (*Casmerodius albus*) with long, white necks and snowy egrets (*Egretta thula*) with elegant, feathered plumes coming off the head. And colored birds too: white-necked herons (*Ardea coci*), great blue herons (*Ardea herodias*), roseate spoonbills (*Ajaia ajaja*) with their pink bodies and red rumps, and a few neotropic cormorants (*Phalacrocorax olivaceus*) with jewellike turquoise eyes.

I motion to Gaspar and Lúcia to stay put for a while so we can watch the frantic pace of the colony's late-afternoon behavior without disturbing them. Everywhere we turn the rookery is a bedlam of activity: birds landing, birds taking off, birds flying, courting, feeding, preening, and mating. At first it's impossible to focus on any one point of action.

Then, through my binoculars, I follow an adult jabiru as it breaks away from a group riding the thermals. The powerfully built bird keeps its two-meter wingspan perfectly straight as it glides past trees brimming with bird life. The big bird tilts the broad wings up and slightly back, catching the wind and bringing forward the half-bent, long legs. The long, heavy beak is lowered and the wings tilt further back, flapping, causing this bomberlike stork to stall out over the crown of the tallest tree in the colony. It comes to rest in a modest nest already overcrowded with family.

It is a rare and funny sight: both parents home and three huge fledglings in a space too small for the adults, let alone five enormous birds. This is unexpected, too, because the scientific literature says that these largest of storks shouldn't be here at all. They're supposed to establish solitary nests far away from such social colonies of other species.

A denuded tree also catches my attention. It is so jammed with birds it would make a New York tenement seem spacious. Practically every limb is occupied with nesting and roosting birds. Near one nest at the top, an adult wood stork lands, collects itself, and steps into the nest, which contains two fluffy, gray chicks. They have down as thick as sheep's wool; gawky, oversize heads; big, twinkling, black eyes; and long, yellow bills. The mouth line runs right up the beak to the facial skin, giving the distinct impression of an intelligent smile.

With the stimulation of the parent's presence, these little chicks became animated, banging their beaks against the adult's, with good result. The parent promptly regurgitates a minnow-size fish, which plops to the nest floor.

Within seconds the youngsters gulp down that and two other fish, and the adult flies away, leaving them momentarily unattended. One of the chicks watches the adult depart, then hunkers down, wedging its body between its sibling and the woven nest material, disappearing from view.

The parent is probably off on another one of an endless number of fishing trips that both adults undertake throughout the two-and-a-half-month nesting season. We haven't seen wood storks working the Paraguay river because it's too deep and lacks the concentration of little fish that their beak-snapping method of hunting can successfully exploit. For that method they have to find drying shallows much like what we saw along the Transpantaneira. That was more than 160 kilometers southeast; the storks are powerful fliers, but that's far for a fishing expedition. They could, however, range up to 80 kilometers away to locate a suitable pool.

The astounding thing is just five short months ago the Pantanal was completely flooded here, dispersing the birds. Then, as predictable as the sun itself, the place dried out, leaving seasonal pools chock full of trapped fish. The storks won't have to venture very far at all.

Unlike southern Florida's beleaguered wood storks, which are steadily losing ground to pasture, sugarcane plantations, orange groves, flood control, and Miami, the Pantanal's interior remains amazingly untouched by human interference, supporting great populations of those storks and other wading birds.

The little chicks in the nest are pretty big eaters and will need considerable food indeed; according to one estimate, a family of two adults and two offspring needs more than 240 kilos of fish before the chicks are flight-ready. If we conservatively estimate two thousand pairs of adults nesting here, that figures to be nearly 450,000 kilos of small fish just for this colony's nesting period. And there are other colonies in the Pantanal. It's a remarkable indication of this region's biological richness.

About fifteen meters in front of us, a great egret arrives at its nest, creating the very picture of domestic chaos. Three frizzy-headed chicks clamoring for food literally attack the adult. They jab at the adult's head as it lowers its long, elegant, white neck. One suddenly takes hold of the parent's bill in a tiny pincer grab with its beak. The huge bird is held hostage and spreads wide its wings in surprise until it begins to regurgitate. Then the fight moves among the siblings to gain the parent's slimy reward.

The storks seem to prefer the most precarious points on the tree for landing—the uppermost thin branches—bending them with their considerable weight. One bird bows an amazingly narrow limb down until it absorbs the full impact, near the breaking point; then the branch releases its kinetic energy, tossing the bird back into the air. Its elegant wings unfold in a high-wire balancing act. The bird bounces a couple of times until the action dampens.

Down several branches, a stork hops onto the back of its willing mate. Gracefully, outrageously, with the male balancing on it mate's back, they spread their beautiful, black-edged wings straight out, at the same time touching beaks; then, hitting their beaks together harder, the birds come in contact. For a moment the mounted storks resembled a two-headed biplane, their wings held out perfectly parallel throughout fifteen seconds of bird love.

As I hurry to photograph them, Lúcia calls me over. Through the binoculars she is excitedly watching a young fledgling trying out its wings. The chick stands up and furiously flaps its wings in a static test. Despite the outpouring of energy, the effort is barely enough to bring the chick even with the lip of the nest. More beating of the wings and there's daylight between the nest and its big feet. It's airborne! At the same instant the bird clears the nest, a strong gust of wind blows it over the side.

Down . . . down . . . down it goes, tumbling out of control, doing only what it has just learned — flapping its wings — then hitting branches and thudding to the detritus litter on the floor of the colony. I can't see if the hapless chick survives the fall because instantly it is set upon by black-headed vultures waiting on the ground.

There's a sudden flapping of black wings; half a dozen hulking birds mob the white chick, tearing it to pieces. One of the vultures has been victorious in dismembering the largest part of the chick and hops away from the group to down its prize. We gaze at each other, speechless.

This was a food fight, jungle style, and a stunning demonstration that however gardenlike the Pantanal may appear, it's ruled by a wild animal economy, where an untimely accident is simply another's lucky sustenance. But that ecological saw in no way quiets my queasy stomach as I watch the little bird come to an early end.

In a few minutes we trudge closer to the base of the nest

tree. It's a real garbage dump. White bird wash douses everything: plants and tree trunks, even the dirt. I kick aside the top
layer of fallen twigs and find long, white, pink, and brown
adult feathers discarded from preening, fish bits, and what
looks like chicken feet. Gaspar confirms they are the remains of
other chicks that have fallen overboard or met with some other
fate.

Lúcia points to a couple of trees, right next to a nest tree,
that have a number of caracaras in them. They are waiting pa-
tiently for the adult storks to err long enough to allow them to
pick off a hatchling.

As we walk around the area, José points his machete to a
long, green, iguana lizard resting on the limb of a nest tree.
Has it just been up there taking lunch? Or is it waiting for
sundown before it climbs up? While the young birds remain
flightless they'll be easy pickings to a whole host of Pantanal
predators. Troops of coatis can sweep into the nests—or a
jaguarundi, anaconda, or even a column of army ants—and
devour the flightless chicks. That's the law of the land. But
these colonies are ancient, resilient, and as long as there are
food and sufficient habitat, a marvel of fecundity.

At times the mated storks return home to an empty nest—
ravaged by predator or storm—and will be stimulated to begin
the entire reproduction cycle all over again. With a little luck
they can raise an entire new clutch to first flight before the torrential rains begin.

Documenting this stork metropolis makes me curious about
how long this rookery has been here. Everyone I ask at the
ranch says it has always been here. Does that mean twenty
years? A century or more?

And how many birds are resting here? Years ago I made
several visits to Florida's Corkscrew Swamp Sanctuary, the last
thriving wood stork colony in North America. In the 1988–89
nesting season only 755 pairs mated in Corkscrew. This rookery is many times greater, covering an area at least a kilometer
long and several hundred meters deep.

More questions. Where do these great birds go in the rainy
season? And does that pall of smoke from the dry-season forest
and grassland burnings have an effect on the birds and their
nesting?

Here is one of the Pantanal's wondrous secrets—perhaps tens of thousands of wood storks—one of a number of giant rookeries virtually unknown, unstudied, and unprotected.

But before I can think of any more questions, Gaspar is yanking our shirt tails and pointing to his watch. It's getting very late and the pilot will be more than a little upset if we have to sleep on the floor of that old ranch house.

We board the plane reluctantly and take off as the sun is setting. I keep my fingers crossed that Sr. Ganchão knows his way back. But I don't care. A blood-red sun is fast slipping out of sight, hypnotizing me while the images of the rookery dance in my mind. Within an hour and a half, like a huge homing pigeon, we are circling Poconé's dark airstrip, preparing to land in a dim afterglow.

eight

Poconé Gold Field

Why can't Brazil's gold be in the deserts of the northeast instead of here?
—*Adelberto Eberhard, conservationist*

Heading into Poconé after our plane ride, we stop several times along the road to shoot pictures. Locals walking to town figure it's a good chance to hop a ride, and in no time our Bandeirante takes on the appearance of a Mexican truck. A lank, old man flags us down in front of his field shack. He has an Asian-looking face, grandfatherly white beard, and a rope belt holding up his raggedy pants. He picks up a little cooking pot and gently places half a dozen eggs in it, then sprinkles dirt over them to cushion against the bounces and climbs in back.

Two little black kids with big, twinkling eyes and great grins get in as I jump out to shoot a huge marsh deer (*Blastocerus dichotomus*, the largest deer on the continent) with eight-point antlers. The magnificent, reddish-brown deer has just emerged from thick shrubs and regally stands its ground, staring back at us and barely twitching its tail in nervousness.

I tell Gaspar that I'm surprised to see one so trusting; in the United States deer are shot at so much that they seldom stay in an area with people. He says big marsh deer are becoming harder to find here; they're not hunted for their poor-tasting meat, but to make folk medicines. A yearling's spike antlers,

135

for instance, are used by some Pantaneiros and natives as an aphrodisiac.

A few more kilometers up the road stands a young white woman in pedal-pushers wearing the unmistakable badge of a tourist: freshly sunburned skin. She, too, is following the deer. In broken Portuguese she explains she's German and hitchhiking the Transpantaneira alone. The two little kids watch her climb in and gaze joyously at her pendulous breasts. As we bounce along, they roll their eyes in glee. After we drop her at the rural bus station, the two boys say she's the same person who was lost on the road last night. They saw her knocking on doors of *fazendas* asking shelter for the night. Did she get in? Or did she sleep by the road? They didn't know.

We're so tired from the exhilarating plane ride and trek to the stork rookery that we decide to stay at the same hotel Gaspar and I stayed at when we began the trip. In fact, we get the same room I had going out. Nothing's changed. The toilet still doesn't flush properly. While I'm carrying in the gear, Lúcia's scoping out the room and reports that it has a fairly decent selection of wildlife, enough to occupy a naturalist for several days.

There's a giant grasshopper on the blue bedspread, a kind reminiscent of tobacco-spitting ones in Wisconsin. A toad about six centimeters long hops into the corner of the room; we run around the room trying to catch it, then it leaps to safety under the bed. In the bathroom a tiny frog about 2 cm long is stimulated by the bare-bulb light and hops high up the wall out of reach.

A small lizard looking like a rubber facsimile is stuck to the upper part of the bedroom wall near the air conditioner. And when I go to inspect it, it does a couple of pushups, opening its mouth wide and practically terrorizing me. Several little, black beetles about the size of apple seeds crawl on the floor, and when Lúcia steps on them in her thongs, it makes a sound similar to shelling peanuts.

Then there's a muffled shriek from the shower stall. "Victor, will you come here a moment?" Lúcia calls out. "What's the matter?" I ask, unpacking fresh clothes. "There's a spider about the size of a dinner plate in here, and he doesn't want to share the shower with me," she explains.

Lúcia insists I take a shower with her, and I say sure; but I can't understand why she's so worried about a little spider. When I get there, I gulp. The thing looks like a dark Alaska king crab hanging from cables. It moves to inspect one of its webs with the calm movement of a road warrior after Mad Max. I make the manly gesture by placing Lúcia between me and the creature.

Immediately we start fighting each other trying to keep from being pushed to the back of the stall where the creature hangs in anticipation. I try to comfort Lúcia and belittle her description. It's not the size of a dinner plate, I console, but more like a porthole.

There are also numerous tiny, pale-red ants scaling the walls and bigger, dark-brown ones near the bathroom mirror. Some diaphanous-winged flies wriggle in the upper-corner spider webs; one that's not completely entwined makes a feeble buzzing sound with its wings.

Out of the shower, we get ready to turn in. I flip the lights off and we crawl into bed. Hungry female marsh mosquitoes force us to take refuge beneath the covers with just our noses sticking out. But Luce has forgotten her skin lotion, and when she turns the light back on, she's horrified: two cockroaches the size of cigar butts race across the floor. Luce shivers, "Ooochh! I can't stand those things." As they beat a hasty retreat to the shower, Luce grabs one of our "clean" towels rank with mildew and stuffs it over the shower drain as they tumble below. She theorizes that there's a roach hatchery below.

In the morning, I feel a tightness in my temples and can open only one eye. Lúcia has slept holding onto my head with a paralyzing grip.

After paying our bill, we load up the Bandeirante and discover it won't start. Dead battery, says Gaspar. At about the same time we hear a heavy-engined vehicle coming down the road. "It's a gold miner going to work," says Gaspar. A sleepy-eyed man is at the controls of a Case bulldozer. Gaspar seizes the moment and hails the fellow to push-start our truck (which has the forestry services' old "IBDF" logo on it).

There is more than slight irony here because neither man can stand the other. Maybe the gold miner doesn't like seeing his enemy—the forestry officer—at a disadvantage. He lowers the bulldozer's huge shovel, catching the Bandeirante under the tailgate, and guns the engine. The diesel comes to life with a belch of black smoke; then we load up and head over to the bank to change some dollars.

When we drive up to the Banco do Brasil the curtains are drawn, and a small piece of paper taped to the window says "*Greve*," strike. Another bank strike throughout the country. There are fifteen people standing in line in front of the glass door, but the armed guard won't let anyone in. The strike is for salary increases to try to keep up with inflation—the only legal basis for a strike in Brazil—and it's been on for a week.

Cab drivers sitting under a sprawling fig tree in front of the bank playing cards don't have enough money to change a few of our dollars. They recommend trying the gold-assay offices in town. Sometimes they buy dollars. We have nothing to lose; without some cruzados novo we'll be stuck in Poconé for days.

There are several assay offices facing the town square, all doing a brisk trade. Tough-looking miners hang around their doors. We go to a little snack bar down the street from one and get a *misto quente*—toasted cheese and ham sandwich—fresh juice, and coffee.

Half a dozen miners inside are downing shots of *cachaça* and talking heatedly about their gold works. Gaspar walks to one of the booths away from us and sits some distance from the men, but one of them recognizes him and immediately changes the subject. Even out of uniform, Gaspar's despised on sight.

The Assay Office

After breakfast I ask Gaspar to stay with the truck on the far side of the town square. I believe it's for his own protection—the way those miners glared at him. He doesn't want us to go into the assay office on our own, but I'm confident nothing will happen to us in a public area. The storefront is painted bright yellow over stucco, with red letters reading "Mattos

Metal." Frosted-glass windows are installed around the open doorway, and several bikes are leaning against a utility pole in front.

Inside the office is a cramped room, very busy and resembling a shoddy bank. A glass partition and wooden counter separate the back of the room from us. On the counter between the cashier and a man with a torch is a large, old-fashioned double-pan balance. Five black kids in bathing trunks and beach thongs, probably miners' helpers, crowd around the left end of the counter with noses pressed up against the glass, watching the skinny man in welding goggles apply the torch to a thick, iron ladle.

The flame envelops the ladle in a brilliant, sodium-yellow ball of fire, illuminating the corner of the room and painting the man's dark goggles with orange light. The ball of metal in the ladle has melted into a fiery liquid; I've come close to the window, too, pushing in beside some of the kids. On top of the shiny liquid float impurities that the man burns away. He then pulls the ladle away from the flame, and the liquid glows yellow. Within seconds it cools to a dull yellow, and he dumps the metal disc onto the counter, sending up blue smoke as hot metal burns into the wood.

A short, white woman with frizzy, brown hair and wild, darting eyes picks up the thick disc and tosses it gingerly from hand to hand. She then rubs it with a cloth and pops it onto the pan of a jeweler's digital scale sitting on the back counter. Electronic red lights flicker, spinning through numbers in a mineralogical wheel of fortune and stopping on 1 . . . 8 . . . 7. "That's 18.7 grams," she says, handing the disc through the cashier's window to a bearded fellow in turquoise swim trunks.

The woman says at today's rates the yellow-metal disc is worth 532 novo cruzados, slightly more than U.S. $250. She asks if the owner will accept payment half in novo cruzados and half by check; the bank strike has reduced their supply of currency. "*Tá bom,*" the man says, okay, and he hands the thick, gold coin back through the cashier's window. As she counts out the cash, I ask the man how long it took him to mine that gold. "Last week," the young man says, grinning.

Another miner, also in swim trunks, steps forward and hands over a silvery ball about the size of a quail egg to the

man with the goggles. He puts it into the crucible, spoons on
some boric acid, and applies the flame.

Lúcia walks up to the cashier and asks if she will change our
money. When she asks how much, Lúcia and I talk together in
English; we're wary about flashing big bills. We tell her about
a couple of hundred and then haggle over the exchange rate.
The place is now full of curious miners, who turn from the assayer to look at us.

Another man right next to us is receiving a stack of money
from the cashier. Lúcia jabs me in the ribs and uses her great
big eyes to draw attention to half a dozen little glass vials resting on the counter next to the old balance. Inside the vials is
poisonous quicksilver—mercury—being sold to miners to concentrate gold dust. It's been outlawed throughout Brazil for
months. Unfortunately, it's the same with many other laws. It's
one thing to outlaw a practice in Brasília and quite another to
enforce it way out here.

The man next to us pulls from his pants pocket a wad of
bills as thick as a triple-decker sandwich and begins wrapping
the new ones around it. I see an opportunity to photograph the
mercury and ask if I can take a picture of his money. He
laughs, and I hold his hand still on the counter a short distance
from the vials. A slight tilt up with my ring flash and snap—a
timely still life of a fistful of money and illegal mercury in the
shadows. The thick roll, the man's proud to say, has several
thousand dollars' worth of cruzados novo, money he will use
this week to pay bills for his gold operation.

The man's name is Miguel. Our interest in his newfound
wealth is disarming, and he begins talking to us with great enthusiasm about gold in Poconé. Miguel is in his late forties,
short, with a big gut; walnut skin shows around a graying
beard. For this area he's pretty well dressed: straw Panama hat,
prewashed denim jacket, overalls, and worn, black, congressman's gaiters. The outfit is set off by a necklace and bracelet of
Poconé gold.

Miguel says in the early 1980s he was living in São Paulo
when Guido, a childhood pal, called him to come back to Poconé and help in his election campaign for mayor.

"I grew up here," says Miguel. "We knew each other from
school. Guido promised if he won I would become the com-

missioner of security." Guido did win the election and soon after appointed Miguel manager of security. I wasn't sure what
that meant in a sleepy little town, but visions of rural Mexican
officials came to mind.

"It was pretty quiet," Miguel continues, "until gold was
found here in 1983. I mean rediscovered, because in the
eighteenth century gold was found here by *bandeirantes* exploring the region around Cuiabá. When that happened, the
town had only four big dump trucks. Within twenty-four
hours after the word got out, there were 1500 available" to
take the gold-laden dirt to be processed. With so many trucks
and earth-moving equipment roaring into town it wasn't hard
to imagine the noise, confusion, and traffic jams that suddenly
materialized.

The mayor directed Miguel to organize this boom-town
fleet. Which he did. And he continued to do so for several
years until the mayor ran in the next election. Guido lost that
election but saw a golden opportunity to expand his considerable mining activity (he had hired men to work his digs
throughout his administration).

Armed with other investors' money, Guido expanded his
claim into one of the larger holdings in the Poconé gold field.
Again he asked Miguel to come help him—this time to manage
the men in the field. As the operation manager, Miguel explains, "I take care of all the expenses here and pay wages to
the miners." Wages equal about U.S. $35 per week—four times
higher than the national minimum wage. At this rate, even
these lowly workers are very protective of their jobs, making it
difficult for us to document the place. "I have much to pay,"
says Miguel. "We use a lot of electricity here; it's brought in to
run lights and motors. We need parts and fuel for our trucks
and bulldozers. It comes to about U.S. $5000 a month."

Suddenly he offers, "I'm going over to the mine right now.
Why don't you come with me?" I'm hesitant. Gaspar has
warned us about the miners; they're not to be trusted. Worse,
he's waiting for us on the other side of the town square, thinking we'll be back in minutes. Miguel seems to sense our reluc-
tance and insists, "It's just ten minutes away." Curiosity gets
the better part of my judgment, and Luce knits her eyebrows
together in doubt. "Okay, twenty minutes, but that's all," she

says. We pile into his lime-green Fiat, which is dusted in red dirt, and leave town.

As we bounce along the dirt road I'm trying to remember our plane ride over the gold field; I'm not sure, but it feels like we're going another way. The road begins to wind, there are fewer houses, and those we do see are of sod construction with naked children playing in front among free-ranging chickens. The road narrows, crowded by a jungle of pale-green sugar cane towering a meter above our little car, blocking the view. I don't have a clue where we are. Luce senses the danger—that we may be going for the wrong kind of ride.

We pass a short, bare-chested man with a bright-red stocking cap walking toward us. Then a dump truck appears from around a bend, heading toward us and kicking up dust. The road starts to rival the Transpantaneira with great potholes that Miguel navigates poorly, banging the Fiat's oil pan many times. Several minutes go by as we work our way down the sugar-cane corridor; then it abruptly stops. And so do we.

The Gold Field

Before us is a large area about the size of ten football fields cleared of plants, trees, and soil, leaving only the iron-red earth and clay. Little, red mountains piled fifteen meters high with ore-bearing earth are scattered throughout the site. Most adjoin large, rectangular pits about the size of an Olympic swimming pool, with one end gradually inclining to the deep end, six meters down, enabling bulldozers to shovel the earth easily.

Miguel stops on the edge of one of the deepest pits. It's very narrow—less than two and a half meters across—close to thirty meters deep, and empty. At various depths there are logs bracing the walls. "We do this because at another site the walls turned to mud, collapsing on the miners below and killing them," says Miguel.

He points to a dark, wavering line running through the clay from north to south. "We discovered this rich gold vein not long ago. It's so rich we don't use machines. The men are able to go right to the ore." Several thick fire hoses hang down the walls of the pit, sucking water from the bottom. "This is hard work this time of year," he says. "We don't know when the rains will come. And when they do, they'll flood us out."

Miguel walks across the road and peers into a small pool of water. "That's another pit," he says, "but it's much deeper than the first one you saw. I flooded it because cracks were starting to develop. We'll leave it alone until the dry season next year; then we'll pump it out and begin digging again."

We walk through the gold field. Dump trucks and bulldozers roar by us; screaming electrical motors power ore-processing machinery, and gasoline engines connect squirting water pumps to many long hoses that snake in and out of the pits. I can hear the shouts of truck drivers calling to miners above the blaring noise. They're yelling to several hardened-looking men standing in the shade of a wooden lean-to beside a narrow pit. They're the next shift going down in the pit. By far this is the busiest place in the field.

There are several hundred men laboring in the broiling sun. We carefully step to the edge of the pit to see a man in a mud-encrusted bathing suit step into a large, wooden bucket and descend into the depths. He's being lowered by a man standing on a rickety, wood platform who simply uncranks a hemp rope as you would on an old well.

At the bottom, the man steps from the bucket into shin-deep, yellow water. All the miners down there wear only trunks—no safety hats or equipment. Some are barefoot. Buckets piled high with gold-laden dirt are hauled up and then dumped into wheelbarrows.

Other men stand near the pit hawking cold pop and popsicles from Styrofoam coolers with "Kissou" painted on the front. The miners take turns coming up to buy some relief; with the frozen sugar water in plastic tubes hanging from their mouths, they step into the bucket for another ride down.

"The heavy equipment," says Miguel "is used only to remove the surface dirt. That vein is very rich. It's best that men do it by hand." I ask how rich it is. "In the beginning each dump truck took seven or eight grams of gold per load. If the gold is just four grams per load, nobody wants to do the mining because it won't pay," he notes.

Today he's taking between four and six grams per truck—on

the first washing. The truck backs up to a metal slide and dumps the earth into a wooden hopper. There several men with high-pressure hoses wash the dirt into a sluice gate, where the slurry of dirt and water forms a fast, red river.

The water runs into an electrically driven centrifuge and spins wildly in a grave-size hole. The heavier dirt with the gold is thrown to the rim of the centrifuge while the waste water passes into another pit. There it's sucked into a black, plastic hose and sprayed onto a growing tailings mound fifty meters away. At this point the water runs off, leaving behind the settled-out diggings. Eventually these tailings hills reach considerable heights. And there they'll remain. Big, barren, and red.

Miguel points to a mound and adds, "Not long ago we discovered that if we processed each truckload a second time we found two to four more grams of gold." That doesn't sound like much until Miguel says his operation runs twenty-four hours a day, with 125 trucks during the day and another 125 trucks through the night.

I start noodling around with some of Miguel's numbers. I figure an average of 6 grams of gold per truck. That yields 1500 grams every twenty-four hours. With Sundays and holidays off, this mine produces about 36,000 grams per month. A recent newspaper quotes the price of gold at 28.5 cruzados novo per gram, so that's 1,026,000 cruzados novo a month. The current *mercado negro* (black market) exchange rate is 2.10 cruzados novo per dollar. That yields a tidy $488,571 a month, or $5,862,857 a year, just for Miguel's operation. And there are more than five hundred such digs working the region.

I ask what's the biggest single piece of gold he's found there. Miguel replies, "We don't have it like Serra Pelada [the famous gold field in the state of Pará, where many baseball-size nuggets have been unearthed]. All ours is placer gold, or it goes through the grinder. But," he beamed, "my biggest take in a day was .5 kilogram of gold, worth U.S. $6785."

How do they get the actual gold if it's all dust? Miguel ushers us over to a padlocked wooden shed. Inside there's a holding tank about the size of a kid's backyard plastic pool, and it's filled with red water. On a board across it is a miner's gold pan. Miguel demonstrates. He places a cupful of mud containing the gold into the pan, adds a little water, and pours in some liquid mercury.

He agitates the pan in a circular motion with hypnotic repetition; the mercury has the property of attracting to itself only the particles of gold. Then he drains off the water through a hole in the center of the conical pan. He pours the remaining quicksilver into a rag and squeezes out the excess water. Finally, he unwraps the rag, revealing that conglomeration of mercury and gold that's taken to the assay office.

Miguel's holding tank for the mercury waste water sits there. He's not telling for how long or what's done with it. Careless handling and disposal of this toxic heavy metal may be polluting the water-based food chains so important to the Pantanal's ecosystem. The use of mercury is rapidly becoming a serious problem here.

There is so much mercury being used in Poconé out in the open. I had thought it was used only in the big digs in the northern reaches of the Amazon. From what I see, the frequent handling of mercury by miners and assayers demonstrates that they don't believe it's harmful to the environment or to themselves. A University of Mato Grosso professor in Cuiabá told me that if figuring the amount of gold is difficult, estimating the amount of mercury is practically impossible.

Public health officials make guesses by resorting to estimates of gold mined. Then they extrapolate from that figure to determine the mercury in use. Their guideline is: for every gram of gold mined, the miners require three grams of mercury to concentrate the placer gold. But even an educated guess about how much gold is produced around here proves to be nearly impossible.

By federal decree, miners in Brazil are required to sell their gold only to the government at a slight discount from the international rate. Of course, the miners don't like that sort of discount, so they try to sell it on the black market or smuggle it out of the country — for the higher prices and also to avoid taxes. The gold is secreted out of the country through Bolivia and Montevideo, Uruguay, to points around the world without the government ever knowing.

To estimate the amount of mercury used in Poconé, I do some more noodling based on Miguel's gold-production figures.

If his operation produces 432,000 grams of gold a year, then he uses 1,296,000 grams of mercury annually—or almost 1300 kilos of the stuff. The staggering numbers don't seem possible. Watching Miguel and the assayer nonchalantly using mercury brings to mind the tragedy of Minamata Bay and Niigata, Japan. From the mid-1960s to mid-1970s more than twelve hundred people in both cities died from mercury poisoning. It took the Japanese years to figure out that mercury in the form of industrial waste was contaminating the region's most important food: locally caught fish.

Minamata's plight was documented by the late *Life* magazine photographer W. Eugene Smith. His book *Minamata, Words and Pictures,* published in 1975, presented stark pictures of this little-known environmental affliction. I recall the haunting image of a dying woman being held by her mother, an image referred to as an ecological Pietá. The Japanese call the disease *itai, itai* (hurt, hurt) because the mercury attacks the central nervous system and inflames bone joints.

According to occupational health and epidemiology researchers I interviewed before coming here, spotting mercury poisoning is not easy, especially for health workers untrained in this area of occupational hazards. Precise testing of water and biological samples in the field is practically impossible. The nearest lab able to analyze for heavy metals is located in São Paulo. Water and tissue samples require immediate processing by gas chromatography equipment, tools that are only now being planned for a future health lab in Cuiabá.

Assayers in Poconé and all the people in the enclosed offices may well suffer from acute toxicity by inhaling the vapors day after day or eating contaminated food or water, to say nothing of the locals fishing the streams containing mercury run-off. It may show up as a lung condition or, if toxicity has reached a dangerous level (measured at fifty micrograms per liter of urine), there can be inflamed gums, tremors in the hands, and erethism—the "mad hatter" syndrome.

The Mad Hatter's behavior in *Alice in Wonderland* was based on the nineteenth-century occupational disease contracted from handling mercury. The mercury was used in crinkling felt for fur hats. Workers with this stage of mercury poisoning exhibited personality extremes from shyness to irritable dispositions. I

remember the nervous woman cashier in the assay office with
the wild stare in her head.

Is it possible that a biological time bomb is ticking away as
the mercury enters the Pantanal's waterways and passes along
the food chain? Can what happened in industrial Japan happen
here in remote, wild Brazil?

As we leave the busy gold field three young boys are playing near one of the tailings ponds on the edge of the mining
area. The pit has thick, ochre-colored water about three meters
below the surface. Playing follow-the-leader, the kids peel off
pretty good jackknife dives into the water. The littlest boy
doesn't have a bathing suit on and sheepishly covers himself
when he sees Lúcia walking by. He quickly dives back into the
water and waves to us as we look on, speechless.

Gaspar is understandably miffed with us for disappearing
with a miner and doesn't calm down for several miles as we
leave town in the truck. He points to a number of abandoned
digs on private property. They aren't hard to find; all we have
to do is look for a red hill where the earth has been thrown up
and worked over. Miners had approached the ranch owners,
offering to cut them in on the gold profits. Of course, what
they failed to mention was that when the mine played out, the
ruined land would be theirs too.

Walking through one site sends shivers through me. There
are crippled, barren trees. Not a blade of grass or any other
living thing stirs amidst the barren, red moonscape.

nine

Arne Sucksdorff,
Swedish Pantaneiro

When people see his movies . . . they never forget.
—*Antonio Gonçalves Filho, Brazilian journalist*

*W*hen we return to Cuiabá, I take Gaspar's suggestion and
call Arne Sucksdorff, the man whose Pantanal pictures adorn
forestry service offices in Brasília, Cuiabá, as well as several
airports, tourist agencies, and hotels, including the one I'm
staying in.

Although his photographs have become virtual icons of the
region, and he's been working for more than thirty years to
save the Pantanal, Sucksdorff is known mostly to older people
familiar with the problems here. And like the largely overlooked Pantanal itself, this multitalented artist has also been
forgotten in his native land, Sweden.

Sucksdorff lives in a comfortable tropical home on a hill in a
quiet residential street on the outskirts of Cuiabá. The home's
front yard has been lovingly landscaped with many bushes and
flowering tropical plants. As Lúcia and I pull up in the noisy
Bandeirante, a young Brazilian woman comes out onto the veranda. She walks down the path, opens the iron gate, and ushers
us up to the veranda, where we are to make ourselves comfortable. "Sr. Sucksdorff will be out in a moment," she says.

Around us are hanging plants, two swaying hammocks, and

148

a cage housing an Amazon parrot. An overweight black Labrador gets up from the red tile floor and comes over to investigate us, sniffing our feet and issuing a perfunctory nervous yip before settling back down near one of the hammocks.

A gardener in the front yard is weeding some plants, and several children play in the street. I'm looking at the parrot trying to decide if I should stick a finger in the cage when a tall, pale man shuffles from the living room out the front door.

"Hallooo," he says in heavily accented English, offering a big handshake. Sucksdorff is a tall man—at least six-feet-three—but slightly round-shouldered from hunkering over a desk. His hair is sandy brown, long, and combed back over his head, revealing a deeply receding hairline. He's wearing large, oval glasses over pale-blue eyes and smoking a straight pipe. Dressed in old bermudas and sandals, he's at one with the comfortable furnishings on the veranda. It's hard to believe Sucksdorff is in his seventies.

It's difficult partly because of his deceptively high energy level. At one moment, I think I'm going to have to lean over and catch him before he falls. Then he begins talking about the Pantanal and it's clear he's been through a lot. But as the minutes turn to hours, I barely put questions to him before he's taken the thought and is off and running about his abiding love of the Pantanal—and it's hard to catch up.

Sucksdorff came to Brazil in 1962 after having accepted a United Nations assignment to teach a course in filmmaking at a university in Rio. Through friends he heard about the Pantanal, made a visit, and spent twenty years in and around there. I make the mistake of calling the Pantanal a swamp early on in our conversation, and he is quick to correct: "It's a flood plain, not a swamp. The Pantanal has none of the drawbacks of a swamp, no stagnant water. This is a paradise. No disease, no malaria. The weak and sick [animals] are eliminated and cleaned up before illness can spread. It's fabulous."

So enthralled by this region, Sucksdorff disappeared from Sweden, becoming immersed in the machinations of Latin life, leaving behind his wife and children and beginning another family in this unlikely place. In Brazil he completed another feature film, *My Home Is Copacabana,* an unprecedented view of life in Rio as seen by homeless children, presaging *Pixote,* the famous film of street children in Rio. Critics in Sweden wrote him off for producing non-Swedish subjects and living abroad, and today few Swedes know what happened to the filmmaker who was seen as a peer of Ingmar Bergman.

The frustration of being a Scandinavian accustomed to living in a clean, orderly society is constant. Bureaucracy, extremes of wealth and poverty, extremes in education, economic chaos, and loss of political will through rampant corruption are all elements that Sucksdorff has had to deal with for three decades.

There have been compensating factors, such as living for many years in one of the most beautiful and remote regions of the Pantanal. He discovered an area with a profusion of animal life that had seldom seen humans. When Sucksdorff talks about the wildlife he lights up, along with his pipe, puffing away enthusiastically. After sipping some cold beer together, he invites us inside to see the project he's working on.

Inside there's a large living room with few furnishings. The adjoining dining room has a wealth of photographs on the walls and dining table. All are landscapes, aerials, and close-ups documenting his time in the Pantanal.

Sucksdorff wrote a book about his experiences in an area not far from Poconé called Paraguayzinho, Little Paraguay River, one of the sources of the larger Paraguay River. Here he and his new Brazilian wife, Maria, came to live with the Pantanal's wild riches for many months. A photograph taken during that time shows the couple feeding a catfish to a young, giant river otter at the water's edge. The otter is standing on its hind legs, like a dog, begging.

Lúcia is disbelieving. "You weren't afraid of the *ariranha?*" She relates an incident at the Brasília zoo during her childhood. A child fell into the giant river otter exhibit, and a policeman went in after the child. He fell and was subsequently bitten on the arm by one of the otters. The bite later became infected and the policeman eventually died, leaving everyone in Brasília mighty fearful of giant river otters.

Sucksdorff protests, "That's nonsense; these animals aren't so aggressive." He points to the begging otter in the picture. "I trained this 'wild' one myself. In a matter of days it was catching fish and bringing them to us."

In the picture Sucksdorff looks the part of Robinson Crusoe:

barefoot with rolled-up pants; knife tucked in his thick, black belt; swept-back, blond hair falling into his smiling face; and the ever-present, long-stemmed pipe in the corner of his mouth. He doesn't have to explain a thing. The picture is a sensational moment out of many spent in the Pantanal, which he calls Eden, Paradise, over and over in our conversation.

The pictures bring to mind a wetland version of Argentine writer W.H. Hudson's classic *Green Mansions*. It's the story of a young revolutionary fleeing to the South American jungle to escape authorities and meeting an unearthly beautiful and natural creature named Rema. (In Sucksdorff's case it was Maria, a native Cuiabano and trained agronomist.) Together they discovered the secret places in the rivers and forests where the animals became their friends.

Sucksdorff's magical ability with wild animals dates back decades to his childhood days in Sweden on his father's farm outside Stockholm. There he would venture into the woods and take the time to observe nature. After his formal education in Sweden and Germany, he returned home to Stockholm with an Arriflex movie camera to shoot a wonderful and widely acclaimed film, *The Great Adventure,* produced in 1953.

The film tells the story of two young brothers on a farm in central Sweden who catch a young river otter and bring her home. One of the boys lets the father know about the hidden animal. When the father finds out, he warns the boys that the otter will have to return to the forest. Sucksdorff's camera reveals the subtle parade of the seasons and the growing urges in the animal, as well as the boys' desire to hold onto what they've caught. They tame the otter through the winter, but when spring arrives, and when their guard is down, the otter escapes to begin its own great adventure of discovering the world of the Swedish forest.

This was Sucksdorff's first feature film, running ninety minutes and costing just $50,000. It won wide acclaim, receiving the Grand Prix award at the 1955 Cannes Film Festival. Reviewers have often compared his films to Robert Flaherty's classic documentaries *Nanook of the North* and *Louisiana Story*.

According to the Swedish Film Institute in Stockholm, in the 1940s and 1950s Sucksdorff was regarded as an up-and-coming young talent in Swedish cinema. His films shot in black-and-white are powerful studies of nature and the power of innocence. Their stark beauty is still impressive today, as I found when I viewed four of them in the Swedish consulate offices in Chicago. They have none of the cute, sanitized nature depicted in Disney films that were produced nearly twenty years later.

The degree of technical finish and painstaking labor used by Sucksdorff to achieve uncontrived wildlife scenes are legendary. One report had him shooting more than 30,000 meters of film just for a fifteen-minute program. It was this fanatical attention to painstaking detail that eventually led to international recognition and acclaim. In 1949 he won an Oscar for his short film *Rhythm of the City*.

But Sucksdorff is reluctant to bring up those artistic successes of the past. Now he devotes his complete energies to his photographs and to reworking his book about his time spent along the Little Paraguay.

I ask about the photo murals decorating public places. "Yes, they're mine," he admits. He had gone to the head of the forestry service, offering to donate the images if they would distribute them in an effort to get the message out about the Pantanal. It's odd that, even in Brazil, this place had only been known to adventurous outdoorsmen.

Sucksdorff says there's a great deal to be done. He contends that the main problems facing the Pantanal are not within the region "but around it. You must go and see the Chapada dos Guimarães. It's wonderful," he says. This is the plateau where many of the Pantanal's rivers begin. "It's absolutely criminal what the farmers are doing to the water there. They are using agrotoxins—tons and tons of the poisons are being sprayed onto their soybean and corn fields. They don't even protect the people who are doing the spraying. I read a study that claims 40 percent of those people are condemned to death because they don't take any precautions whatsoever.

"And worse, now they have mercury poisoning right here. Have you been to Poconé? Those gold miners are going to die from mercury poisoning. These waters carry those poisons into the Pantanal to the fish and animals. Why even the tapirs eat fish here and get the poisons. It's terrible. And the authorities are absolutely corrupt. They say much and do nothing."

He's very agitated by telling this to us. He lights his pipe
again, sucking in deeply.

Aside from chemical pollution of the Pantanal's headwaters.
Sucksdorff complains that there are more insidious types of
problems. "We have tremendous problems here. The worst is
education. I've been to America, and it's like Europe—you have
to study hard in college. Here students barely do four hours a
week. They're always interrupted by teachers' strikes. With
raging inflation, teachers must strike regularly to make sure
their salaries get adjusted. These strikes can go on for months
at a time, and nothing gets accomplished in school. Teachers
are so badly paid and badly educated themselves that they can't
maintain their own family. It's impossible.

"And you can't talk with a professor intelligently about
Charles Darwin because Darwin was an atheist, and you can't
talk with children here about him either. Oh, no, you can't talk
with children about biology." It's ironic here, on the doorstep
of some of the greatest wildlife than can be seen.

"People can have twelve children in the family, and not one
knows about reproduction," Sucksdorff continues. "I have an
American book [sent by the Watch Tower Bible Tract Society]
that the students use in the classrooms here. People send them
down from pro-life groups. They abuse scientific facts, manip-
ulate everything, and cheat the people."

I ask why the government allows such materials to be dis-
tributed here. "They don't have money for regular textbooks,"
Sucksdorff declares. "I protested this [to the governor]," he says
vehemently, "and told him this can't go on."

Sucksdorff's fierce love of the Pantanal reminds me of
professor Helmut Sick, the famous ornithologist in Rio. So
many Europeans and North Americans come to Brazil and become enraptured with the profusion of nature. The vast
majority of local people see this and wonder why.

"You see, we have here professional politicians," he mumbles. "Nothing gets done. Nothing works here without money
making an economy of value. They don't realize what they
have: a little East Africa. They just don't understand how
tourism could be very important for them. So I open my
mouth."

He talks about many types of pollution, the defrauding of

the Indians, the killing of animals: "These are crimes against nature. It's an ancient attitude stemming back hundreds of years to early colonial days.

"It's like what happened in Australia. Portugal released prisoners and undesirables and sent them over to South American labor colonies. They went in with the sole purpose of finding wealth . . . gold . . . diamonds . . . emeralds . . . and take, take, take. And it's still true today.

"They've got a good new constitution. There's even a place for the Pantanal as part of the recognized national heritage. But crimes against nature must carry serious penalties, and they must physicalize these laws with men and equipment. But there's no money, and little tax money returns here.

"With so much economic chaos and corruption, it's almost impossible to have good conservation. I think about the only way for doing this now is to have outside groups come here and buy some of these lands and administer them as private national parks. I like some of your country's environmental groups, like Audubon and Nature Conservancy. Yet [others] have been so concerned with other priorities, and they do so many studies I think they don't understand what's going on here."

The house has now become filled with the sweet smell of his Dutch aromatic smoking mixture.

Even though Sucksdorff says he knows the governor and several congressmen, he's the kind of person to take things on himself, and the Pantanal is no exception. For example, when the wholesale killing of caimans here had finally gotten him angry, he took the law into his own hands by chasing outlaws into the marsh. He learned that these hunters were following the orders of some very wealthy and influential people. He also believes—as do other people—that many highly placed public servants are involved in drug trafficking, mostly cocaine, brought in from Bolivia.

In the late 1970s Sucksdorff started making a lot of noise about these things here, writing letters, getting stories printed in the local papers, and calling officials. And finally he got results. But it wasn't what he expected. While he was away on a trip in the Pantanal, hired thugs came to his house and shot his housekeeper in his bed downstairs. When Sucksdorff returned the next day, he found the man dead with the gun between his legs. Upstairs, Sucksdorff's wife had been brutally raped and beaten, leaving her a psychological wreck and in need of intensive therapy far away in São Paulo, which left Sucksdorff alone to care for his children. "She's not the same anymore," he says disconsolately.

For a long time after that attack Sucksdorff had an armed guard watch his house at night. His disrupted family life and the deteriorating conditions in the Pantanal have created an intense burden, and managing such a burden has been difficult.

For his thankless work he's had that vicious attack and many death threats. But that was more than seven years ago, when local attitudes were more extreme. Of late he's had a slightly more optimistic attitude. "People are coming around," he says. "There is some hope for the Pantanal's future." In June 1989 Sucksdorff participated in a symposium on the Pantanal in which research and enforcement agencies from both Mato Grosso and Mato Grosso do Sul met to discuss common issues. It was the first such meeting in the history of the two states.

In his senior years Sucksdorff's long-standing commitment has, of late, received a small measure of appreciation. In 1988 at São Paulo's Museum of Image and Sound, curators held a Sucksdorff retrospective; they showed many of his Swedish films and exhibited much of his Pantanal work. Sucksdorff takes pleasure in seeing the Pantanal come to light and continues to envision its future. "There is not a single organization here devoted to the Pantanal," he says. "One day I would like to build a Pantanal foundation that conducts research."

ten

Skins and Other Games

You can have all the technology in the world . . .
but it's the grunt that holds the fort.
—*Frederick Forsyth, novelist*

To save time Lúcia has gone ahead to Brasília to make interview arrangements with high-ranking officials. But, before I
leave Cuiabá, Gaspar asks me to come with him back to his
headquarters on the edge of the city. There is something I
should see.

We walk down a wooded ravine behind his office to a very
large, red-brick garage that houses earth-moving equipment.
The building has a two-story, black garage door that he unlocks and slides back; we step inside. As my eyes adjust to the
dark, the smell of rotting meat attacks my nostrils. The stench
is so overpowering that we both turn our heads away.

Littered all over the garage floor are black-plastic garbage
bags stuffed full with animal skins in various stages of decay.
Steel leg traps, wicker fish traps, monofilament fish nets, rusted
small arms, and other paraphernalia of capture are strewn
helter-skelter over piles of dry cat skins.

Teeth, claws, feathers, bones, and other animal parts crunch
underneath our feet as we try to move about the place. Gaspar
bends over a pile of skins and begins tossing them about, apparently looking for something in particular. A huge, orange-

and-black jaguar hide with its head still attached, maybe a dozen rag-size ocelot skins, the skin of a giant river otter, a howler monkey skin, and a pale rolled-up skin of a seven-meter giant anaconda are shunted aside until he comes up with a necklace made of brightly colored toco toucan beaks.

He says good populations of big animals used to live in the Pantanal: giant river otter (*Pteronura brasiliensis*), crab-eating fox (*Dusicyon thous*), bush dog (*Speothus venaticus*), giant anteater (*Myrmecophaga tridactyla*), and giant armadillo (*Priodontes giganteus*). Today they are all listed as endangered. Waving his hand over the area he says, "Bye-bye, Pantanal."

It's been like this since 1967, when most "big game" hunting in Brazil was officially outlawed. Some say hunting was encouraged by many ranchers. It was a way to reduce livestock predation while helping poorly paid ranch hands. Certainly, as the large cattle ranches declined in productivity, organized poaching grew into a profitable Pantanal industry.

Protection became *politica*—politics. Gaspar shrugs his shoulders in resignation. The garage full of skins is held as a show for journalists and politicians to demonstrate that something is being done about poaching. In fact, in 1989 the Brazilian Congress passed a law permitting officials to burn these skins to make room for more. Gaspar says most of these skins are old and amount to *nada*—nothing. Nobody really knows how much poachers are taking.

About six years ago the respected newspaper *Estado de São Paulo* estimated that U.S. $100 million in caiman skins alone were being hauled from the Pantanal annually. In 1985, *Veja* (Brazil's equivalent of *Newsweek*) published a story that 70,000 skins were confiscated from São Paulo's international airport. The cache included maned wolf, jaguar, anaconda, and caiman. This shipment was reported by São Paulo newspapers as a fraction of the twenty-one metric tons comprising 526,000 skins that had been already sent to Germany.

Even for a country as economically besieged and dominated by the faraway cities of São Paulo and Rio, the caiman slaughter in the remote Pantanal caused outrage. It forced then-president João Figueiredo to order Operation Pantanal, in which the army would interdict skin hunters.

"These hunters are well organized," Gaspar says with respect.

They have good equipment. He hands me a confiscated high-power focusing flashlight, made in China and smuggled in from Paraguay. He picks up a rifle and aims it, gripping the light under the barrel. Shine it on a *jacaré*'s eyes and . . . pow.

Two or three men shooting for several nights can pile up a lot of skins that way. Gaspar holds up a thin strip of caiman skin. They take only the softest flank piece, perhaps 20 percent of the body. The rest is trashed. Then a small plane lands at one of the several hundred remote airstrips. The poachers are long gone by the time the army arrives.

"*Palhaços,* [clowns]," Gaspar says, laughing bitterly and now chain-smoking. It sounds like the Keystone Kops. In a face-saving gesture, the government assigned him to guide the military. "In truth, I was volunteered," he clarifies. Being a federal employee, Gaspar could be loaned for the military operation.

The colonel in charge regularly designated Gaspar point man on the river patrols. "It wasn't so dangerous . . . then," he says modestly. "I knew many of the people doing the hunting. Someone would tip me off when a group would be going hunting." Then, like a marshal heading off to a gunfight, he would walk nonchalantly into their shacks and take away the fire arms.

His quiet derring-do won him recognition around the area as a man to be avoided. Eventually a number of angry hunters had their fill of his heroics and put the word out: kill Gaspar. He took to wearing a *pistola* and hiding a .45 under his pillow.

Today there is another agency on the scene to control poaching—the Policia Florestal, the forestry police of the Mato Grosso state government. This police force was created to do the job that the army failed to do: enforce the ban on hunting and control illegal fishing and range fires.

But Gaspar has grown cynical about these much-reported efforts as his role has diminished. "So many years of experience," he says. Dealing with local crooks, corrupt authorities, and being low on the chain of command are taking their toll on his spirit. Worse, his monthly paycheck (about U.S. $90) is quickly eaten away by inflation and a growing family at home. His love of the Pantanal is being put to an acid test as enforcement and a measure of prestige are being transferred from his agency to the forestry police.

He asks, "Remember that army colonel who first came in here to stop the *coreiros* five years ago?" I nod yes. "He's retired now, living here in Cuiabá. He's got another job, though." What's that? "He's still called the colonel, but at night he's colonel of the skin hunters."

What about the new forestry police? Aren't they doing anything? *"Falam muito, fazem nada,"* Gaspar says. It's another Portuguese lesson in reality: "Say much and do nothing." Even though he is admired by his educated colleagues, Gaspar senses much futility in what he does. Exhaling deeply, he dreams aloud, "Maybe I'll leave IBAMA and become a dairy farmer like my father. At least I'd be my own boss . . . and my family will survive. Maybe I can make a little money too."

He takes a long drag on his smokes. "Go ahead, take a look at the police operation in Cuiabá. They like gringos," he says, smiling cryptically. Before we leave I give him a Brazilian bear hug, my father's fishing gear, and my binoculars.

The Forestry Police

Early the next morning I make arrangements to visit Captain P. M. Pfeil, chief of the newly outfitted Mato Grosso forestry police. The station is on the outskirts of Cuiabá off the main highway. Several Quonset huts comprise the offices, mess, communications, and billeting facilities; there is also a long, open shed with a galvanized-metal roof full of offroad vehicles and motorboats.

Captain Pfeil is a surprise. At just thirty-four, he's a fifteen-year police veteran. He's five-feet-nine with quick, clear blue eyes, closely cropped hair, and a brush mustache. Several men in blue military jumpsuits with infantry rifles stand guard outside his office and snap to attention when he greets me.

Inside his office the shades are drawn to help the whining air conditioner in the losing war against the Mato Grosso sun. On top of his "out" tray is a popular weapons magazine. Its cover is a riveting close-up shot of a Magnum pistol against a bright-red background. Captain Pfeil talks enthusiastically in clear Portuguese. While he talks he extends a radio antenna and taps it into his other palm.

"Our force was created three years ago," he says, "to enforce state and federal laws regarding illegal skin hunting and out-of-season commercial net fishing." He knows Gaspar and adds, "The forestry service oversees similar issues; but they only report, we enforce." He pokes the air with his antenna for emphasis.

On a wall map of the region he points out seven posts strategically located around his section of the Pantanal: Cáceres, Porto Cercado, Caracara, Isla Diamon, Barão de Melgaço, Poconé, and Porto Joffre. Poking again at Porto Joffre, he says, "My jurisdiction ends here." The larger sector of the Pantanal to the south belongs to Mato Grosso do Sul.

"There the rivers are different," he notes. "They have shallow banks and large beaches where the *jacarés* gather, offering easy shots day or night. Down there bands of hunters move fast. Light airplanes are used a lot around Necolândia just inside Brazil.

"Our last big operation here was three months ago, forty kilometers south of Poconé on the Pisame River. Four men were captured with more than 250 caiman skins. They are now in Corumbé Federal Prison awaiting trial. The skins were transferred to the forestry service in Cuiabá, where they are documented and later burned."

Captain Pfeil says defense lawyers used to offer a ten-cruzado *suborno,* or bribe. That's all? I smile sheepishly. He smiles, too, recalling that when he first began work, when a man was arrested, "I would get a mysterious phone call asking what was going to happen to him. The person talking would know everything—where he was arrested, his name, the offense." Suggestions were made for an expeditious release. "No. No more. Now there are better attitudes in government. Depending on the judge, those men could get from one to three years in jail," he says.

Who are these poachers? "Our *traficantes* are unorganized and shoot with old rifles. They are mostly local Pantaneiros. For the most part they use the big *rêdes* [monofilament nets] to take the valuable predatory fish—especially *dorado* and *pintado*—during the spawning season."

"I have 105 soldiers, including one female, and they are divided into detachments. They are always on patrol or stationed at posts," he says. "In addition to basic training, our recruits receive special courses in the appropriate environmental laws and how to work with tourists along the Transpantaneira Highway."

How's the soldier's pay? Captain Pfeil says, "To start, they are paid about U.S. $92 a month. High-risk bonuses for dangerous operations are added." Even in this tropical climate, where clothing is minimal and fruits and river fish cheap and plentiful, local residents say you can't support a family on the forestry policeman's salary.

Captain Pfeil rises and invites me to tour the grounds. Out back there are three silver Brazilian offroad vehicles. They are top of the line with Recarro seats, powerful diesel engines, and radio telephones. All brand-new. We head toward the long, corral-style shed with the galvanized-metal roof.

We stroll inside. Captain Pfeil proudly points to a military troop carrier and two canopied patrol boats with machine guns forward and sixty-five-horsepower outboards aft. Also new. "There's more," he beams. "We've got fifteen seven-meter boats driven by twenty-five-horsepower outboards already parked at their bases." At the end of the shed is a big red tube on wheels. "That's an ultralight plane," says Pfeil. It flies ahead of the patrols to spot skin hunters.

"Yolanda," he calls out. In seconds a short woman dashes from the radio shack and comes to attention in front of us. She's dressed in a blue beret and a tight, gray jumpsuit. She salutes. She's the pilot.

I ask where all the expensive gear came from. "Banco Mundial, the World Bank," says the captain. It's for establishing real enforcement in the field. I am amazed. In all the times I've come to the Pantanal, enforcement has always been the catch-22 to stopping the skin trade.

Officials constantly decry the wholesale killing of so many animals here, but they say there simply isn't any money to buy the equipment necessary for law enforcement. And here, right in front of me, are nearly a million dollars in the latest police matériel and salaried soldiers—enough to wage a proper campaign against the plunderers. All this gear makes an awfully impressive image.

When is the next operation? Captain Pfeil pauses a moment,

then talks softly, "You must understand, a patrol runs fifteen days. Each one uses 10,000 liters of gas. Today a liter of gas costs 162 cruzados novo." I did some quick calculations. That converts to more than U.S. $3700 for one patrol. "We simply don't have the money for gas." No gas money?

As the captain walks me out to the parking lot, we pass one of the barracks. Pfoom. A softball-size cooking-gas tank goes sliding down the polished floor and plops off the door ledge, hitting the sand near Pfeil's boots. The men in the barracks have been playing soccer. Suddenly it's very quiet.

I don't say a word and keep walking, only to pass half a dozen more soldiers sitting on a bench in the shade near the radio hut. They're all nicely uniformed and intently watching a portable television, which blares, "La-de-la-de-lay, oh ho ho. La-de-la-de-lo, oh oh oh." It's Xuxa (pronounced Shoosha), the stunning blonde Brazilian superstar. She's scantily clad and singing the opening of her morning kiddies' cartoon show.

Captain Pfeil quickly senses the awkward situation and offers, "Next time you come through Cuiabá, we'll take you along on a patrol." I grin and ask, "How about this weekend?" He doesn't bat an eye and calls out, "Lieutenant Adarildo, come here." A short, mustachioed soldier in jungle camouflage steps away from several men and salutes Pfeil, "Yes, Captain?"

"This is Sr. Banks," Pfeil says. "He wishes to see our patrols in action. You have room for him tomorrow, don't you?" Pfeil isn't really asking a question. "*Tem!*" the lieutenant snaps. I have room. "See you at your hotel at 5:15 A.M. *Tá bom?*" Great. Now what am I in for?

The Cuiabá Professors

It's Friday night, TGIF for Federal University of Mato Grosso professors. A number of them have become alarmed about the declining environmental situation in the Pantanal and have invited me to get together after work and talk. Domingues and Marcos are geology teachers at the university and have offered to take me along to the meeting. Both come from Brazil's large Arab community, Syrian and Lebanese émigrés, living in the far southern states of Rio Grande do Sul and Santa Catarina.

We drive through the darkened, narrow streets choked with workers going home for the weekend and end up at a small open-air café—Restaurante Accacia—not far from the university. Within a short time there are about fifteen professors, friends, and their children happily gathered here. The men are enthusiastically talking and drinking strong München dark beer. At times the talk is interrupted by a brief macho ceremony. Shots of yellow *cachaça* are downed with much gusto, chased by beer. It's a Latin American boilermaker. Platters of *lambaris*—little river fish—are brought to snack on. They are fried whole and served on a bed of lettuce with cut limes. They look like tropical fish that would be in a pet store back home. But here they're salty, crunchy, and perfect with beer.

Most of the teachers, including Domingues and Marcos, are geologists in their mid to late thirties. A few are agronomists, mathematicians, and sociologists married to other professors. They have a litany of complaints, such as not enough money to support research and the fact that when they do complete a study for the government, the recommendations are rarely implemented.

One agronomist says he wants to conduct research in bio-controls, pesticide alternatives for the booming agro-industry surrounding the Pantanal; but the university receives money from pesticide manufacturers and therefore isn't interested in funding new ways of controlling pests in Brazil. "Watch television in Cuiabá any morning and you'll see commercials persuading farmers and ranchers to use many chemicals in raising cows or growing soybeans and corn," he says, shaking his head in disappointment.

More alarming, says Domingues, is that the Pantanal and its watershed appear to be in for an intense period of development. Domingues puts on the table a symposium paper with a map of the Pantanal; as he talks, he marks points where development or prospecting is being undertaken.

He draws a map of South America and marks an X in the center. "The Pantanal and Cuiabá are the *coração*—heart—of the continent. Together they occupy a key geopolitical position for the whole world," Domingues says. We guzzle a little more

The Pantanal

beer. "Do you know Porto Velho? BR 364 is the only main road from here to there. That's the door for access and occupation of the northern Amazon.

"You see," he continues, "Brazil is like Africa. We have many important undeveloped resources. Some are renewable, like water, trees, and sun: our *cerrado*—or what's left of it—is being eyed for germ plasm research.

"Yes," he says, a bit intoxicated by the weight of the conversation, "I think the East-West conflict may be resolved right here." He smacks at the Pantanal on the map. "And that will determine our North-South relationship.

"You see, the Pantanal soil is poor; the flood water replenishes the nutrients." He makes digging actions with his hands. "But, below, it's very, very rich. Some pretty big foreign players are conducting much research here." He points to the map. "In the southern Pantanal, the Soviets have received permission from Bolivia to do mineral research. BP, British Petroleum, is active in southeast Paraguay, and the British Geological Survey has joined with Bolivia to explore just across the frontier from Brazil. But it's all the same land. It's the Pantanal.

"North, in Alto Paraguay [the headwaters of the Paraguay River], the Ambrosian Bank—the financial group that invests the Vatican's money—is searching for minerals around Araputanga. BP is also there in cooperation with T.V. Globo, Brazil's very successful news and entertainment network. And there are the South Africans. Have you heard of DeBeers? They're here too.

"Mato Grosso is blessed with great deposits of copper, *plumbum*—what you call lead—antimony [tin], iron, limestone, vermiculite, manganese, diamonds, gold." He breaks off and passes around more *cachaça*.

"Sarney [then Brazil's acting president, promoted when president-elect Tancredo Neves died in surgery] has talked privately with the Japanese and Swedes about opening Pantanal and Mato Grosso," says Domingues, "from the Pacific. They've proposed a bold development to establish a Pacific Zone of Exportation. A corridor across the Andes would be built to take out minerals and hardwoods. Bolivia and Peru will join Brazil

164

in the talks." He waves his hand over the map. "For the moment, it's just talk.

"But," he fingers the map, "Manso isn't. Manso is a tributary of the Cuiabá river, a major stream that feeds the Paraguay. The headwaters gather strength seven hundred meters up on the Chapada dos Guimarães, the plateau seventy kilometers northeast of Cuiabá. The government is planning to build a hydroelectric dam there because Cuiabá doesn't generate its own electricity. It comes from Goiânia, more than six hundred kilometers to the east. The Manso dam will power the further expansion of Cuiabá.

"There'll be a big *lago* [lake] behind the dam that will divert water away from the Pantanal . . . *ruina,*" adds Eduardo, another geologist, who asks if I know Koko Taylor's Chicago Blues. "The only reason why they haven't dug up the river is . . . " Eduardo rubs his thumb and first two fingers together, "*dinheiro.*" They are looking for money from the World Bank.

Domingues continues, "Getting land for such projects and mineral rights isn't so hard. The *fazendas* are huge and owned by only a few *patrãos.* These *fazendas* are precapitalist, how do you say . . . feudal systems. The landowners have held these lands for ages. They even still have slaves. The 1980 Nobel Peace Prize was given to Adolfo Perez Esquivel, a sixty-year-old Argentinean architect who came to northern Mato Grosso, for his human rights organization work. He documented that there are workers who incur large debts to some of these owners. Unable to pay off these debts, they try to work them off; but in the end they are compelled to remain on those remote farms for years. If they escape they're recaptured. White slaves. Yesss." People at the table bob their heads in agreement.

I'm not sure if it's the spirits or spirited conversation, but my mind is saturated: A lot of energy goes into maintaining my pidgin Portuguese, and now I have data overload and start to drift from the heady talk . . . until a tiny voice says, "Don't call me *senhor.*" Huh?

"It's *sen-horr* in Portuguese, not like Spanish," the voice says, getting much louder. Some of the professors are laughing. I look up to find who's talking, and the voice is coming from another professor. I don't remember meeting him, let alone speaking to him. He's tall, with big ears. He's dragging on a cigarette and leaning back in his chair at the end of the table. His wife, also feeling the effects of the liquor, is slumped in her chair. She picks up her head, thoroughly enjoying the rising tension.

This guy continues talking very deliberately at me, each word spit from a snarling voice. "I've been in your country, at a meeting last year in Santa Barbara. An American professor there thought I was Mexican. He couldn't understand my accent." I try to ignore the man and am talking with a visiting Pakistani teacher, but he keeps interrupting. "Why are you attacking me?" I finally demand.

"You're from Chicago, aren't you? I've been to Chicago," he says. "Why don't you leave the Pantanal alone and go back to your own city. We'll take care of it ourselves. You're just like all the other gringos."

Instinct takes over. My leg muscles tighten, teeth gnash together. This is my first ugly American, Latin style, in eight years. Brawling with a geology professor is not high on my list of probabilities. My heart is banging away in my chest so violently that I rock back and forth.

We're glaring at each other, unable to move—two junkyard dogs, hackles up, about to dust off an ancient territorial imperative. Domingues's wife senses that the situation is about to explode and comes over to me, saying "He's been drinking a lot. I think we should go."

The Northern Patrol

Promptly at 5:15 A.M. the next day a Chevy Blazer, with an aluminum boat on top and "Polonoereste" stenciled on the side, pulls up to the hotel. The lieutenant hops out and shakes my hand. I'm wobbly from last night's drinking bout, but I've got company—everyone in the patrol is glassy-eyed. With the lieutenant are four men. All of them are dressed for jungle warfare: camouflage fatigues, Vietnam-style tropical boots, commando knives, and automatic rifles. They're silent as I climb in and take my seat over the transmission hump in the middle.

To break the ice, I point out our groggy state and ask if the forest police has a TGIF too. Nobody laughs. Try something else; the ice is thick. I notice they're looking curiously at my long, black trumpet case that holds my trusty 560mm telephoto lens. I tell them I'm from a big city in the States, Chicago, and point the case at the Lieutenant, shaking it Tommy-gun-style and uttering rat-a-tat-tat. You know, Al Capone. Their eyes go wide. One of them says, "Oh. Al Caponeee." Then they burst into laughter. The guy at the wheel floors the gas pedal and we're off, heading east from Cuiabá.

Lieutenant Adarildo asks for the map. In the rearview mirror I see two of the three men in back are already asleep. We're going east to the village of Barão de Melgaço, which is on the Cuiabá River about seventy kilometers upstream. On the map, the river's course is tortuous, like an intestine.

The radio is playing the Bee Gees in English. The driver, a private, hums along, without a clue as to the song's meaning; the speedometer needle shows a steady 120 kilometers an hour. Without warning, he jams on the brakes. "A body!" he yells. There in the tall grasses, indeed, is a body. A young man, fully clothed, with binoculars on his chest and a backpack at his side. He doesn't move.

The private leans on the horn. The boy in the grass starts, rubs his eyes, sees our police truck, and sits bolt upright. Asked what he's doing, the boy says, "I was bird watching at dawn, then sat down to wait for friends. I must have fallen asleep." The private whispers in an intimidating way, "I wouldn't do that again. You might be mistaken for a *contrabandista*." The boy nods his head, now clearly frightened. Scaring the daylights out of the bird watcher agrees with the policemen. They have a belly laugh, lighting up cigarettes. The private points the Chevy out on the road and floors the accelerator.

About half an hour later we pull up to the river bank. The river is low, maybe fifteen meters down from us. The soldiers muscle the long boat and outboard motor down the steep embankment.

From the river's edge, the forest appears thick and imposing, but it's an illusion. Here the gallery forest follows the river and takes its nourishment from it. But farmers eager to increase their acreage have trimmed the forest back so that it's now a thin, green veil hiding great fields of corn, soybeans, and rice.

It's after 8:00 A.M. by the time all the gear's in the boat. One of the men is assigned to take the truck downriver to meet us. The men are sweating a lot. The early-morning sun is already fierce in a cloudless sky. A couple of tugs at the starter cord brings the outboard to life, and we're finally moving with a fresh wind in our faces.

At this point the Cuiabá River is about a hundred meters across and less than seven meters deep, cradled by eroded banks. The clay-bearing soil in the banks has been sculpted by powerful forces. Torrential downpours, uprooted trees, and other debris driven by currents have gouged the bank; caimans and capybaras have left crafted holes and slides too.

The river water is muddy from a distance, but up close I can see clouds of silt billowing in the current— like when cream is first poured into coffee. When we round an elbow bend, the currents bounce off the submarine features, churning the surface.

Ahead, a man is fishing from a dugout canoe tied up to a fallen tree. We pull alongside and the lieutenant questions him about hunting and fishing. The man is old, with a long, white beard, straw hat, open shirt, and tattered trousers. Several flat, silver fish lie in the bottom of the dugout canoe beside his bare feet. Despite the man's meager catch, one of the soldiers sweeps under the canoe with a paddle, "making sure the fisherman hasn't hidden anything overboard," he says.

The old man says a couple of nights ago there were some people working around the next bend. Here the river widens, exposing a sandbar that has a camp set up on it. Two more dugouts with fishermen bob easily in the current. The lieutenant points to the camp and the private runs the boat onto the sand. A boy and an older man stand on the sandbar awaiting the patrol and showing no emotion—which makes me think they're petrified.

They are commercial fishermen who've been out for two weeks trying to put together enough of a catch to return to a nearby village. There a broker will buy their fish and market them in Cuiabá; a few of the fish may even reach restaurants in São Paulo. In the water are two huge wicker baskets more than a meter tall and two meters across. These are live wells to keep the catch fresh. The tall soldier with his army cap on backwards takes a paddle and stirs the baskets. Many *pacú* churn the water, splashing us.

The lieutenant also finds a large, tin icebox and pops open the lid, asking about illegal net fishing. Shoving aside cracked ice, he sees hundreds of fish; some have been in there two weeks, their skin wrinkled. They'll be sold to a broker on the dock of Barão de Melgaço, and he, in turn, will market them in Cuiabá days later. Fresh fish indeed. The soldiers measure a few of the *pacú* and *dorado,* making sure the fish are keepers.

Before we depart, the lieutenant gets two large *pacú.* There's been no exchange of money—sort of a gift.

We motor upstream to search a dead tree floating off the east bank. One of the men finds a line hidden in the foliage with a long, narrow, plastic net drifting five meters underwater. As we pull it on board there are about a dozen half-dead fish, mostly piranha and catfish, caught by the gills in its mesh. The lieutenant says the gill net is illegal, unsheathes his commando knife, and cuts the monofilament net into pieces.

The lieutenant wants more information about who has been using the net. We haul out downriver, meet the truck, and follow a dirt road northeast through foothills covered with brush, then descend to a small hamlet named Poco nestled between one of those hills and Lago Saco Grande—Big Bag Lake. This marshy lake is about eleven kilometers long and more than a kilometer wide. A tributary of the Cuiabá River rises up three hundred meters on the high plains of the Chapada dos Guimarães sixty-five kilometers away, then flows through this wetland on its way to the Pantanal.

There can't be more than fifty people living here, but the officer needs directions to find a fisherman's house. "This fisherman," says the lieutenant, "has been caught once before taking fish during spawning season and has since become a local informant, keeping tabs on illegal activities for us."

On our way over, the driver overtakes two teenagers riding bicycles. He thinks they could have been using the net in the river. The lieutenant nods approval, and we slow alongside the boys to question them. The boys say they don't know anything and pedal past the rolling truck. Then the private yells, "Stop." The riders are maybe eighteen years old, skinny, and no more than five-feet-nine. Both are bare-chested and shoeless. One has a machete tucked in his pants.

The lieutenant walks around to the driver's side and lights up a cigarette. The boys are standing there. One smiles nervously. "What are you smiling for?" the officer asks. The boy shrugs. The lieutenant says again, "Someone's been working the river at night with nets. We've come to Poco to find out who." The boys exchange nervous looks with each other. Then the private shouts at them, "It won't be funny if we take you in." I fear he's going to slap them around.

Through the windshield I can see only the back of the officer's camouflage uniform and the two shirtless boys with their hands behind their backs. "Don't let me hear you're doing this, because you'll go to Cuiabá. Okay?" They just stand there. Then the driver bellows in their faces, "And I'll come to get ya." They get back on their bikes and pedal away fast.

The fisherman's house is a wood and concrete structure painted two shades of green and nestled in a grove of fruit trees. There are no glass panes or screens on the windows, only heavy slat shutters. A cat is sprawled on the cool, concrete floor by the open door. The soldiers in the truck stand around the vehicle and light up cigarettes as the officer steps into the doorway and calls for the *senhora*.

A middle-aged woman with fine, shiny-black skin, beautifully sculpted features, and a turquoise bandana comes from the kitchen. She says her husband is down by the water and should return soon. The lieutenant orders one of the men to bring in the *pacús,* suggesting it would be nice to have lunch here. It isn't really a request. The woman doesn't bat an eye and says she'll make a very special dish. The shy daughter passes around *cafezinhos.*

I step outside, where the men have found shade under one of the tamarind trees and have begun eating some of the fruit. Tamarind (*Tamarindus indica*) is a strange fruit, more like a long, brown, pea pod. Inside the thin, brittle casing is an amber meat surrounding a seed that tastes like a sour apricot. They suck the seeds, then spit them out.

Guinea fowl (*Numida meleagris*), domesticated West African birds resembling dwarf peacocks, have also found relief under another tamarind tree. They've gone the soldiers one better by resting in a cool, dirt pit and trilling the heat away.

Back inside, the lieutenant has pulled up a chair in the center of the room, crossed his legs, and is holding out his left arm, grasping a burning cigarette between his thumb and index finger. He's not smoking it. As a result, the ash is growing very long and crooked. He's begun questioning the fisherman, who's just returned to the house. The old man, who appears to be in his late sixties, says there have been men catching fish on the marsh. But he isn't sure if they've been using nets. The lieutenant decides that after lunch they'll launch the boat on the marsh. The old man will take them to the spot.

The meal is ready, and the main room of the house is packed with eleven people. The food is delicious, drawing praise from all. The *pacú* have been cut in large chunks and simmered in a spiced broth. The gray flesh is mild, yet rich from its own interstitial fat. Rice and *farofa* (grated manioc) are also served, as is homemade hot sauce. Everyone's enjoying themselves immensely despite the tremendous heat, and no one feels uncomfortable about the lieutenant inviting himself in. Except me.

The lieutenant wipes his mouth and suggests that I would probably find the boat ride on the marsh uninteresting. He tells the private to show me around the river town of Barão de Melgaço.

Maybe the lieutenant senses my uneasiness with his way of doing things, or perhaps he's going to do some serious interrogation and doesn't want me around. I'm glad to break away to see the countryside instead of the faces of frightened people.

Half an hour later the private sits a bit taller as we drive into town. We roll slowly past a table of women drinking beer along the quiet waterfront. His eyes stray to them as one of the women returns an inviting grin.

Barão de Melgaço is a plain little village except for its impressive quay on the Piraim River, a northern tributary of the Cuiabá. All kinds of watercraft are tied to piers and run up on muddy banks. There are twenty-six-meter, wooden river steamers, a couple of small diesel tugs for barges, supply boats, several abused cabin cruisers—one sunk at the pier—and one skiff with outboard.

The river steamers are odd-looking craft. The hull is a narrow, wood barge. The deck and superstructure, also made of wood, seem to have been slapped together from one big, long box sitting on top of the hull. Window and gangway openings are simply cut through the box's walls.

Several blocks along the waterfront, we pull over to watch some children swimming fifty meters offshore from a small beach. I'm stunned. "Aren't they afraid of piranhas?" I ask. "Piranhas don't attack here," says a young man whom the private knows.

The man has come from São Paulo to try his hand at the fish brokerage business. He likes being away from the big city, and he likes getting out to meet the many types of people who fish these waters. As we talk he ushers us into his fish hut. It's situated among boat and engine repair shacks on the waterfront about fifty meters above the water. Inside, the strong ammonium odor of heat-spoiled fish is breathtaking.

He points to his pride and joy: the walk-in tin cooler. One of his helpers opens the door and steps onto a white mountain of cracked ice. Holding my breath, I step in as the boy shovels aside some ice, exposing dozens of large, aging fish. They won't let me leave this stinking cooler until I've taken a picture of the fish—this I gladly do, backing out of the room. Not until I see the picture weeks later do I realize that, in the one hastily taken frame, I've inadvertently captured the many fish commercially sought here: *bagre, barbado, caracú, dorado, jáu, pacú, pacupiva, pintado,* piranha, *piraputanga,* and *traíra.*

Returning by the riverfront road, we find that the women drinking beer have parked their Chevette so that it blocks our way. The private maneuvers our vehicle right up to the table and lays on the horn, mustering his sexiest smile. One of the women holds up a beer.

The private's eyes twinkle as he talks with them. The women are in their twenties. Two are dressed in tight short-shorts and halters and the other in a *tanga* bikini and open shirt. All puff away on Minister cigarettes. They are here on a brief holiday from Cuiabá, where they are "program girls," prostitutes, at the massage parlors. One sees I'm not Brazilian and complains, half-joking, "Not another gringo."

"Other gringos come to see you?" I ask. "Oh, we have many come in these days," she says. "Japanese men come in groups. They're so little. [The other women laugh.] Chinese. Russians too."

Russians? "Yesss. They're the loneliest. They want a good time . . . " She lowers her voice and sticks out her belly, mimicking a big man, places an arm around her girlfriend's neck, and says, "Come with me to Buzios [a resort area near Rio] . . . but they don't want to pay." Everyone laughs.

The private is leaning against one of the girls, then glances at his watch and snaps out of it. He's got a look like the lieutenant will kill him.

We jump in the truck and take a shortcut over a hill to get back to the village. As we descend, the air becomes thick with smoke. On the other side of the hill a field is burning, casting a pall over the valley. The private lights up a cigarette.

In front of the fire stand a bare-chested man and his three nearly naked children. This is another *sítio,* smaller than Tutu's. Thousands are scattered throughout northern Brazil. With this country's economic chaos, the *sítio* is the poor man's refuge, last hope, and tiny imperial domain. It's his stake in the wild and crazy action of Brazil's breakneck development.

The man has a few hectares cleared and maybe half a dozen gray cows. Funny, the animals are standing virtually on top of the fire without the slightest agitation as they chew their cud.

Closer to the fire, I can see it's not a single blaze. Spots of fire flare up and burn back. The grasses are burning, singeing large tree trunks and consuming smaller ones completely. The fire moves rapidly, almost at the speed of a walk.

Stalking the fire's far edge is a big savanna hawk (*Heterospizias meridionalis*). The beautiful raptor is unafraid of the flames, smoke, and noise; apparently it knows that the fire is driving critters out of the grasses and is taking its pick. The hawk walks, then freezes, as a huge grasshopper goes arching out of the smoke a meter in front. The raptor takes a flying leap as the insect launches into a couple of short hops as if on a pogo stick. The hawk sees me and flies to a distant, charred stump.

On the other side of the road a dog lazes in the shade while a few chickens scratch the ground in front of a wood and palm-branch shack. The bare-chested man sports a weather-beaten straw hat cocked over his right eye. A big grin breaks through his stubby beard as he leans back against the wooden fence. His dirty offspring eye me with suspicion as I gradually close in on their father with my camera.

Before snapping the shutter, I point to the fire and ask the private, "Aren't you going to do something about this?" He smiles and says, "There's nothing wrong." I take the picture: the beaming farmer, his suspicious kids, the oblivious cows, and the approaching fire behind them.

We rejoin the patrol an hour later and reach Cuiabá well after dark.

I'm beat from this police patrol and plop onto my bed back at the hotel. The evening paper, *Estado do Mato Grosso,* has a cover story featuring the former forestry chief in Mato Grosso. He claims that more than 50 percent of the state's *cerrado* grasslands and forest have been or are currently ablaze.

My eyes simply won't follow the text anymore and I fall asleep. When I awake from my nap, I decide to splurge this last night and treat myself to a nice meal at Casa Suiça, Swiss House, supposedly one of the city's best restaurants. It's located on the outskirts of town.

A taxi takes me past concrete homes crammed against one another. There are many outdoor bars, neighborhood watering holes where locals gather nightly to drink beer and shoot the breeze. We pass a couple of "saunas," where men can purchase an hour's companionship and a happy rub for about eight dollars. Then we catch one of the main highways leading out of town.

The restaurant is located on top of a hill named Pico do Amor—Love Mountain—which overlooks the city. It's a smart and clean oasis, a costly facsimile of a Swiss chalet created by its European owner. I sit outside on the expansive veranda filled with tables decked out in red-and-white checkered tablecloths. A cool breeze threatens to revive me. Here the local gentry come to feed on quite different meals of schnitzel, brats, steak tartar, rabbit stew, smoked fish, and chocolate fondue washed down with the best domestic and imported beers—all pretty pricey.

I settle in with a liter bottle of domestic dark beer. Its creamy, strong taste is easy to take as I watch crowded buses strain up the hill. They're taking Cuiabá's laborers home to the outlying shantytowns. I order a green salad, thinking the crunch of crisp lettuce will be appreciated, but what the waiter brings is neither fresh nor green. Instead, the platter is full of cooked carrots, sliced boiled potatoes, pale canned peas, a couple stalks of canned heart of palm, and a boiled egg, all swimming in a thick mayonnaise and pickle relish dressing.

Another large beer, please. Mulling over my day's adventure, something seems screwy with the forestry police. They've been outfitted by the World Bank as a powerful military unit. Not even the biggest skin-hunting organization would dare take them on in a fire fight. But patrols and actions are few and far between. No gas money, they say! So they stay at their headquarters polishing equipment and watching Xuxa.

The lieutenant and his men—talk about relishing your job. They are having a pretty good time running around the countryside terrorizing the local peasants. And over what? A few stinking fish. Yet no one stops the farmers from burning their land. The farmers in this region have done much to change the land. They've cut down the forest to the river's edge, speeding erosion. They've laced their lands with heavy doses of herbicides, pesticides, and fertilizers that wash into the streams and threaten the great fish stocks in the Pantanal waters.

According to Dr. R. L. Welcomme, a senior fisheries biologist with the Food and Agriculture Organization of the United Nations, the Pantanal supports one of the most important freshwater fisheries left on the planet. He theorizes that the farmers around the Pantanal know their practices are having a serious negative impact on water quality. As a result, they encourage a well-publicized enforcement of hunting and fishing regulations to draw attention away from their destructive agriculture. If that is their strategy, it's working like a charm.

This little chat with myself, lubricated by a third tall beer, has worked up a good deal of anger and frustration, not the sort of feelings to have in a restaurant. I'll end up eating for satisfaction. The waiter recommends something light — carpaccio? Italian, great.

When the platter arrives, I'm not sure what to say. The meat is sliced thin enough that the light from the table lamp shines through it in a cool, red glow. The meat is raw. I dump on a mixture of olive oil, minced garlic, basil, oregano, salt, and mozzarella cheese, lamenting my long-gone diet of fish, pasta, and salads. I wolf it all down, mopping up the blood with crispy rolls, order another plate, and say good-bye to Cuiabá.

eleven

Back in Brasília

> We have an attitude problem here. People watching television
> learn to care more for elephants or lions than the jaguar or
> giant river otter . . . . they like Africa better than Brazil.
> —*Adelberto Eberhard, conservationist*

The trip to the northern Pantanal was as exhausting as it was
exhilarating, and I'm showing a peculiar side effect: a difficulty
in swallowing. Or am I always swallowing so as not to gag on
raw stomach acid seeping up the back of my throat? Is that
from breathing so much smoke? Or is my body reacting to the
fun food I'd downed in the Pantanal?

Anyway, I'm out of movie film. The rest of my supplies and
other gear are stashed at Dr. Carlos Leite's house here in
Brasília. I need some time to recharge my emotional batteries
too, and to check in with private environmental groups. Lúcia
is already here, but she'll soon return to her job in the States
and I'll be off to the southern Pantanal west of Campo Grande.

The climate here is a welcome change. These high plains are
a blessing: free from the Pantanal's sweltering heat and choking
humidity. There has been a long stretch of weather so dry, in
fact, that it is approaching the danger point, where people can
unknowingly weaken from loss of fluids.

Dr. Carlos says the government has been carefully monitor-
ing the humidity levels, announcing on every weather report if
the day is safe for outdoor activities. (I went jogging here, and

although I covered nine kilometers, my skin, which normally is dripping with sweat, was barely moist.) There is a public health law in Brasília, he says, that states if the humidity drops below 20 percent, it becomes unsafe for outdoor work. But Dr. Carlos adds that the government always says it's 20 percent, never less, because they don't want to pay people for a day off.

Brasília is abuzz with environmental news, all of it about the Amazon. Peru and Brazil are negotiating with Japan to finance a paved road, BR 364, that would go from the town of Rio Branco over the Andes to Pucalipa, Peru, connecting Brazil's interior to a Pacific port. This would give the Japanese access to the Amazon's vast stands of hardwoods. Dominguez was right. He had told of an unpublished agreement between Brazil and Peru weeks ago.

In response, the British rock singer Sting had teamed up with Raoni, an Amazon chieftain, to draw attention to the plight of the Amazon and of Raoni's people. Together they were a dynamic duo—one with long hair, macaw-feather war bonnet, and wooden lip disk; the other with long hair, milky white skin, crew-neck sweater, and horn-rim glasses. They traveled to Paris to meet with Francois Mitterrand, who called Raoni's fight to save his home in the Amazon "a symbol of the struggle to save the planet." Sting would take trips to the United States and Japan to further publicize the Amazon.

A litany of environmental events had suddenly turned up the country's ecological awareness. There was the murder of Chico Mendes in the western Amazon. Mendes, a rubber-tree tapper, had become a popular leader in the environmental movement. He had campaigned to ranchers that rubber tapping was less destructive than cattle for the rain forest and longer-lived too. Word of Mendes's murder flashed around the globe. His struggle became an ecological cause célèbre as publishers and film producers fell over one another to lionize his life.

The second major event was the protest meeting held in February 1989 at the town of Altamira along the Xingu River in the northeastern state of Pará. There, six hundred Kayapo Indians were joined by other Amazon natives and outspoken representatives of foreign environmental and human rights groups. They confronted officials of Funai, the federal government's Indian protection agency. They were protesting the

construction of the Balbina hydroelectric dam, which would
flood them from their centuries-old tribal lands.

In Europe, there were huge and angry demonstrations
against the World Bank's policy of funding Brazilian projects
that had a destructive impact on the environment, especially
dams and roads through virgin forest.

Ecology was so hot a topic that on my first day in Brasília, a
taxi driver held up the popular newspaper *Jornal do Brasil* with a
front-page photo of Rondônia in flames and shook his head in
dismay, even though Rondônia was more than six hundred
kilometers from his own home. For a country world famous
for so much wild nature and so little concern for it, these were
indeed surprising events.

But finally the government had had enough. Outgoing President Sarney, preoccupied with the coming presidential election,
did something unthinkable. He interrupted Brazil's favorite
nighttime passion: watching steamy novellas on television. The
country, he said, was engaged in "a fight [for] . . . integrating
Latin America. Our products, our people, our institutions are
submitted to this infamous campaign. The international community put us in the seat of a condemned man. Without doubt
we're stubborn to be free because what they [the international
community] recommend to us is to still be a slave . . . to accept
these powerful international organizations and multinationals
that come here to dictate to us how to defend what is our right
to defend." He declared that global pressure to save the
Amazon was nothing short of the internationalization of the
Brazilian Amazon. "It's not our government that is being
judged," he said, "but the process of our national growth."

Sarney held up documents prepared by the Brazilian space
agency (INPE) and made his case: "Since the days of Brazil's
discovery, five hundred years ago, no more than 5 percent of
the Amazon [forest] has been cut. Developing . . . poor . . . and
Third World countries don't have force (and don't want this
force) to destroy their land. We lament that decision [to con-
demn our development] from those countries who have huge
stockpiles of atomic weapons . . . and have put ozone in the atmosphere that allows holes for ultraviolet rays. Millions of tons
of their industrial garbage is making the atmosphere warmer."

Sarney, General Bayma Denys (chief of the National Security

Council), and José Carlos Mello (secretary general of the Ministry of Interior) denounced these foreign pressures to save the Amazon as "an international conspiracy in an unjust campaign that was cruel and infamous."

In closing, Sarney welcomed the concern of the world about the environment. And he announced that the Brazilian government would set up a special fund so that people worldwide could contribute to the preservation of the Amazon. But, he concluded, "conditional international aid is unacceptable for the 'intelligent' use of the Amazon." Brazil would use that money to protect its own land in its own way.

Within days of Sarney's announcement, the *Exxon Valdez* ran aground, fouling the Alaskan coast. It was hit hard by the Brazilian government and media. In fact, Roberto Marinho, owner of the highly influential T.V. Globo channel, rushed into production a program about world environmental damage on the weekly television special "Global Reporter." Sequences included all kinds pollution throughout the developed world, laced liberally with scenes in the United States: Three Mile Island, toxic waste at Love Canal, and the dioxin spill at Times Beach. Special attention was given to the Valdez spill, including long, uninterrupted shots of lifeless seabirds and sea otters rolling in the deadly, black surf.

When the program airs, Brazilians watching it with us are stunned by the scenes of despoiled North America. "I thought America was beautiful and clean. Why are the Americans blaming us for the greenhouse effect when they've already ruined their own environment?" we are asked. It's a tough situation to defend.

Lúcia is quick to pick up the program's deficiencies. Where's the reporting on Brazil's own environmental sore spots? Burning in Rondônia, Mato Grosso? The severe industrial water pollution of Cubatão? São Paulo's eye-watering smog? The flooding out of native Indians? Mercury pollution by gold miners? Unchecked population growth? The spraying of DDT and 2,4 D? Unenforced skin hunting? Not a word.

One official has dared to stand apart from the president and his men. He's Fabio Feldman, a congressman from São Paulo. Feldman accuses the president of deliberately manipulating the space agency's data for political purposes. According to figures

Feldman's staff has researched, the rain forest is at least 7 percent, and perhaps as much as 12 percent, gone.

For several days after this program is broadcast, I can feel a rare anti-American sentiment in Brasília. Whenever I raise environmental issues with Brazilians I know, most feel defensive, believing that the Amazon is theirs and that foreigners, mostly North American multinational corporations, are taking control of it.

The only other time I had sensed such a derisive mood toward North Americans was in 1983, when President Reagan visited Brasília. He addressed the Congress in Brasília when the military government had agreed to step aside. After announcing there would be a Brazilian astronaut soon, Reagan raised his glass to toast the new democracy and said, "Mr. President and congressmen, a salute to . . . Bolivia." This boner set up a howl of laughter, which was poorly reported back in the United States. In Brazil, it became a good joke. To this day, you can get a belly laugh by raising your glass and saying, "Here's to . . . Bolivia."

I am happy to hole up at the Leite house again. Much is happening there too; Carlito, the eldest child, has become engaged to his girlfriend, Adriana, a tall, blue-eyed blonde he'd been serious about for years. The family is head over heels in joy preparing for the wedding.

Late one evening, the guard on the block awakens me with his periodic whistle-blowing. (Dr. Carlos says it's as much to tell us he's not asleep as to scare away burglars.) I walk to the fridge for some water and hear Carlito in his ham radio shack. It's 3:00 A.M. and he's excitedly talking with another ham operator in Wisconsin via a new amateur radio satellite presently passing over the northeast coast of North America.

"Carlito, don't you have work tomorrow?" I ask. He does, indeed, but couldn't sleep; the idea of marriage drove him to the radio shack. "At thirty-two, it's time to leave my father's house," he says. "In South America it's so expensive to set up your own place. We've been looking and saving for years. I have a good job, but the salary doesn't keep up with inflation."

"You think being independent is everything, don't you?" Lúcia observes. "In America you leave the family and get jobs making money so early. But it has a price too. Everyone's so busy, alone, and the family's about gone. In Brazil it's one big family until you die. With our families, it's the only way we know how to survive."

In the morning I call Nicholas Von Behr, a friend at Funatura, one of the country's new, high-powered environmental groups. He invites me to a meeting about the controversial fires being set throughout Mato Grosso and Amazonia. He says it's going to be a doozy.

In the afternoon, Lúcia goes on business to the Brazilian foreign service and I to one of the congressional buildings at the end of the Esplanada dos Ministerios, those futuristic federal buildings designed by Oscar Neimayer in the 1950s. They look like a little United Nations Plaza sitting on a table with two big, white bowls, one upside-down. An enormous green, blue, and yellow Brazilian flag droops in the slight breeze.

Inside there is a maze of offices and meeting rooms without much signage, forcing you to rely on guards. The conference room is packed, including a roped-off area for local press. The meeting is underway. The lights are dimmed, and a tall man in business suit is at the podium explaining slides being projected to his left.

The man is Dr. Alberto Setzer. He's from the national space agency in São Paulo and has directed the fire study with the forestry service and with assistance from NASA. The program is to report on the scope and impact of burning in the country from July 15 to October 2, 1987.

While the torching of forests and old pasturage is decades old, this is the first time that scientists had actually measured the burning throughout northern Brazil, including the states of Amazonas, Rondônia, Pará, Maranhão, and Mato Grosso, where I am working. They monitored this region using the United States' NOAA-9 weather satellite and confirmed those observations with high-altitude overflights by the Brazilian Air Force. The study concluded that 20 million hectares (200,000 square kilometers) of new forest was in the process of being burned.

Setzer pops up a satellite photo that appears to be a picture of the night sky: pitch black and hundreds of yellow dots. It's not a picture of stars at all, but a night photo looking down on this region. Each yellow dot is a fire measuring at least a kilometer square! They had counted no fewer than 136,930 separate fires during the eighty-eight-day period.

According to Setzer those fires put an estimated 580 million tons of gases and particulate matter into the atmosphere. To help the group visualize such a figure, he says that amount of smoke is roughly equal to a hundred volcanoes erupting concurrently.

In his next slide, Setzer points out the track of this smoke cloud. In a high-altitude, black-and-white photograph, a veil of smoke spreads from north of Cuiabá to the southeast. It covers 1,500,000 square kilometers, causing uncounted health problems to local residents and even closing regional airports up to several weeks at a time. That strikes a bell. This picture accounts for that strange black line of smoke I saw on my flight up to Cuiabá. It was the smoke cloud drifting south.

The smoke was tracked southeast across Mato Grosso, Mato Grosso do Sul (the entirety of the Pantanal), Goiás, passing over Brazil's largest city, São Paulo, then out into the South Atlantic Ocean, where the roaring, high-altitude winds drove it over Antarctica. It required only ten days to cover more than five thousand kilometers.

Setzer concludes on a cautionary note. While the connection between those fires and the weakening of the ozone layer over the South Pole remains to be established, the peak of the fires occurs in August. The seasonal high for ozone-layer erosion occurs right after that—from September to November.

I remember that farmer and his raggedy children standing in front of their burning pasture near Barão de Melgaço, so confident and self-reliant. I wish he could see where his smoke was going. There are thousands and thousands of such farmers ringing the Pantanal and throughout the Amazon Basin. What alternative do they have?

Setzer is asked what will become of this report. He replies that it will be handed over to the president, and it will be up to the government to take action. I imagine what Gaspar would think. He'd probably hold up an inverted "A-okay" sign, the equivalent of giving the finger.

Nicholas introduces me to Fabio Feldman, who's chairing the meeting. He's the congressman who questioned Sarney about the Amazon. Feldman is about five-feet-ten with a wrestler's build. He looks tired for his thirty-four years. He'd been up the night before, preparing for a meeting with the president regarding an environmental decree soon to be announced. He invites me to come talk with him after the meeting.

In a few days, the news programs will be full of reports that President Sarney is inaugurating a major new environmental program called Nossa Natureza (Our Nature). It will establish two new national forests in the Amazon Basin totaling 1,412,000 hectares and three national parks covering 84,000 hectares in the northeast's grasslands and 1,000,000 hectares in the hills of the western Amazon's state of Acre.

I'm surprised to hear the program includes 33,000 hectares of the Chapada dos Guimarães (on the northeast edge of the Pantanal) for park land and 1,504,000 hectares for an enormous biological reserve in the coastal state of Espirito Santo. Although this is a lot of land to set aside, the government still needs money to actually buy the land. For now it's a paper decree.

There are also provisions to control and recover toxic chemicals, with attention directed to the use of mercury by gold miners. And the government is suspending subsidies and incentives for new ranchers to clear vast sections of privately owned forest.

The government is committing 179 million novo cruzados (U.S. $87.3 million) to the program. But there is a glaring omission: the Pantanal. Nothing is designated for it, and yet the Pantanal is one of only three natural-heritage regions in Brazil (along with the Amazon and Atlantic Forest) actually cited in the newly ratified constitution. They are supposed to receive special efforts for conservation.

The Leader of the Green Front

As planned, I go to see Congressman Feldman. His suite is located in the Congressional Annex building in a busy corridor with other elected officials. It isn't hard to tell which office is his: the glass wall facing the hallway is plastered with wildlife posters and decals from many ecology groups in Brazil: S.O.S.

Atlantic Forest, Funatura, Oikos, World Wildlife Fund, Nature Conservancy, Survival International, and the International Union for the Conservation of Nature.

Half an hour later I join Feldman in his private office. Obviously fatigued, he slumps into his chair. "I'm sorry you had to wait, but it's been a crazy couple of days." His telephone buttons are all lit up with calls from the press wanting quotes about his stand against the government.

He's rushing to head off the government from announcing the Nossa Natureza program with an expensive fanfare. "They're planning to spend $3 million to bring in the international press [free] and make a big show of the program. How can you do that in such a poor country as ours . . . at the same time as we're debating in Congress to raise the terribly low minimum wage from $35 a month?"

He shakes his head in dismay, saying, "The president's speech was very lamentable and out of date . . . more like a speech from twenty years ago. I think Sarney is looking for Brazil's Malvinas–Falklands—an issue to rally the people and to use to point to outsiders for Brazil's problems. Today the international community has become that whipping boy. We [the national environment movement] have been lumped into this group too. We are seen as not being very patriotic." He believes this rising nationalism is a direct result of Chico Mendes's murder and the protest at Altamira, which he dubs the "Woodstock" of Brazil—"It didn't do much, but a lot of people watched it."

Feldman cites one more event that I hadn't heard before: a visit made to Brazil by American Senators Albert Gore, Timothy Wirth, and John Chaffee. Feldman wrinkles up his face, recalling the event. "I traveled to the United States before they came down here. I explained it was a time of great sensitivity for us and their trip should be one of fact-finding and quiet dialogue. But when they arrived they ended up confronting our president. They became sharply critical of his environmental policy, even lecturing him on the Amazon, telling him what should be done there."

This first of several visits blew up in the lawmakers' faces. Instead of creating a dialogue and easing the way for one of America's unsung exports—knowledge of conservation practices—the visitors came off as condescending and elitist. Sarney curtailed their meeting, and the Brazilian press had a field day. As the leader of the Green Front, an environmental coalition in Congress, Feldman had his hands full trying to massage all the politicians' bruised egos and encouraging a second visit.

"Survival International has directly attacked the World Bank policy, to get them to stop funding destructive projects," says Feldman. "Denial of such funds would hamper the government's plans for development. That's why this escalating environmental awareness is being seen as nothing less than a national security issue. This first impact has been reactionary, but I'm convinced that ultimately the government will be obliged by foreign pressure . . . and results will be positive for us.

"One of our greatest problems is deciding what we will do after we take emergency measures to slow the fires. It's the same problem as in the Pantanal—deciding what the land is good for. We know, for example, that just as in the Amazon, most of the Pantanal's soil is poor, not very good for agriculture. It's better for fishing and ecological tourism.

"The *fazendeiros* [ranchers] in the Pantanal are not unlike those working the Amazon. They want to make more money from the land, but their management of large farms is poor. Their economic activity is not sustainable, and they don't care. And why should they? In ten to twenty years, with our changing economy, even if the land is left alone, it will have a greater value by simply sitting on it. For them the capital gain is more important than the immediate profit.

"So, you see, the *fazendeiros* don't have to be productive at all. With many of their activities they're not successful in economic terms. The land [both in the Pantanal and Amazon] is poor for agriculture. It needs fertilizers and pesticides, and the markets are far away. [On the other hand] cattle ranching is a simple process. You just throw the animals onto the fields."

I ask how he plans to change all that. "We have to change the culture of government and the culture of this society," he says. Feldman believes there is a way to accomplish this peacefully: by developing a strategy to pull together the country's environmental groups; construct political alliances with Indians, ranchers, and even gold miners; and nurture international relations.

For someone so young, Feldman exudes a singular sense of purpose, even vision, for his beleaguered land. He's quick to point out some surprising accomplishments in the short two years since he was elected. "I was a minority of one," he says, "the only ecologist elected." When he first came to Congress in 1986, he had a real problem: how to bring up environmental issues to what looked like a hostile legislative body.

At first glance, Feldman seems a fish out of water as Brazil's leading environmental spokesman in the country's booming industrial age. He founded the Green Front in Congress; yet he comes from São Paulo state, the most urbanized region in the country, with a burgeoning capital city of about twenty million people. When he was at university he became fascinated by environmental issues, argued the predictions from the Club of Rome (a group of international economists), and became involved with many early ecological groups while going through law school.

"I became the president of Oikos," Feldman says, "one of the first environmental groups here; we represented some of the victims of Cubatão [the chemical-manufacturing and refinery corridor outside São Paulo where oil and chemical fires claimed many lives and destroyed homes].

"At this point our country was finishing the transition from dictatorship to democracy. The end of this process was writing a new constitution, and I wanted to participate; so I ran for election. When I took office, I created the Green Front; today we have eighty members in Congress." His key to success, he says, is accomplished by "making alliances. You can't easily place our ecological movement on the left or right politically; it cuts across the entire political spectrum. After all, who would be against nature?"

Feldman thrives on championing the underdog. And he's had plenty of experience, having been raised as another minority — one of just 300,000 Jews living in a largely Catholic country of 150 million. I think it might be a tough game. "Yes, it may seem that way," Feldman adds. "It all depends on your point of view. My Jewish upbringing and education gave me some feeling that makes it possible to have a simpatico relationship with nature and minority causes. Oh, yes, it's a tough game, but it's the only game I enjoy playing."

Despite Brazil's enormous territory—it's greater in area than the forty-eight contiguous United States—he maintains a positive outlook: "I know we have this terrible range-fire problem, but you know, three years ago you never heard this even mentioned. Today you look at television or read the paper and it's everywhere." He leans forward out of his big chair and says, "Maybe I'm dreaming, but in five years I think Brazil can be the leader of the Third World in environmental issues."

Back at Dr. Carlos's house Lúcia is wearing a long face. I cajole her into telling me what happened over dinner at a Japanese restaurant that had recently opened in the city. As we guessed, the place is deserted; Oriental food is still something of a novelty here. Over hot sake, Lúcia is practically in tears telling about the Brazilian foreign service and its disorganized efforts to return home most of its senior staff living abroad. The official reason why people are being returned to Brazil is for belt-tightening measures.

It doesn't sound unreasonable, I think. People have to come back home; the country is in severe economic crisis. What's wrong with that?

Lúcia had gone to visit a girlfriend who had lived abroad in the foreign service and then been sent home. She had lived ten years in London, where she specialized in cultural promotion, and then dutifully accepted her return post to Brasília. She was in a state of shock. In London she had earned U.S. $2000 a month. When she returned, her pay dropped to U.S. $250 a month. And there hadn't been an apartment provided, as was promised; she begged an old friend to let her live in her apartment until things got straightened out. That was five months ago. The job they gave her was a nightmare too. Since her return, she food-binged, putting on twenty kilos from stress. And there are many stories like hers.

There is also a huge scandal breaking. One of the foreign-service officials has embezzled health insurance and retirement funds amounting to more than U.S. $11 million; yet no one has been charged. The foreign service is becoming a joke, with the lower-level people the butt. Lúcia vows to protect herself by taking legal measures.

Brazil has just emerged from a shadowy dictatorship, every bit as feared as those in Argentina and Chile. For Lúcia to try and protect her job, and do it formally — with lawyers, no less, and not through the informal system of friends and favors — will be gut-wrenching and without guarantees. It takes courage, and I'm very proud of her.

Silently we watched the chef prepare our sushi. He takes a small handful of vinegar rice and makes a little mound in his palm. Then he licks his index finger and runs it down the ball of rice, lays a piece of raw tuna on top, and arranges it nicely with others he's made the same way.

"Did you see that!" Lúcia whispers in English. "Uh-huh. You gonna eat it?" I inquire. "Yeechhh!" she manages to say while holding her hand to her mouth to keep from gagging. The chef places the platter between us. I don't know how she does it, but she manages to convince the man that we've changed our minds and want to order something hot. Within minutes a Japanese man sits down at the sushi bar, and the chef gives our plate to him.

José Carlos Mello Speaks to the Issues

Thus far I've talked only with pro-conservation officials. Before I leave for the southern Pantanal, I want to interview José Carlos Mello, one of the government's most ardent spokesmen. He's receiving much press for espousing Brazil's right to develop its wilds. Mello is secretary general of the Ministry of Interior, considered the most important departments behind finance, making him a mighty difficult man to see.

I can only find a two-year-old government telephone directory. None of the numbers I try are correct. I mention the frustrating time I'm having to a friend in a nongovernment organization. He laughs and says that his boss's secretary has a little black book that they constantly update. It not only lists the most recent telephone numbers of key officials, but it also has the names of all their personal secretaries and notes on how to deal with them, including their favorite interests and family status. Without that book, "why, we'd be like gringos here," he laughs.

Lúcia offers to give his office a call, gets through, but is put off five times with excuses. Out of exasperation she hands me the phone and says, "You try!"

On my first try I'm connected with somebody's home; even though I dial the right number, the phone system often burps and rings up an absolutely random number. My second try gets to the right office, and in Portuguese I introduce myself as a North American writer. Before I can finish the sentence, the person says, "Just a moment" in broken English and puts me through to one of Mello's secretaries.

The interview is arranged for late Friday afternoon, three days away. Meanwhile, Lúcia will be going to Rio to see a lawyer to begin her legal process; the lawyer says her appeal is promising.

In the intervening days, I try to learn more about the secretary general by talking with other politicians and journalists. José Carlos Mello hails from the state of Santa Catarina in southern Brazil. People from this region are very European, having strong continental roots—mostly Italian and German—dating back more than 150 years. Many have a condescending attitude toward their less educated compatriots in the northeast—much the same as northerners in the United States used to have for southerners. Mello is a former professor of transportation and economics and a seasoned politician. He held numerous appointed positions in Brasília for nearly ten years before accepting Sarney's appointment to the Ministry of Interior.

On Friday I search out the Ministry of Interior. It's located in one of the nondescript rectangles forming a corridor on the Esplanada dos Ministérios in the government complex. As soon as I leave the elevator on the fourth floor, I enter another world: the inner sanctum of power. Piped-in opera music, glass and chrome architectural accents, polished marble floors, richly grained wood paneling, subdued lighting, and enough white-jacketed aides and waiters to outfit a cruise ship.

I anxiously await my turn in the spacious anteroom, reviewing my notes, scribbling additional questions, and watching several elegantly dressed men being ushered past a room with three secretaries into the secretary general's office. An hour and a half goes by; eventually some of the help begin saying their weekend good-byes, and I think I've been forgotten. It's well after 6:00 P.M. when I'm introduced to Secretary General Mello.

Mello rises from behind his vast desk, greets me warmly, and apologizes for the long wait. I ask how long we have, and he says about ten minutes. Mello is in his mid-fifties, stands about five-feet-nine, and is impeccably dressed in a dark-blue, double-breasted, pinstripe suit. His nearly all-white curly hair, beaming cherub grin, and great reservoir of self-confidence bring to mind the late David Susskind.

As I ease into the chair, Mello sees me flip open my notebook and set up my tape recorder, and he assumes a formal attitude, a reflex probably acquired from months of having reporters jam microphones in his face. I say, "You're becoming quite famous for your 'ecological conspiracy' theory."

He smiles beatifically and says, "Today there exists in First World countries an hysterical attitude about the question of protecting Brazil's environment." He hands me a *Newsweek* magazine opened to the "Letters to the Editor" section. He points to a letter stating that in Oregon the virgin forests are being destroyed very rapidly—nearly six thousand acres a month.

"In Brazil," Mello continues, "nobody has done something like that or what Exxon did in Alaska. France conducts nuclear tests in the South Pacific in open skies. The Japanese just killed 250 whales. These rich countries are aggressive toward nature every day. Now I don't know why Brazil is the attention of the whole world. It makes us think that this is an escape. Instead of defending Alaska [or] the Oregon forest, which demands practical action, they turn to something easier, more comfortable to defend . . . something twelve thousand kilometers away. I believe this is disingenuous and hypocritical.

"In my opinion, we have today two serious environmental problems worldwide. First, the destruction of the ozone layer. Second, the greenhouse effect. They are irreversible to people's health and animal and plant life. The ozone is destroyed by chlorofluorocarbons, CFCs, used in refrigeration construction and aerosol sprays. The United States is the largest consumer of these, followed by Europe and Japan.

"Brazil uses ten times less [CFCs] than the United States. Already we have some laws in several states [Ceará and Rio Grande do Sul] that prohibit their use. Brazil has nothing to do with this problem.

"As for the greenhouse effect, it's caused by the burning of fossil fuels." He pulls from a stack of papers a United Nations report and reads, "'Eighty-five percent of the carbon dioxide comes from burning by First World countries. And 25 percent of this is produced by the U.S.A. In Brazil the energy consumption per capita averages 800 kilograms of carbon burned. In the U.S.A. it's 9600 kilograms per person, more than eleven times greater than in Brazil.'

"It's the United States and the First World rich countries that are ruining the environment. In Europe there is not one living first-growth tree left. Yet the First World wants our best wood . . . you have to kill ten trees to get one of the best. I'm telling you it's egotistical for them to come and tell us how to handle our environment. It [the environment] will be decided by Brazilians.

"There has been too much emphasis on saving the Amazon," he says. "For example, that road to the Pacific, BR 364. Do you know that that road is already there? It was financed by the World Bank in 1975. This new project is to pave that road. And do you know why the United States is screaming so loud to the Japanese not to fund BR 364? It's not to protect the Amazon hardwoods. It's grain. They're screaming because this road would open a Pacific port twelve thousand kilometers closer to Japan. And that would make our grain more competitive with that of the United States. Their stance is hypocritical."

Mello contends that the country's development isn't so dependent on the Amazon, at least for now. "Why, we don't even know what we have there," Mello adds. "Soon we will explore its natural resources for rational exploitation." Rather, he says, it is the vast *cerrado* grasslands in the country's central western area that are currently being torched and plowed under at record speed, but who cares about grasslands?

I tell him that I saw many gold miners around Poconé freely using mercury and skin hunters working the open lands of the Pantanal. He snaps back, "We prohibited mercury in December 1988, but enforcement has been a problem. There are millions of miners and so many rivers—it's a big problem. Little European countries like Switzerland—the size of Marajo Island [in the Amazon Delta]—think it's easy to physicalize [patrol] our land. If the United States can't control Mexicans coming across its borders with all its men and advanced equipment, how can we control everything here?"

Mello has an urbanologist's eye for issues. He believes the greatest problem facing Brazil isn't the destruction of its incredible wilds, but "the pollution of our urban centers," where 75 percent of the population lives. He points to Britain's restoration of the Thames River as a great example of cleaning up a polluted urban resource. "But it came about only after society's infrastructure—public health, education, housing, and transportation—was functioning," he adds.

Mello has been talking at a great pace for nearly an hour, going way past my allotted ten minutes and making it difficult for questions.

Why can't Brazil appreciate what it has? Why are they in such a hurry to turn this paradise into a tropical New Jersey? With its lion's share of South America (nearly 49 percent), Brazil is rushing headlong into development, eager to finally take its place among the world's leading nations. Like the United States in the mid-1800s, this mammoth, rich land has its own Manifest Destiny.

Political decisions to become more independent had been put into motion decades before: close off imports and encourage home-grown industries through subsidies and government ownership. Steel, cars, soybeans, petrochemicals, intermediate-technology airliners, cheap armaments, and computers are all going concerns, helping to make Brazil the seventh-largest economy in the world. And certainly after the Falklands–Malvinas War, Brazil has been wary of close reliance on the United States.

There has been a price for rapid development. Foreign money has fueled this extraordinary economic engine, requiring U.S. $120 million a month for interest alone. As a result, the land is being plundered for mineral riches at breakneck speed. Aside from not paying back those loans, what can they do?

What about the debt-for-wild-land swap being talked up so much abroad? "I don't like this debt-for-land idea," says Mello.

"It's a very new concept being tried out in Costa Rica. They set aside a million dollars' worth of their debt for a little bit of forest." He hunches up his shoulders, shrugging off the idea. "That's nothing in terms of our land . . . and our debt. Besides, a specific proposal along those lines does not exist today.

"To achieve their economic development, the United States and Europe destroyed their nature and environment. We can take our lesson from that. In the last forty years we've become very aware of our environmental problems. For example, lead in gas—we stopped that last year."

And what of the country's unchecked population growth? Mello admits they have their hands full with the poor and uneducated people of the northeast. "But the birth rates are definitely declining in our big cities. They're equal to the birth rates in bigger cities of Europe."

Mello has concluded his oft-repeated official stance. We sit in silence for a while. Then he begins talking about the differences between the United States and Brazil, not in harsh tones, but the way a close friend might describe his own strengths and weaknesses. I'm not sure if I'm sensing envy or simply Mello's own cultural affinity for American-style drive and accomplishment. He seems almost apologetic. Referring to a famous book, *Bandeirantes and Pioneers,* he compares Brazil to the United States.

"Look, you must remember that Brazil suffered an odd colonization," he says. "Portugal was a tiny, resource-poor, Catholic country choked even then by bureaucrats. They sent undesirables here, and whatever was found of worth, they took back to Europe. Eventually Dom João VI [King John VI] brought his throne here, and with it fifteen thousand noblemen and their aristocratic habits. They influenced our mentality. You know we're the only country in Latin America that has never had a revolution.

"Your colonists came to escape religious persecution. The big land always challenged them to find new places to settle. And," he paused and sighed, "in the United States they were never ashamed to work with their hands."

Everywhere I turn in Brasília, the media, environmental groups, government officials, and even friends who have seen me come and go to the Pantanal over the last eight years, look at me as if I'm a bit mad. It is lamentably obvious that the Pantanal has been forced to the side of the main-stage Amazon show. But I am convinced that if the Pantanal has become a side show, it is most certainly part of the same circus.

twelve

South to Campo Grande

Here we have good environmental programs, a decent
attitude toward the Pantanal. It's frustrating, because in
the north, where the waters are born, they don't do much.
— *Mato Grosso do Sul official*

I'm catching a Varig flight from Brasília to Campo Grande,
the southeastern city bordering the Pantanal. Campo Grande is
the second of four stops on the way down to São Paulo.
There is one advantage to the long flight though. Sitting by
the port window as the plane makes its trajectory south is mes-
merizing. The light is fine, and there is only a modest amount
of atmospheric haze. As a result, I'm treated to a high-altitude
Pantanal geography lesson.
We're tracing the Pantanal's eastern edge along the Chapada
dos Guimarães, a plateau that rises dramatically some thousand
meters above the steamy lowlands. These fabled tablelands and
their rocky buttes and bluffs bring to mind Utah and Wyo-
ming.
It's here that many of the Cuiabá River's feeder streams rise
up, prompting Professor Domingues back in Cuiabá to warn
"the conditions of these highlands are responsible for the Pantanal's past, present, and future." Both he and Arne Sucksdorff
told me that the once expansive grasslands have been simplified
into an upland Kansas. Kilometers and kilometers of uninterrupted "green gold"—soybeans.

The once crystal streams and waterfalls destined for the Pantanal now carry an ominous burden of soil. According to R. L. Welcomme, of the Food and Agriculture Organization of the United Nations, it's only a matter of time before the great stocks of fish will suffer a decline and so, too, all the animals (and people) depending on them. Welcomme considers the Pantanal's rich waters one of "the last great unexploited freshwater fisheries on earth."

The Chapada dos Guimarães is one of two raised topographical features in Brazil's flat, central western region. About three hundred kilometers further west is Chapada dos Parécis. Together they form a physical barrier separating the Amazon River Basin from the Paraguay River Basin. Gaspar told me there is a humble marsh on the Chapada dos Guimarães where streams slide away from each other. One flows north as Rio das Mortes, then into the Amazon and the Atlantic. The other, Rio São Lourenço, tumbles off the plateau south, eroding pre-Cambrian shale and siltstone on its way to the Paraguay River, which joins the Paraná River then flows past Buenos Aires and into the South Atlantic.

Many rivers make a steady procession past my window: São Lourenço, Piquiri, Taquari, Aquiduana. All have dramatic, serpentine courses winding their way east to west.

I recall a conversation with Dr. Newton de Carvalho, one of the few hydrologists who knows the Pantanal well. He spent fifteen years studying the ebb and flow of its waters and installing flood-telemetry devices throughout the region. He told me that the Brazilian highlands forming the edge of the Pantanal below me are actually mountains that have worn down over the millennia. They are among the oldest rock formations on earth, dating back to when all the continents were one, called Gonwanaland. They contain many diamond deposits.

In comparison, the Andes, which are 100 million years old, are geologic newcomers. When the Pacific Plate crashed into South America and tossed up the Andes, the region that is the Pantanal was pushed down slightly so that it filled with water and sediments and became a real inland sea. It's not hard to find shiny black fossils of marine animals buried in the shale and sandstone. That sea dried up millennia ago, leaving behind a sediment pan that has filled in the original seabed to an average depth of a hundred meters above sea level. As a result, there are few deep places left to store great amounts of water. Thanks to the slight pitch of the land and strong sun, the floods are seasonal, producing the current wet and dry hydrologic cycles.

As we fly further south, the high country becomes the familiar checkerboard of farmlands to the horizons. It's odd that so much of these grasslands are in soy production, because the soil is incredibly nutrient-poor. One of the few soil studies conducted on savannas found even less concentration of key elements — calcium, phosphorous, sulphur, and nitrogen — than in the Amazon. Nevertheless, intensive farming on the Pantanal's rim has been growing since the 1970s. To maintain soil fertility, farmers increasingly must rely on a wide variety of agrochemicals, including fungicides, pesticides, and ammonia fertilizers.

Nearly all of the villages I can make out below, including the larger towns of Rondonópolis and Coxim, are conveniently situated on the rivers for drinking water, fishing, navigation, and waste disposal. With so much chemical run-off, farm erosion, and urban effluent, I wonder how long the ecosystem can absorb this load and still support the great concentrations of wildlife.

On this flight is a group of tourists, twelve in all, taking their second leg of a new type of travel in Brazil called "eco-tourism." Behind me is a heavyset man wearing a navy baseball cap with "Alaska the 49th State" in stitched gold braid. He's from a small town in California.

"We've come from the river [Amazon] an' we're going to a place 'sposed to be good for birds . . . the Puntenel," he says. I ask him and his sunburned wife how they liked the Amazon. "The river's so big . . . amazing . . . and where the two branches meet . . . wonderful . . . but it was hard to see animals . . . too dark. We're hoping to see animals here at a ranch outside Campo Grande," he adds.

There's a likable Oklahoma rancher, well-traveled, with a goatee. He says, "This country [pointing down at the window to the grasslands] reminds me of home."

Campo Grande — the name means in effect "vast open land" — is a breath of fresh air. Another cold front has arrived, this one swept up from Antarctica through that natural causeway of the Paraná and Paraguay rivers between the Andes and the high central plain. The wind is snappy, the temperature a bracing 16°C (60°F), and the locals are shivering.

The drive into town goes past a large military base at the end of the airport. The cabby informs me that several thousand soldiers train there. It's necessary, he says, because of all the illegal activities taking place in the frontier region between Bolivia and Brazil, three hundred kilometers to the west.

This town of 220,000 inhabitants is light years away from Cuiabá—and not only in climate. I arrive at lunch time. The thoroughfares are clean and full of recent-make cars stuck in traffic. Maybe it's the wind, but surprisingly the air is free of the heavy diesel fumes so prevalent in Cuiabá. Policemen stroll along busy sidewalks crowded with well-dressed shoppers. The first impression is that Campo Grande is a steadfastly middle-class farming community, sort of the Des Moines of Mato Grosso do Sul.

I go to talk with Dr. Nilson de Barros, secretary of Mato Grosso do Sul's well-established environment department. His offices are housed in a two-story concrete building on Avenida Calogeras on the edge of town. De Barros, a Pantaneiro and practicing veterinarian, has within the last eight months been installed as secretary after his predecessor's untimely death. He's immensely proud of the cowboy lifestyle here. "It's two hundred years of living with nature in a unique ecosystem . . . the most important wetland," he says.

His confidence and enthusiasm for this region is contagious. It occurs to me that with such love for the Pantanal he should be four hundred kilometers north in Cuiabá, where the rivers slide off the highlands and the officials seem to have a different attitude toward the Pantanal.

He laughs. "Just look at a map," he says, pointing out that in the sister state of Mato Grosso only 10 percent of the Pantanal lies within their territory. "Here 33 percent lies within our border. We are preoccupied with the Pantanal. I love Mato Grosso, but she's no good." He draws a battle line on a piece of paper: fishermen, cattle ranchers, and cowboys on one side; agribusiness and gold miners on the other. It's a classic conflict of land-use values.

There are considerable differences. The northern state not only has other interests aside from the Pantanal, but its political structure has been described as being aligned to the "old ways." Leaders in Cuiabá are closely associated with the former military dictatorship.

When the former state of Mato Grosso was divided in 1977, Campo Grande became the new southern state's capital, and elected officials had to start from scratch to develop government institutions. Even though the Pantanal occupies considerable territory in both Mato Grosso and Mato Grosso do Sul, to date there have been no serious cooperative efforts in protection, pollution, or resource management.

De Barros's organization has established an extensive program dedicated to environmental education for youngsters seven to eighteen years old. They have school programs, a living *cerrado* state park complete with guides, and a wildlife hospital. They've produced public-service television announcements and an inventive highway signage program along the southern Transpantaneira Highway, which runs east to west connecting Campo Grande and Corumbá.

The other part of de Barros's program is curative. "In some parts of the high country more than thirty tons of soil a day is eroded off farms," he says. "It ruins the water here. You can go to the Taquari River and take a glass of water that is 50 percent sediment." Twenty years ago you could see the bottom in five meters of water. His department is developing efforts in soil conservation and attempting to replant a denuded watershed with native grasses.

I also talk with one of de Barros's technical specialists, who offers some pretty stunning details on public-health problems of the nearly one million people who rely on the Pantanal's waters. He says epidemiology studies are practically nonexistent. Why is that? "If we were able to find such problems as viral hepatitis, typhus, amoebic dysentery, and salmonella, among others, we wouldn't be able to afford a solution," he says. "Right now it's better if we don't know they exist."

Around Cuiabá, in Mato Grosso, the drinking water is filtered and dosed with chlorine, but once it gets to homes, the pipes and holding tanks recontaminate the water. At the fish market, kids often clean fish for buyers with river water that flows right next to raw-sewage outfalls.

Also in the north, meat processors and dairies dump waste

directly into the streams. Here in the south, sugarcane plants that make fuel alcohol for cars periodically have "accidents" in which high-oxygen-demand distillates are released into the water. In 1985 more than 450,000 kilos of dead fish were found floating in the Miranda River. The deaths are believed to have been caused by one of the six alcohol refineries sited along the major rivers.

The researcher adds that in 1989 the environment department made water quality tests on the Miranda River west of Campo Grande by sampling commercial fish species of *pacú* and *pintado.* They found small amounts of mercury present that had likely come down from the north. But there are more than seventy thousand miners working with gold in Mato Grosso, and the researcher says, "Here we are controlling mining better than in the north. After Serra Pelada [the immense gold mine in the state of Pará] became famous, it became a symbol for all South America . . . the one great chance." Mato Grosso do Sul officials saw this gold rush and swore NIMBY (not in my backyard).

Other highly toxic chemicals are in use too. When grasslands are burned for pasturage it not only stimulates the growth of new grasses, but also of non-nutritious weeds. To control them, "there are many kinds of herbicides used, some outlawed in the United States, like a mixture of 2,4-D and Picloram used by farmers," he says. The mixture, called Agent White by the American military, was used during the Vietnam War as a potent defoliant. Some people even allege that 2,4,5-T, better known as Agent Orange, has been used here, too, as an herbicide.

The researcher says that in 1985 dioxin was sprayed on a pasture near the town of Miranda (about 200 kilometers west of Campo Grande) by a relative of the mayor. The rains washed the residue into the river, resulting in an estimated five hundred metric tons of fish killed.

Mato Grosso do Sul has a law to monitor toxic chemicals, but there are no real fines. As a result, there's a growing international campaign to sell chemicals to farmers. He shows me a book listing Monsanto (United States), Dow (United States), Bayer (Germany), I.C.I. (Great Britain), and CIBA (Switzerland), among others, all doing heavy marketing to farmers in both Mato Grosso and Mato Grosso do Sul. He says you don't have to see this list to know. All you have to do is watch the morning farm reports on television here to see the onslaught of agrochemical commercials.

I want to know the extent of the problem; so as I had done in the north, I go to the market and buy half a dozen local fish—piranha, *pacú*, and *traíra*—that had been caught in the area. Back at the environment department I take over their tiny coffee kitchen, cutting open the fish and taking samples of fat, liver, and flesh. I have with me a new portable pesticide-indicator field test that environment- and food-monitoring groups are beginning to use in the United States. I make a real mess of the sinks, mixing up fat and reagents in my little beakers, while the staff gawks.

The tests are not quantitative. They merely indicate the presence of certain organophosphate herbicides and pesticides. And 40 percent did. More precise laboratory tests would have to follow. Nevertheless I give the testing gear to the department. I think it will be helpful to test soil, plants, fish, and beef right in the field.

So many kinds of agrochemicals and waste flowing into the waterways paint a bleak picture, I think. But then why hadn't there been major epidemics and outbreaks of waterborne diseases? Were the communities around the Pantanal simply lucky?

Modern sewage treatment is, of course, unheard of around the Pantanal. With all of the human waste pumped into the rivers from cities with booming populations, as well as the wastes from slaughterhouses, alcohol distilleries, and dairies, this biomass reaches alarming levels. The waste is acted upon by bacteria and algae, utilizing a great amount of oxygen dissolved in the water. This reduces the oxygen available for fish, threatening to suffocate them. "But just when it seems the waste water is going to kill tons of fish, the rains begin," the researcher says with a grin.

Indeed, the people of the Pantanal are very lucky to be living in and around such an enormous wetland. For centuries this immense flood plain has had a remarkable capacity to cleanse much of the natural and manmade organic waste that flows into it. Apparently, the flood plain is not only a fabulous bird and fish factory, but also a natural sewage-treatment works.

It's able to dilute much of the waste to less toxic levels and recycle the silt and nutrients.

Later, when I return to the United States, I ask Professor Howard Odum, one of the pioneers of wetlands research, about the damage being done in the Pantanal. For twenty years he and his colleagues have studied the remarkable capacities of wetlands. He affirms that you can "regard a wetland as a sewage-treatment plant and put a fence around it if you like . . . [after all] sewage-treatment plants in North America are just ecosystems in a concrete box." After I describe the wide array of pollutants flowing into the Pantanal, Odum says many communities around the world are beginning to appreciate the value of their marshes to handle those kinds of waste.

What about heavy metals, such as mercury? "We were invited to Poland last summer," he says, "to a place where lead pollution from mines now runs down through a marsh. It's been very effective in taking a lot of toxic materials out — nearly 50 percent. The marsh is just not big enough to absorb it all." In Florida his colleagues ran toxic-metal experiments in freshwater marshes and found that mercury was "bound up in lignum and peat when the water levels were maintained."

Odum has consulted in Brazil, too, near Itabuna, along the Atlantic Coast. Just as in Mato Grosso do Sul, there are alcohol plants that dump distillate waste into the rivers. "They made a mess of the [waterway] . . . until they put the waste back in the cane fields and a regular wetland. They had good results," he says.

I brightened on hearing this. In fact, Odum is very optimistic, saying it's a matter of measuring what's going in one end and what's coming out the other. "If they could get some wetlands set aside as a catch basin," he thinks, many pollutants could be managed safely, including pesticides.

Odum believes "the ultimate root of Brazil's conservation problems has been bad economic advice [by banks and developed countries] . . . to use cash crops instead of keeping their resources at home." But he is convinced there is hope for the Pantanal's future. "Nature's trick in protecting itself has always been the wetlands," Odum says. "They even protect other ecosystems."

thirteen

Down on the Farm

What is your favorite Pantanal animal?
Why . . . the cowboy, of course!
—*Manuel de Barros, poet and rancher*

The last decade has been a considerable challenge for Pantanal ranchers. As I have already seen in the north, some ranches, like Descalvado, have fallen on barren days. Or, in the case of São João, keeping back the annual floods has led to a failed experiment in intensive agriculture. In both cases, the owners have left their ranches to live in cities as far away as São Paulo. Their children have become urbanized, less interested in carrying on the family farm.

Some of these huge properties were created by enterprising ancestors. These eighteenth-century poineers placed a survey marker in the ground and walked a horse for days, tracking an immense boundary before returning to the stake. These land claims, though controversial, are honored to this day.

Currently, some of the pioneers' distant descendants are opting to break up some of the ranches, preferring condominiums in São Paulo. The nearly three-centuries-old business of cattle and horse farming isn't making enough profit for other ranch owners. Once the ranches averaged 100,000 hectares (220,000 acres). Now a number of them have been subdivided into smaller ones of 5000 hectares (11,000 acres) each or less. When the floods came, the cows used to be able to migrate to higher ground; today that's more difficult. And the smaller land units are not very efficient.

The impact on wildlife can be serious. Smaller farms means fencing off territory of widely ranging larger animals, such as the caiman, capybara, giant anteater, and peccary. It would limit foraging behavior and could have disastrous results, especially in flood time, when access to high lifesaving ground could be prevented.

Several ranch owner associations have been formed in the last few years, including one out of Campo Grande, in an effort to support the ranch owners and their increasingly threatened way of life. Workshops and other educational efforts are offered to improve cattle management, teach nondestructive agricultural technologies, demonstrate fish farming, and conduct experiments on the commercial farming of capybara and caiman (as has been done in the Orinoco River flood plain of Venezuela).

One of the recent ideas has been to supplement cattle ranching by inviting tourists into the hinterlands to see wildlife living in close proximity to the ranches' feral cows and horses.

Poussada Caiman

When I was in Brasília making plans for my southern journey into the Pantanal, I heard about a ranch once called Estância Miranda, one of the most famous in Mato Grosso do Sul. Now it is called Poussada Caiman, a working cattle ranch 20 km from Miranda. It offers adventures in eco-tourism, the hottest upscale approach to seeing wild Brazil today. Guests can explore this wildlife-blessed property the same way many naturalists, including zoologist George Schaller, have done for years.

But this place is no backwoods hovel. The four-hour drive from Campo Grande gives no hint of what's to come. I ride through familiar parched cattle range, the same as I've seen on the ride to Corumbá, punctuated by palm or fig trees. There are American rheas—those South American ostriches—and many ant mounds, I think.

Driving over a few small bridges and up a hill, I enter the

ranch proper and drive by a wonderful, shallow lake and a luxuriant marsh, then past the cowboy village, which consists of some twenty cottages where the workers and cowboys live.

We pull up at a literal oasis in a desert of yellowed grass. There is a big, rambling *casa* built from large, quarried stones and native woods. It could easily be situated in Taos or outside Tucson. What sets the ranch apart is the welcome greenery landscaped to shade the big house with flowering bushes, vines, and tall trees.

It creates a mighty attractive mini–green belt in the middle of nowhere, attracting an impressive array of tropical birds. When I get out to stretch my legs, I easily spot songbirds, parakeets, Amazon parrots, stunning black-and-orange orioles, doves, and a friendly black currassow (*Crax* species), called *mutum* in Portuguese and the size of a wild turkey.

I've seen these *mutums* dash across the Transpantaneira up north without much luck photographing them. I quickly follow this one around the grounds behind the house, where it assumes a peculiar hunched-over position, with head down and wings held tightly to the body, and utters a low-pitched, gentle "whooo-oo-wha-oo-woo" call. Then the bird flies up to the edge of the garbage dumpster, looks around, and hops in!

If the landscaping is an oasis for the birds, the big house is the same for humans. In its U-shaped, friendly confines there's just about every deluxe hotel amenity. And in the central outdoor area there's an inviting swimming pool.

Inside, the old family quarters have been converted to accommodations that cater to twenty-two guests. The common room is a rustic but well-appointed space, easy on the eyes and body. There are vaulted beamed ceilings, a polished, Italian-tile floor, an imposing stone hearth, comfy leather sofas, an intimate bar at one end, and deeply appreciated air conditioning. Long-distance phone lines, satellite-dish television, and plenty of ranch beef served in the adjoining dining room complete the amenities.

More important, the ranch has developed a program of morning and afternoon outings in specially built open-air vehicles or in boats to explore a number of trails and sites on the ranch. There is a staff of well-informed and enthusiastic guides — Sylvia, Roberta, Ronaldo, and Marcia — to ease guests into the spirit of discovery. They're genuinely serious about studying the wildlife and communicating their knowledge in a caring, unhurried manner to a wide variety of guests.

Poussada Caiman is the brainchild of Roberto Klabin, the thirty-five-year-old heir to the Klabin fortune (made in wood and paper products). Roberto is an intense, high-energy fellow, eager to develop his part of Estancia Miranda into an exciting showcase of *cerrado* and Pantanal wildlife. "I researched this concept very carefully," he says, "seeing exotic hotels in Bahia and the Amazon. I also went on safari in Africa and was impressed at the way they've built luxurious lodges in the wild, right next to the animals."

There were few examples to follow in Brazil. "In the beginning it's been a tough process of study and selection," he notes as we drive out on a truck converted for open-air sightseeing. The experience is indeed as close to an East African safari lodge as can be found this side of the Atlantic.

Klabin is planning new trails, activities, and possibly a bigger facility for more guests, but he says, "My guides [who are college graduates and veterinarians] are giving me other ideas." They want to do research on the ranch and keep the tourism modest, preserving the delightful intimacy that is as hard to find these days in mass tourism as spotting a rare bird itself.

Roberto proudly notes that "I've set aside 7,000 hectares (15,400 acres) as an ecological reserve, where no development, cattle management, or anything else will take place. It's a tough balance too," he reminds. "Caiman is also a real cattle ranch. Some of the old cowboys have a hard time adjusting to the idea of having city people, many of them foreigners, running around here."

A serious ranch indeed. There are about sixty working cowboys here who cover 53,000 hectares (117,000 acres), down from 250,000 hectares (550,000 acres) when the family divided the ranch after Roberto's father, Samuel, died. Some of these men have lived here virtually all of their lives. Together they form a subculture unto themselves, remaining remarkably unaltered for several hundred years. Bloodlines can be traced back to a mix of Guató, Terena, and Bororo Indians, Spaniards (who brought horses to the Pantanal), African slaves, and Portuguese.

The ranch provides the cowboys with simple cottages,

monthly wages (about U.S. $50), rice, coffee, as much beef as they can eat, and health and spiritual services from circuit-riding professionals. In return, the cowboys spend their able-bodied years in the saddle, working far-flung herds until they simply can't anymore.

Farm mechanization at this ranch has made considerable in-roads. By my count there are two bulldozers, a road grader, four diesel dump trucks, five tractors, two jeeps, two Bandeirantes, two custom-made tourist trucks, and a self-contained welding and repair shop. Still, there are nearly a hundred horses on the ranch; it's tough to replace nature's own four-on-the-floor.

Roberto has played his eco-tourism business hunch well, being the first to offer such an outback-style program of wilderness adventure and luxury accommodations. And it seems to be paying off handsomely. Other tour developers are scrambling to convert more ranches along the lines of Poussada Caiman. The question is: Will this long overdue tourist interest in the Pantanal curb the despoilers?

More Big, Blue Birds

The ranch here is not at all like the wild lands of the northern Pantanal. Managed pasturage dominates the environment. Rolling hills and bottomlands are the only places where patches of forest remain.

Here and there tall palms dot the pasture with slender, straight trunks and short crowns of palm leaves. They're *bocaiuva* (*Acrocomia* species), at least fifteen meters tall and lending the grasslands a distinctly tropical character. The trunk is less than a third of a meter in diameter, and the growth scars are much smoother than those of the *bacuri* palm in the north. The trunk is topped out by those stubby palm leaves, the lower ones are yellow with age. Emerging from the center of the palm foliage are the tightly bunched clusters of palm nuts — green, hard, and grape size. This is the main food that hyacinth macaws survive on in the southern Pantanal.

The cowboys and staff of the ranch hear of my love of

hyacinth macaws—of which this region has a goodly number—and suggest that I may want to hang out around a stand of those trees lining the grass airstrip on a hill at the outskirts of the ranch compound. At the top of the hill there are corrals for cows and calves, the ranch's lumber mill, and the airstrip. The landing field is covered with grasses and maintained in near fairway condition by a herd of champion goats.

Unlike the ranch lands in the north, where I've seen precious few of the blue parrots, here they've developed a remarkable tolerance for ranch activities. Cows, goats, chickens, and horses meander under hyacinth-roosting trees. Kids with clanging milk pails pass right beneath the birds with not so much as a ruffled feather in response.

Amidst this farm business two big hyacinths sit atop a *bocaiuva* tree eating its fruit. I shoot some frames; then they start to growl. They get louder. I fear I'm the disturbance and back off ten meters and sit down behind a bush. Three more fly in, flapping their broad wings as they stall out onto the crown of a large, old, fig tree. Now there are five of the big, blue birds—all growling. I can't believe it; these birds are ganging up on me to drive me out. So I pick up the gear and back off a greater distance, but they don't settle down.

More hyacinths are coming, this time screaming while in flight from the outlying forest on the far side of the airstrip. They course low over the airfield and then rise up, wheeling around the big fig tree. I try to photograph them flying with the long lens, but it's practically impossible with their speed and the sun behind them. At right angles to the light their beaks shine, and the sun puts fire in their black eyes.

An instant later the dark purple over their stomachs and underwings has turned golden from the setting sun. Around and around the fig tree they fly, screaming, until I hear a high-pitched hiss. Then I relaize it's not me that's provoking this ruckus, but a pair of raptors that have alighted in a nearby tree. They're smaller than the macaws and smoky gray in color.

The hawks are certainly no match for those big birds and definitely way outgunned at the moment with this growing flock defending its territory. A dozen . . . eighteen . . . twenty-five hyacinths are wheeling overhead, circling the tree. My shoulder sockets ache from tracking them through the big lens.

The birds are getting tired too. As they fly overhead, I can see their beaks agape and the thick, black tongues flopping up and down from the exertion.

One of the hawks is emboldened and leaves its mate, landing in the same fig tree as the macaws. The exhausted parrots then labor into the air and circle closer and closer to the hawk. Finally the gray hawk utters another piercing hiss, yielding the territory, and flies off, joined by its mate.

It's too dark for pictures as I watch five hyacinths fly up to the palm leaves, where one of them hangs upside-down by a single claw in a lighthearted moment after the raptor incident. Another flies up, knocking the first one into the air. Then the first bird comes back up in a wild flap as the two play a game of aerial "chicken" to see which one can hold the lowest part of the frond without falling off.

It's been a pure joy watching these big, gregarious birds. And I want to learn more.

The next morning I'm up at dawn with the little kids who are going to the corrals to milk the cows.

At first light, the big parrots aren't so noisy; I can see them coursing in low over the pasture to the feeding trees. I've hidden behind a bush near the air field among the calves. I hear the hyacinths fly in; they make a sound like crinoline rustling as they flutter their big wings. But I don't know which trees they've landed in. I scan all the nearby tall fruit trees and can't locate one. Yet I'm still hearing the flapping of wings.

I discover four of them on the ground outside the corral, right beside the water tank for the calves. They appear to be eating corral dirt for minerals. Another flies in and perches on the fence. He's a sentinel while the others waddle on the ground sipping the water that leaks from a crack in the concrete trough.

With their crescent-yellow cheek patch, the birds always appear to have a grin on. But that's a mask. They're as tough as junkyard dogs.

In the next few weeks I make many outings across the savanna pastures, chasing those alluring macaws in their daily routine with my movie camera, tripod, and long lens. I put everything down, set up, and film them. Then they fly off, with me puffing in pursuit, ready to set up all over again.

Exactly where the birds roost at night is still a mystery, but it's a reasonable bet that at morning's first light they'll be coursing in to that grassy hill beside the airstrip and alighting on those tall *bocaiuva* trees. There they assemble to munch those favored palm nuts and to socialize a bit, engaging one another with their beaks.

Then they fly several kilometers across pastures to a vale where a permanent marsh trickles through the lowlands. I don't find this out so easily. I climb through barbed-wire fences, tiptoe through pastures with feral cattle, scan the birds' flight path with binoculars, and lug the gear over my shoulder in their direction.

Scattered in the fields are many mounds, each with a remarkable little bird—a burrowing owl (*Speotyto cunicularia*)—perched on top, right in broad daylight: Not only is it a treat to see owls in daylight, but these small raptors have ungainly chickenlike legs and a well-developed chest. Their heads, though, are complete business, with classic large owl eyes and sharp beak.

The hyacinths have settled onto a dead tree in the bottom-lands. They're easy to spot—seven long-tailed, blue macaws sitting on dry limbs. The sun begins to dry the air considerably, burning off the dew and ground fog.

The birds sit well apart from one another, preening and nibbling their claw nails. I'm able to sneak up close enough to use my 560mm lens hooked up to a motion-picture camera, effectively doubling the focal length. It's difficult to rig this equipment in a hurry. I keep my fingers crossed that they'll stay a while.

This morning roost is different from Tutu's grove and even the airstrip. Here the macaws are right out in the open and can see any danger approaching, including me with my optical bazooka. Thus they take their morning respite without fear of surprise. There's not much tension and certainly no growls. One is even secure enough to close its eyes and doze off on a limb, tucking a leg up into its belly feathers as the warm rays of light edge up the birds' long bodies. Occasionally a macaw will leap over to where another is perched and they'll lock beaks in a parrot buss. One seems to be without a mate; yet it, too, socializes, moving over and touching others in the intermix of individuals.

Then one flies down to the muddy ground. Another flutters down. There they waddle, tipping left and then right, dragging those magnificent tails through the dirt. They use their beaks like clamshell dredges and dig up some of the gray material and begin eating it. For grit? Minerals?

The others do the same, while one appears to keep a watch out as they had done at the corral. When finished, they fly up to three young palms on the edge of the mineral patch. One thing, though—none of the trees has any leaves left. In fact, one is a leafless trunk pointing into the sky. Two birds cling to the pole and chew away at the top as, I guess, they've done for months, leaving the tree dead. They've left a great pile of dead leaves, feathers, bird wash, and unfinished foods below.

The macaw's beak is like a cross between a ninja weapon and a Swiss army knife. Watching for a few minutes, I see the beak used as a brace (like a third leg), a preening tool to split quill sheaths, a tweezers to pull out feathers and smooth barbules, and as a clamp, pickax, climber's tool, and seed cracker.

And what a tongue. It has yellow stripes running along the black sides. It flicks out to test and taste everything the clamshell beak and claws bring in.

The macaws demonstrate a close bond with their mates as well as with others in the group, showing affection and aggression to nearly all eventually. (One seems to be odd bird out, though, and barely tolerated.) They appear to have understood and exploited their environment so well that they have much time left over for what can only be regarded as leisure and play.

I may have watched the birds too long because I begin to think I can identify individuals among them, based on specific behaviors and vocalizations. I'm convinced they display personalities. Other social animals of the Pantanal—the American rhea, capybara, caiman, and wood stork—seldom show a similar level of intelligence. Only the monkey and river otter demonstrate this. After days of watching these curious animals, the term "birdbrain" seems a downright compliment.

When I told people back at the ranch about the flock of hya-cinths mobbing the hawks, I realized right off that I'd been smitten by a compelling disease: parrot fever. I simply can't see enough of them. In a way, these macaws are a perfect symbol of the Pantanal itself: the biggest of their kind, poorly under-stood, and very much in trouble.

The scientific literature on hyacinth macaws remains surpris-ingly scant, with only a handful of studies conducted in the wild, most done more than fifteen years ago. Yet among exotic-bird collectors these big, blue macaws remain the most sought after of all parrots.

I asked one well-known hyacinth breeder in the United States what makes these birds so much in demand among col-lectors. Because they're the biggest parrot? No. Because they're an uncommon blue color? No again. A special personality trait? Maybe. The man contends that they're heavily sought today because "These birds are becoming rare and expensive. The more scarce and costly, the more pressure there is to have one of them."

According to Carlos Yamashita, a Brazilian wildlife researcher I know and one of the few people to have conducted a popula-tion survey of these birds, "There are more mountain gorillas left in East Africa than there are hyacinth macaws left in South America." Yamashita estimates that in their last haunts—north-east Brazil, the Pantanal, and eastern Bolivia—there are only about 3500 left in the wild. Although other researchers ques-tion such a low figure, the warning flag of endangerment is up.

There is more irony. While hyacinths are in decline through-out their remaining habitats, there is a growing population whiling away in pet cages and zoos around the world. Accord-ing to one authority, there is at least a number outside Brazil equal to or actually surpassing the remaining wild population.

Worse, conservationists seldom have reason to dialogue with hyacinth breeders. Even though importation of these birds has been banned through CITES (Convention on International Trade in Endangered Species of Flora and Fauna) for years, the pet trade is seen as part of the pressure threatening the wild popu-lation. Fraudulent papers of origin allow illegal exportation.

Yet some hyacinth breeders in the United States—where the largest percentage of the estimated 5000 to 7000 hyacinths reside—have developed some impressive reproduction techniques for a bird notoriously difficult to breed in captivity. One report cites a pair that fledged eight young in one season—a phenomenal success. There might be interest in developing a recovery program for hyacinths in which breeding techniques and other knowledge could be shared. Perhaps at Poussada Caiman? Maybe someday a captive breeding program could be initiated in Mato Grosso to support the wild population—that is, if a secure habitat could be found.

Several years ago, forty hyacinth macaws were discovered in a small plane at Campo Grande's airport. Apparently some had gotten loose while the plane was aloft, creating havoc in the cockpit and forcing the pilot to land. Most of those birds were confiscated by police and housed in a zoo in São Paulo. Some died. But enough survive that could become the core of a recovery effort.

There are many studies that could challenge researchers, such as mapping the birds' social interactions within flocks, groups, and pairs. The late Dr. Bernhard Grizmek had developed an ingenious experiment in East Africa to test pairing and aggressiveness among rhinos. He constructed a balloon shaped like a rhino and walked it out in front of himself on the Serengeti. I wonder what would happen if I made some lifelike, inflatable, blue macaws and set them in one of their roosting trees. Would they be attacked and reveal a flock or group leader?

Furthermore, Charles Munn, a research colleague of Yamashita's, wonders how the birds are able to live primarily on the saturated fats of palm nuts and not succumb to clogged arteries.

The head guide, Marcia, and I drive out in a jeep to observe a nest tree. The tall, African-looking tree with a broad crown is rather thick and rises more than twenty-five meters above the pasture, just ten meters from the dirt road we're on. About fifteen meters up and center in the trunk is a hole the size and shape of a football. The edge of the hole is swollen, like puffy lips, and light colored, a natural aberration of growth, expanded and hollowed out by years of wildlife tenants.

As our jeep pulls up, the noise brings a blue-headed parrot to the hole, and instantly it's up and out from the nest, perching in a nearby tree and screaming at us. Its mate hears the commotion, and soon both adult hyacinths are putting up a loud defense.

I'm afraid to stay longer for fear of driving the birds away at a time when there could be young in the hollow. "We looked already; there are no chicks in the nest," Marcia says.

Someone had climbed up several weeks earlier and taken the hatchling. She says bird collectors use a variety of techniques aside from raiding a nest. Once a nest tree or feeding site is located, collectors typically coat a limb with a sticky balsam, trapping the unsuspecting bird. Or they risk killing the bird outright by wounding it with an arrow or small-caliber fire arm, enabling the capture.

The staff and cowboys at Poussada Caiman have an obvious economic interest in keeping these birds at the ranch to impress the tourists. Protection of known nest trees remains a weak link. Ultimately it's up to the Pantaneiros themselves—ranch owners and cowboys alike—to recognize and appreciate these creatures for what they are. Nothing short of a change in attitude will save them.

The Old Hunter

An older man is pointed out to me as one of the most knowledgeable about life here on the ranch over the years. His name is Sr. Celistano and he's now retired. I find him in the small village behind the main house where the cowboys and their families live. He's playing with the cowboys' children on the veranda of his bungalow.

Sr. Celistano is in his sixties. He's tall and lanky with wrinkled, walnut-colored skin. He wears a baseball cap and blue workshirt. He's very quiet—and somewhat reluctant to talk about the old days. His eyes brighten when I ask him to help me film some of the water life on the lagoon.

In the late afternoon we shove one of the new skiffs into the water. It's without a motor; so Sr. Celistano grabs an oar and sits precariously on the edge of the gunwale, sculling with it off the stern. He keeps his eyes on the horizon, working the oar with short, powerful "J" strokes. He's not saying much, deferring to the gringo.

Sr. Celistano is in his environment now, filling his chest with authority as we glide among the weed-choked shallows, following the wooded shore. Most of the plants are water hyacinth; many have beautiful, pale-purple flowers. The sun dances on the black water in hypnotic fashion.

As we round a bend we surprise a pack of capybaras grazing on the water plants. The largest adult gives a warning bark and they beat a hasty retreat, splashing through the shallows into the forest.

Sr. Celistano has lived and worked on this ranch for more than thirty years. I think to myself that it must be tough to have been a cowboy, forever in the saddle, and now no longer able to ride.

"Cowboy life thirty years ago must have been interesting," I say. "Yes, it must have been, but I wouldn't know, *senhor*," he says with pride. "I was a professional hunter." A hunter? "Yes, *senhor*, I hunted jaguars for the *dono*." "You mean Roberto's father, Samuel?" "Yes, the same."

Whenever the ranch hands found a carcass of a calf or noticed bloody scratches on the cattle, Sr. Celistano would be called over. "I used to go after the cats with packs of dogs to run them down," he says. The dogs were brought to the scene, given the scent, and then set free on the trail. "Sometimes they would run for hours. We'd follow on horse."

I ask Sr. Celistano how many jaguars he killed. "Beginning in 1966, over nine years, I shot eighty-eight. Then the federal government prohibited hunting," he says.

Eighty-eight? "Yes, *senhor*," he answers. "All of them taken here at this ranch. My largest was an *onça pintada* that weighed 195 kilos." What an animal that must have been. There was no emotion in his voice—just an old man's recollection of bygone days.

Gator Gulch

By now Sr. Celistano and I have drifted down to where a stream exits the lagoon in a small but pretty falls. The sun has dipped behind a stand of trees, filtering several brilliant beams that cut across the stream and illuminate a marsh.

We beach the boat and climb an embankment, where the lagoon forms a little spillway. On the western bank sit thirty or forty caimans sunning themselves on bird-washed rocks. Several more float in the slight current at the far end of the pool. In the dark-chocolate water about a meter from the far bank, a white common egret slowly stalks fish. This elegant bird stands not more than two meters from three caimans piled on top of each other on a little island of grass. It doesn't so much as glance at the reptiles. Its attention is fixed on spearing little fish.

With three or four major rainsqualls a day for the last several weeks, the spillway has swollen into a two-tiered cascade that drops about six meters, creating a respectable little rapids. A dead tree to the right of the falls holds a gathering of a dozen cormorants preening and drying their wings. The dying light paints the tree tangerine and lights up the birds' green eyes. Two Ringed kingfishers land on some algae-covered rocks to one side of the falls, chattering in anticipation of the easy fishing ahead.

Sr. Celistano says, "I'm going to have to go now. It's getting late — time for my dinner." He pats me on the back. "Have you seen the *jacarés* at night?" Yes, I answer, telling him about the great pool near the *posto* with hundreds of caimans and their eerie eyes.

"No, no. They are different in this stream at night. Stay here and you'll be rewarded," he says cryptically. I wonder what caimans do here at night that's so different. And I'm nonplused about how to get back. I'm a couple of kilometers from the ranch house. "Take this trail back when you're through," he says, patting me on the shoulder and paddling away.

The sun has gone, too, lighting the cumulonimbi in a high-altitude alpine glow. Mosquitoes and no-see-ums spread out from the dank forest to feast as I set up my tripod in a tongue of brushy land that forms the right bank of the falls. I hunker down, waiting for something to happen.

A couple of small, sparrow-size birds with thick, black beaks, yellow breasts, and charcoal backs land on the rocks not far from the kingfishers. They watch the kingfishers for a few seconds, then scrutinize a tiny rivulet that spills over a large boulder along the far side of the falls. Suddenly one of the yellow birds wades into this microstream, grabs something, and retreats to its rocky perch. Its companion does the same.

The pink dusk reflecting off the clouds bathes this pool in a cool light, turning the black surface to silvery-rose, then gray. From my angle now I can make out what the birds are so excited about. Fish the size of minnows are leaping from the boiling water, flashing their shiny skins in short little arcs in an effort to navigate the rapids upstream. This is *piracema,* the spawning migration.

More and more fish begin leaping. Larger fish the size of perch take a less dramatic route up a trickle of water into a stepped area blanketed in thick moss. The flow of water is just enough to cover their gills, making this seem like a procession of small, peeled bananas wiggling upstream.

The news spreads quickly. The cormorants see the smaller birds' success and dive into the action. One by one they fly down from the tall tree and glide into the water. Others on the rocks see their kin in the water and paddle over.

They surface-dive into the whitewater. Now all the cormorants are working the pool below the falls. When one comes up empty, it checks the others for their luck. One surfaces with a fish in its beak, flashing the good news. This draws still more of the big water birds right to that spot and into a diving frenzy.

In short order the caimans get the message too. One big adult raises up on all fours, climbs over some of the other sunbathers, and noses into the water. At first it simply orients toward the falls, maybe thirty-five meters away, and stays in place, invisibly dog-paddling with its legs against the weak current. Then more of the big caimans follow suit, crawling over one another and creating a moment's fracas: objecting jaws and reptilian hisses. Soon, nearly all have slithered into the water.

At about this time, I hear a strange noise not far from me in the woods. It sounds like a ripe watermelon being dragged across gravel. Emerging from this little spit of land is a bumpy snout connected to a meter-and-a-half-long body. A smart caiman is making an overland shortcut to the falls when it spots me not five meters away. My eyes go big. So do its. Then it bursts into a saurian scurry for the water.

Silently, with only a few visual cues, the caimans swim into a V formation led by a big one. Slowly they cruise upstream, driven forward by their powerful tails swishing back and forth. They are half submerged, pushing a snout-bow wake.

A last glint of sunlight lights up the top of the cormorant tree. The dying light and the caiman action have pushed the birds out of the water. Now all of them are safely perched in the tree, preening, many with their wings propped open to catch the last warmth of the day.

At the base of the rapids the light on the water is now silver and foam. A long, dark figure eases right into a rushing eddy, the snout inches from the falling water. How the caiman manages to stay put in the considerable force of water isn't clear. The tail doesn't move. Maybe more dog-paddling.

The smaller ones follow suit, lining up shoulder to shoulder and staking out their watery claims, which will be worked through the night. Then the big one opens its jaws in a toothy smile and stays that way as the torrent of water races through its mouth. In short order fifteen reptiles have their jaws open in the falls. More are stacked up behind them, somewhat broadside to the current.

Although the sun is down, high overhead a flock of egrets flies, returning to roost; they're bathed in gold by the last rays of sunlight. Now the light is too weak even for my fast film. The best of this caiman behavior will be happening very soon. I decide to try something I had done before in Asia. I attach my powerful flash to my 560mm telephoto and prefocus the distance in an attempt to capture the caimans fishing.

These reptiles are now living fish traps, snapping whenever they feel the slightest bit of flotsam (or fish) hitting their cavernous mouths. When one does, the effort from snapping its jaws shut shoves it back into the current for a second; then the creature has to paddle back into place. Near shore, the juveniles pile on top of one another in a Gordian knot of bodies and mouths.

Dozens of snaps are required before success, giving me good opportunities to shoot film. I'm sure many frames will be out of focus. But when I get the film back later, it is stunning—the foaming bubbles, caiman jaws agape, pink mouths with water stroboscopically frozen in time—it looks as if the caimans are roaring through the water at sixty knots.

The pictures that really send a wave of goose flesh over me are the ones with the flash and the close-up shots of their toothy, frothy mouths and those gator eyes—lit up with an eerie glow like refrigerator bulbs. That night I stay late photographing this seldom seen event until my batteries go dead.

A Strange Old Man

This ranch is so large that each day I try to explore a different section or walk another trail, away from the everyday traffic of horsemen and ranch workers. One late afternoon I'm returning to the ranch near some of the outlying cowboy cottages. I come to a long, converted horse stall, which is located right in front of the ranch slaughterhouse. The end stall has been converted to a sleeping room with a split door. A short, old man leans out as I walk by.

"Yank, eh?" the man mumbles to himself, loud enough for me to hear. Odd. He uses "Yank," not "gringo," which is the universal euphemism for northern strangers.

"Uh-huh," I confess. "Who are you?" He unbolts the bottom half of the stable door and steps out of the shadows. He weaves a bit, in poor balance, and sits down on a stump. The vapors of *cachaça* waft over.

The man is a physical mess. He's short and stocky, no more than five-feet-four. He's barefoot and wearing worn, blue Bermudas. His toenails are awfully long, gnarled, and split; I don't think they've seen shoes in decades. A web of blue and red veins seemingly lifted from a road map work their way from the tops of his feet, with thick state roads and federal highways around the ankles. His calves and upper legs bulge like long, lumpy worms trying to find a way out. The knees stick out arthritically.

Yet it is from the shoulders up that his decrepit nature takes on alarming proportions. On the right side of his neck is a swollen lobe about the size of a cut grapefruit. The man's skin has a cadaverous pallor, odd in such a sun-drenched land. His nose is grossly enlarged and deformed; its thickened skin also has blue and red blood vessels running through it, a condition that's often a telltale sign of heavy drink and smoke.

An awful, long, red scar works its way from under the left side of his nose across the cheek, nicking the eye and disappearing into his hair. His eyes are pale blue, clouded from age, and glassy from drink. His hair is dirty white and streaked with yellow from scratching his nicotine-stained hands on his head, which he does while smoking as we talk.

"My name in Waldimir," he mumbles. He chokes off his words, swallowing their pronunciation; yet I can make out this man's Portuguese without a hitch. The sounds come out stiff, the effort of someone not quite at home with the language.

Years ago, he says, he simply came to this ranch and asked for work. And the owner let him stay. "What did you do here?" I ask. "I was the gunsmith. I'm very good at making and fixing guns." He worked with Sr. Celistano at a time when hunting was considered the right thing to do.

But Celistano wasn't the only professional hunter who pursued the jaguars (and pumas), says Waldimir. There was another man, a Russian who had come to Mato Grosso in the 1930s. His name was Sasha Siemel. He was a civil engineer who had come to Brazil to meet his brother, Ernst, who was engaged in constructing some of the first roads into South America's hinterlands.

What happened to Siemel is legend. He became involved in a brawl with a man and ended up pistol-whipping him to death, or so Siemel thought. Fearing the worst, Siemel and his brother took off into what they called, in those days, the Great Swamps of Mato Grosso. At first they did what Waldimir did: repaired ranch owners' weapons. Then Ernst went to work on a civil-engineering project in the south. Sasha was impressed by the Indians of the Mato Grosso and sought them out to learn their secrets of how to hunt and subsist in those Great Swamps.

Sasha became friends with one Indian in particular who was adept at killing jaguars in the ancient native way of hunting—not with rifles, but one-on-one, armed only with a *zagaia*, a heavy spear. This blood rite awakened something primeval in him, and he set out to master the hunting of Mato Grosso's big cats with a spear. This he did.

Sasha became well known to the plantation and ranch owners for his primitive, yet deadly accurate hunting technique. He also became an expert archer, using the native longbow. He was hired by cattlemen in the Pantanal to rid their lands of the jaguar "problem."

Sasha continued his spear-hunting for nearly three decades, working many of the places I'd visited, including Descalvado, Amolar (in the national park), and this ranch. Ernst was killed in a bar fight. Sasha later married Edith Brey, a woman from Philadelphia who shared a number of his Brazilian adventures before retiring to the United States.

Later, I mention to Sylvia, one of the tour guides, that I had been talking with Waldimir. She looks at me in shock. "That awful man's always drunk. He just stays in his room for weeks at a time. People say he has a strange background. They think he's a Nazi."

fourteen

A Hot Time in Old Corumbá

> [In Corumbá] . . . the sun devours the yellow streets . . . the heat
> comes up in a haze . . . a vast, heavy stillness broods over the
> terraced town. By day the porous stone sucks in the hot savagery
> of the tropics, and breathes it out like an evil odor at night.
> —*Julian Duguid*, Green Hell

The city of Corumbá is an important gateway between
Bolivia and Brazil and the jumping-off point for the southwestern Pantanal. To get there from Campo Grande travelers
are faced with poor choices: a plane from which you can see
nothing, a cattle-passenger train that requires a numbing ten-
hour nighttime milk run, or Mato Grosso do Sul's version of
the Transpantaneira Highway. The latter is also called the
Transpantaneira Highway; it's 429 fun kilometers of thin
asphalt (that has split open like an overcooked sausage), gravel
the size of tennis balls, and fine dust.

My handy and infallible *South American Handbook*—the 1982
edition, now bound in aluminized duct tape from years of
use—informs me that this trip requires two crossings of the
Paraguay River. Both are accomplished by unreliable, but expensive ferry boats, which are often flooded out or in various
stages of disrepair.

I quickly imagine myself going down another all-weather
"highway," with its tank-swallowing potholes, holding onto
my fillings as I ogle great gatherings of animals. How can I refuse such romance? I make arrangements immediately to drive.

In the course of making the rounds of officials in Campo Grande, I meet a man who is in charge of developing recreational facilities for the state. He and his colleagues are in the process of proposing Mato Grosso do Sul's first Pantanal park in an area not far from Corumbá called Necolândia, named for a man who first built a ranch there. We work out a deal where I will get the loan of a vehicle to Corumbá. From there a speedboat will take my driver and me up the Paraguay River. We will then transfer to a jeep and visit the site of the proposed new park. I will get the vehicles and driver if I pay for all expenses, including fuel; he will get copies of some pictures I take in the area to help his project along. Of course. Deal.

The vehicle is a 1975 Chevrolet suburban wagon that's green as the color of money. And that's what it's gonna take — wagons full — because there's a six-cylinder engine with pistons the size of coffee cans. And it drinks only gas — not alcohol or government-subsidized affordable diesel. The price of gas here rivals prices in Europe. Renaldo, the driver, says, "The wagon's a pig . . . but a fast one."

Renaldo is twenty-two years old, a Tom Cruise lookalike in T-shirt with a winning grin. Despite the promise of choking heat, he wears tight blue jeans. He dons mirrored sunglasses, lights up a Hollywood cigarette, and we're off. Eh, not exactly. He's got some friends who are going to Corumbá — can we give them a lift? Ah-ha, the old get-the-gringo-and-turn-the-wagon-into-a-Mexican-truck routine. I know that one. Before we can escape town there are six of us. At least I refuse to take the chickens.

Off to Corumbá. It's 5:50 A.M. I tell Renaldo that I've made appointments with scientists at the agricultural research station there and the commandant of police. "Today's Friday; don't forget that TGIF comes early here," I note out loud. Renaldo thinks a moment. "It'll take us . . . six hours. No problem," he says, flooring the wagon. In seconds we're screaming down the highway, zipping past buses stopped to drop off passengers, donkey carts, stray dogs, and bicyclists. The speedometer oscillates wildly anywhere from 115 to 145 kilometers an hour depending on what's standing in our way. Which reminds me to buckle up, but there aren't any seat belts.

The road is not like the primitive Transpantaneira in the

north. This is a major paved highway carrying lines of traffic to and from the Bolivian frontier. It's built a lot higher than the northern road too: from six to ten meters above the surrounding lowlands. It was done to provide a measure of safety from the great floods that inundate the region. Since the Pantanal slopes gently north to south at only two centimeters a kilometer, the flood waters have a slow velocity, allowing them to accumulate at this end and stay longer than in the north.

This is border country, like the national park region, only with roads. Or like the United States' Rio Grande border with Mexico minus the fence. Thousands of Bolivians come across to find some relief from their abject poverty. On the legal side, dyes, handicrafts, and natural gas come into Brazil, and all kinds of manufactured goods — cheap electronics, furniture, household items, fashion wear and shoes — leave.

According to investigative journalists with whom I've talked, in the last several years the growing interdiction pressure on Colombia has forced cocaine traffickers, especially the Medellín and Cali cartels, to seek alternate routes. This poorly enforced wilderness frontier has proven to be an increasingly valuable outlet for drugs to be moved into Brazil and from there to the United States and Europe. In addition, gold and even trailer trucks full of soybeans go out illegally. It's done to obtain higher prices and escape federal taxes.

Just outside the turnoff for Aquiduana, the traffic comes to a screeching halt and is backed up for half a mile. An accident? Renaldo gets out and steps on the running board for a look. "No, it's a roadblock," he says. The military police are stopping all vehicles heading west. As we creep along, Renaldo fishes through an envelope of papers to find the car's documents, and his.

"Do you have a pistol?" he says. No. "Drugs? If you do, throw them out now. These guys can be a real pain." I assure him hospital sheets aren't any cleaner than my bags. It seems they're looking for someone in particular, since it isn't a permanent check point.

"We'll have to watch the truck carefully when we get to Corumbá," Renaldo warns. Brazil has been plagued in recent years by gangs of car thieves working all the way to Rio and São Paulo. Since Bolivia doesn't make its own autos, those on the streets of Corumbá represent a great opportunity for profit if they can be smuggled out. Officials estimate that about a thousand cars a month are illegally fed into the Bolivian "used" car and auto-parts market. For the Brazilian middle class, a car is an exceedingly expensive purchase, ranging up to U.S. $17,000 for the latest Ford Escort convertible tricked out with all the extras.

Owners have outfitted their vehicles with all manner of antitheft devices. At car parks you often have to pay a street urchin to watch your car. But no matter, they're stolen. Some outraged victims have actually tracked their vehicles all the way to Bolivian chop shops, making for some nasty confrontations.

The police at the roadblock are wearing full combat gear — camouflage fatigues and jungle boots — and are armed with what look like M-16 knockoffs and a few machine pistols. Renaldo hands over the papers to a soldier, who motions us to pull over and get out. Uh-oh.

Another soldier searches the wagon while I try to get some information from an officer wearing a black beret. The guy is mum. All I get is that roadblocks are randomly done up and down the highway. Then the officer starts asking me questions. What's a gringo doing in this part of the country? Where am I going? He takes a long look at my passport.

When we get back into the car, the soldiers come together by my window, snap to attention in a mock salute, and shout in eighty-decibel unison, "Yessirr!" in English, scaring the hell out of me. Then they all burst out laughing as we pull away. Too many John Wayne reruns.

Campo Grande has long since disappeared in the rearview mirror. Ahead are miles and miles of smoky, open plain. Flat, dry *cerrado*. Once this was an immense *campo* (countryside) of scattered brushy plants, tall tussock grass, short impoverished trees, and sentinel arrangements of ant mounds. But much of that has long since been simplified by the ax and match. In its place, managed cattle range, along with their favored sweet mimosa and imported grasses.

This is *derrubada,* or cleared cow country, kept so by those controversial burnings. Here, as in the north, most of the bovines dotting the landscape are light-gray zebu cattle with floppy, tubular ears. They're everywhere on this range, standing in the wilting sun; only a few with a bit of sense sit under the spreading arms of stark fig trees and wait out their time.

While better able to cope in this hostile flood plain than their Jersey kin, zebu have gustatory drawbacks. Time and again I find their meat flavorful but tough as shoe leather. It doesn't matter whether it's cut into pieces and cooked with rice or barbecued in lion-size chunks.

At points along the way, green highway signs loom up with specific messages geared to tourists, fishermen, and farmers, asking them not to spoil the Pantanal. They are thoughtfully designed with enormous wildlife images accompanied by a few words about each animal. One sign, for example, has a drawing of a caiman and copy that reads: "I am the *jacaré*. Two million of my brothers die each year; help me save my skin. Preserve nature. Thanks from the heart." Another shows a toco toucan with the saying, "I am the toucan. My freedom depends on your maturity."

In all, I think we drive past eight billboards that, in essence, identify a bird, mammal, fish, or reptile living in the Pantanal, note its condition, and put the environmental responsibility on the people coming through. More address the types of people using the roads: tourists, truck drivers, children, fishermen, and farmers. An agricultural sign reads: "Chemical products destroy life. Apply them correctly. Our nature thanks you from the heart."

The signs were placed recently by Dr. Nilson de Barros's environment department in an effort to make highway motorists aware of the issues as they enter the region. Mato Grosso do Sul seems to have a more positive conservation attitude prevailing in its government.

Suddenly I notice with alarm that the gas gauge has moved speedily off the "F" mark and is beginning a rapid descent to "E" as if the tank had a hole in it. Oh, my dollars. With so much environmental information along the highway, I'm surprised there hasn't been one sign posting the distance to the next gas station.

We turn off a bit too soon to catch the road to Corumbá and the ferry — there are no signs to help us — and end up driving in the lowlands off the beaten path. Near a small lake we stop and inquire for directions at an old, planked cabin. The people living there resemble poor Appalachians. Close to their property we see a big tree with a dark, wet stain nearly seven meters up its trunk. The people say that's where the last flood came up to—about a meter above their roof.

I remember talking with Dr. Newton de Carvalho, the man who placed fifty telemetery stations throughout the Pantanal. He said these floods are seldom sudden and violent like the spring flash floods in North America. He said the town of Cáceres in the north has had dramatic rises, though; between March and February, the level there has been known to go up one meter a day.

These people say the rains are like what I experienced in the Chapada dos Guimarãs—a heavy rainstorm lasting up to a couple of hours, then moving on. Sometimes, too, the rains pour down for a week. It all adds up to 1.7 meters a year.

For the most part, a local farmer observes, the waters are expected here by fish, flowers, birds, and people too. The floods push out most of the farmers for weeks, leaving their domestic animals and cattle to literally sink or swim for themselves.

We've found the main road again, and for the next fifty kilometers I haven't been able to enjoy the landscape much. Instead I've been fixated on the gas gauge. That damnable needle has done a freefall to "E" in record time. Now it's not even bouncing above the red warning zone. It's dead on and we have to fill up now. Only there isn't a service station in sight. The idea of taking a hike in 40°C (104°F) morning heat is sheer lunacy.

The specter of walking on such a day rouses Carlos, Renaldo's friend, who's sitting in the back. He's been asleep in the shade of his jacket, which he's stuffed in the window to block the sun. Carlos, who is returning home to Corumbá, lifts an eyelid long enough for a look around, then waves a forward motion and mumbles, "A little more."

Long minutes pass before we roll into a gas station on the outskirts of Corumbá. While the serviceman pumps the gas, we get some local snacks—little meat pies and cheese bread. We wash the food down with Guaraná, the Brazilian carbonated tropical-fruit drink that tastes like ginger ale. It's made from the guaraná shrub (*Paullinia sorbilis*), which is used as a general tonic as well.

Admiring the station wagon are three Bolivians. Despite the heat they wear new blue jeans, snakeskin cowboys boots, western-style shirts, and straw Stetsons. They stroke the vehicle's shiny sides affectionately, revealing thick, gold, pinky rings. "Nice car," one of them says in Spanish as we walk over. After the inspection, they whisper to each other, then saunter over to us and promptly make an offer: "You take U.S. $4000?"

Renaldo stands there with his arms folded and shakes his head no. One man sweetens the deal: "I have cash now." It's a terrific deal. Dollars are always in demand because they're a popular hedge against Brazil's wild inflation. But Renaldo says no again, and the men walk away.

"What was that all about?" I ask. Renaldo says Bolivians like these old Chevies because they're fast. He points to the large cargo area, adding, "This old guzzler isn't worth U.S. $3000, but it can carry lots of coca." I pay U.S. $35 for the gas and we drive into town.

Corumbá, with a population of 200,000, is located on limestone bluffs high above the Paraguay River. We take the road into town that runs parallel to the river. There are a few breaks between the buildings on our right, revealing a wild lowland. The western bank of the Paraguay is at river level, allowing the water to spill easily into Bolivia, where it forms a large lagoon and an expansive marshland pockmarked with hundreds of ponds as far as the blue haze lets me see.

The local bluffs were quickly appreciated for their strategic position. Forte de Coimbra was built on the edge of town in 1775 to protect Brazil's southwestern flank along a poorly defined national border. The Paraguay-Paraná river system was becoming an increasingly important natural outlet for resources and goods from the country's heartlands. Eventually, disputes over its control led to a series of border wars with Argentina, Uruguay, and Paraguay from 1851 to 1870.

At this point the Paraguay is wide—maybe five hundred meters across—and busy. Barges and steamers ply the waters all the way to Argentina and are laden with meat, hides, forest products, fish, and, surprisingly, minerals. The minerals are mined about five kilometers south of town where there are mineral-rich buttes; the site is being rapidly developed, bringing along all the environmental and economic concerns that rapid development brings to a rural community. Those buttes contain the world's largest deposits of manganese.

The city, however, doesn't look as though an economic boom is on. It's an anemic, colonial place. The air is heavy with tropical humidity and decay. Many buildings are in disrepair, the whitewash streaked and shutters off their hinges. Cobbled streets were wisely planted long ago with broad-crowned trees, which thankfully shade the sidewalks.

We check into a simple bed and breakfast place on Rua Antonio Maria Coelho near the town center. Sra. Regina has just begun renting the few rooms to help supplement her husband's cab-driving income. Sra. Regina sits at a kitchen table with a circulating fan on the floor blowing on her. We're all sweating profusely. "You've picked the hottest time of the year to come. Yesterday was forty-nine degrees [120°F] and it's supposed to go higher today."

The Southern Police

We're late for our appointment with the commandant of the forestry police. Funny, the headquarters on Rua Cuiabá is situated in a nice house in a residential section of town. When we drive up, the only thing that sets it apart is a lot of well-armed soldiers dressed in steel-blue uniforms milling around the house. Two of them stand rigidly at attention in front of the gate; they wear blue helmets with "Polícia" stenciled in white.

Inside, ceiling fans are going, but it doesn't help. Everyone is sweating through their uniforms. The only room that's cool is the commandant's. Major Matias is only thirty-four years old. He's smartly dressed in a navy-blue tunic and riding pants with high leather boots.

The major's aide-de-camp hands him a silver *chimarrão* (cup) full of *chá-mate* (*Ilex paraguaiensis*), a popular herbal tea. It's a traditional beverage sipped communally from leather or horn cone-shaped cups. The aide then gives the major a silver *bomba* (straw) and spoons in some crushed ice. "Our group is a year old," says the major. "I have 280 men in Corumbá, rotated at six outposts at critical junctions in the state. The men undergo a special five-month course of training involving jungle survival, physical training, knowledge about the Pantanal, its fish, jacarés, and the law." He sips from the cup, then passes it to me.

"Come outside," he says, showing the way. His men snap to salute as he walks through what was the living room, where three citizens await his return. A fisherman's pickup truck is backing into the side drive. Several soldiers walk over to it and lift out a large, metal ice chest, dumping its contents onto a blue, plastic tarp spread on the lawn.

"One of our major problems here is the indiscriminate taking of fish — any size, any kind — throughout the year. It's especially bad during *piracema,* spawning, from October through January," says the major. While he talks, three of his men watch the quiet fishermen. They separate hundreds of fish into species. *Pintado,* a few small *dorado,* some good-size *pacú,* and many piranhas litter the tarp. A soldier with a clipboard notes the fish while another randomly measures them and weighs each pile.

The major says that all undersize fish are immediately impounded (and later given to the hospital or orphanage). "To get out of the city," he says, "every fisherman must stop here to be inspected and to obtain a permit. Without it they cannot cross the river back to the main roads [legally].

"We believe that in just one year things are getting better. About 30,000 fishermen work these waters. Last year we estimated 20,000 kilograms of illegally caught fish a month were being taken. Now 3000 kilograms are taken illegally."

Major Matias says, "Of course, our other major problem here is skin hunting . . . for *jacarés.* The hunters are mostly Brazilians working for Bolivian bosses." Operating in groups of ten or fifteen, they camp out and hunt for two to three weeks at a time. They can take 2500 *jacaré* skins, which are then flown out in unmarked planes. The major has heard of a Bolivian military man in Santa Cruz de la Sierra who directs a fleet of two hundred small aircraft. They continually run skins into Bolivia and marijuana and cocaine into Brazil.

I ask about the last action his patrols had seen. "Our last patrol twelve days ago ran into trouble," he says. "We encountered a group of four traffickers. They had killed four hundred *jacarés;* half had been skinned when the patrol arrived." There was a fire fight, and three of the hunters escaped. "But we wounded one. He's in the hospital."

What's the chance of interviewing the man?" I ask. The major thinks for a moment and talks with his aide, who then telephones the hospital. The hunter is in decent enough condition. "Okay."

A Wounded Skin Hunter

The chance to talk with a skin hunter is indeed a surprise. It's a chance to step away from the official line, the sanitized figures and accounts.

Skin hunting has gotten so completely out of control in the last ten years—no matter what state and federal authorities have done—that a few officials have suggested actually legalizing caiman hunting. The sticking point is to convince the illegal hunters that a regulated hunt would benefit them, as well as sustain the caiman population. There has even been an experiment here raising caimans on several farms, as ranchers in Venezuela have been doing. But at the moment, it's cheaper just to shoot *jacarés* in the wild.

I'm eager to ask the wounded hunter many questions and quickly follow Major Matias's officer out the door. The hospital, Society Beneficente of Corumbá, is on Rua 16 November, six blocks away from police headquarters. I am totally unprepared for the scene as we walk up the stairs. The hospital lobby is packed with families coming and going from visits. The walls are gray, fitting the gloom and despair of the people. Some form a line waiting to be admitted to the wards.

Major Matias's aide strolls right up to the nursing station and asks to be taken to the hunter's room. Immediately we are guided past the lines of sad people into the wards. We go upstairs and pass by open rooms with patients housed in field-hospital conditions.

We turn into a room with two beds. The man in the bed near the window has his leg in a cast hanging in traction. An armed officer is sitting beside him. The window is open without benefit of a screen. A number of flying insects work the stifling room. There is a smell, a mix of disinfectant and human waste. The disinfectant is woefully undermatched. I have all I can do to look into the man's face and keep my mind on what I want to ask.

The man's name is Pedro. He's twenty-seven years old and a cowboy on one of the ranches. He was shot in the right leg above the knee. "How's your wound?" I ask. He looks to the officer, then to me, rolling back his eyes. "It hurts," he says. He tries to move to a more comfortable position and ends up just leaning forward and touching his cast. I ask him to tell me about his caiman hunting.

He's been hunting for about five months, going on long motorboat trips down the São Lourenço River with three other men. The head of his group gave him a .22 gauge rifle and one of those focus-beam flashlights like Gaspar had. "We shot only *jacarés,*" he says. "It was easy. Each of us shot fifty to a hundred a night. The police got there about noon and began shooting without warning. My friends ran off. I was the only one who fired back."

Married with two children and working for the minimum wage (about U.S. $35 a month), Pedro is obviously hunting for the extra cash. In many cases, the ranch hands have the tacit approval of the ranch owners to hunt their lands for caimans, jaguars, etc. Despite laws about hunting, it gives the im-poverished workers a chance for more money and takes care of what has been perceived as a wildlife nuisance. As with most extralegal adventures here, if the law moves in, it's usually the little guy who gets caught first.

"Do you know that people want to have a legal, controlled hunt for *jacarés* and that what you and your friends are doing prevent this?" I ask. Pedro shrugs it off in disbelief.

I ask the officer what's going to happen next for Pedro. "After his wounds heal, he'll go before a federal judge for trial. He faces two to eight years in prison," says the officer. Pedro winces in pain.

Off the Track

I walk a few hundred meters from the hospital and feel the sweat trickle between my fingers.

Back at the bed and breakfast place, Sra. Regina is putting out a lunch spread for us, and I don't know how she can cook in such heat. Her husband is butchering a meter-long *pintado,* and the tile wall above the sink is spattered with blood.

Everyone's face is flushed, we're on our second shower in three hours, and it's useless. As soon as I put on my damp clothes, I walk into our room, turn on the air conditioner, and lie on the concrete floor. Its wind is like hot breath on my neck.

"Go with the flow." I recall my promise. But the furnacelike heat has melted my resolve. How does anything get done in such a climate?

I'm worried about the computer. The handbook specifies that the maximum operating temperature is 104°F, and we passed that at 10:30 A.M. We're fifteen degrees higher now, and the mercury is still rising. I turn it on. The machine beeps a couple of times, and the screen blinks its cool, blue light. It's working, but I'm not. I stare at the flickering cursor and can't lay in my notes.

Renaldo comes back with a smile on his face. He's been out picking up girls. He's also made a few phone calls about our transportation. The launch the official in Campo Grande promised is on the river and won't be back for several days. The jeep to Necolândia has broken down. Nothing has turned up except the heat. The boarding house thermometer is pushing 50°C.

My *South American Handbook*'s duct tape is fluid at this temperature, sliding away from its adhesive as I open to a formula that converts Celsius to Fahrenheit: divide by 5, multiply by 9, and add 32. I use a ballpoint to work the numbers. The plastic is soft. Pushing down on the pen shoves the ball bearing loose, allowing the ink to flow out like cream. I come up with 122°F; 50°C sounds better.

Before bed Renaldo suggests that we go for a beer at a corner café and make alternate plans. While there, I decide to take the wagon into Necolândia. Renaldo gets directions, and we agree to travel under the relative protection of the night to avoid the heat and maybe scare up some prowling critters.

Outside town in the predawn blackness, our headlights bring up two blue-green reflections. Renaldo slams on the brakes;

and we charge out of the wagon. I fumble around in my bag to yank out a quick-shot camera. Whatever the animal is, it's big. I use the flash more to see what it is than to take a picture. Foosh! The strobe lights up an equally startled tapir (*Tapirus treestris*). It's huge and elephant-gray. Flash again. Its twelve-centimeter, fleshy nose is turned up, snorkel-fashion, catching our scent and showing healthy, white teeth.

The tapir's poor vision is weakened further by my strobe bursts, allowing us to get as close as the crunch of gravel under foot permits. Then the big beastie makes for us. Enough. It snorts and crashes through the bushes.

The night is soon washed out by the sun, making the critters vacate the premises. It's white hot, and the country's crackling dry. There's no animal life to be seen. A few fishermen are camped along the river, and so is a patrol of policemen—all huddled in the shade.

The only thing we encounter is a dust cloud moving across the range. It's a large herd of cattle, maybe five hundred head, being driven to market. They shimmer in the heat, and the cowboys materialize like Bedouins riding out of the North African desert. In the sun my pocket thermometer has stopped reading at 120°F. There's sweat between my fingers again. I don't like it.

One cowboy hauls up close to us on a critter that resembles a donkey. The man has beady eyes that sit sadly in their sockets. He's dazed. As the herd moves past us, the cowboy moves a little closer. He's silent. I hold up a bottle of mineral water, offering it to him. He shakes it off and asks, "Do you have some *cachaça?*"

There's a time on long trips such as this one when the momentum fails like an overloaded train unble to make a grade. This guy wants rum. And I want out of here. I've pushed hard and fast wanting to peek around one too many bushes. I feel alien here. The animals have laid low in this heat wave, and so have I. There aren't any more to be seen. There's little to occupy my senses and no dreamy lakes to sit by.

No more flow. I go like a crow. Back to Rio. Back to Rio.

fifteen

Endgame

I've lived in the United States. When you have winter, nature
is dead, and I can understand why people want to save what
they have. But here it's green all year 'round . . . yecchhh.
— *Dr. Eliza Caillaux, sociologist*

*D*uring my last days in Rio I talk with Professor Helmut
Sick, the eminent Brazilian ornithologist. His many years here
will help put some of my experiences in perspective, I think.

Professor Sick lives in an apartment in a hilly section of Rio
called Larangeiras, literally "Orangeade," so called because long
ago this area had extensive orange groves. The professor looks
a little haggard. He's wearing a red-checked flannel shirt—it's
21°C (70°F); that's winter for Cariocas—and gray flannel
pants. His living room is small, with a small dining table in the
center. He's been working to revise the twelfth edition of his
landmark publication *Birds of Brazil.*

Bookshelves beside a simple couch are full. The walls display
a number of antique scientific illustrations of birds from South
America, England, and Germany; most are hand-colored and
date from the mid-1700s. The air is so humid and hot that
mold has begun to grow inside some of the frames boxing
these rare prints. Also hanging are black-and-white photographs of Amazon Indians with whom the professor has lived.

Professor Sick's steel-gray hair falls listlessly across his
forehead; yet his demeanor is animated. He makes points

energetically, tossing his head back and staring out the window to another apartment building and a small yard and hills beyond. He purses his mouth, twisting his face up, as he hunts for the right English words. At first he seems to want to test me for my seriousness.

I mention a few other bird people I know and tell him how much I've been captivated by the hyacinths. At first he believes hyacinths are "still quite common." But when I tell him about the recent estimate of their numbers, he pauses. And then he tells me about the similar-looking, smaller Lear's macaw.

"It's extremely rare and endangered today. For a hundred years people thought they were extinct in the wild, but I discovered the place where they still live," he tells me. Sick spent twenty years searching for that one macaw. He made expeditions to remote parts of Brazil to interview natives and cowboys, being perfectly meticulous in his investigations. Then he found them living in northeast Bahia in two separate colonies totaling no more than sixty birds. When he found them in 1979, it was a big sensation.

"The most incredible mystery in South America is how a bird of this size could not be found for a hundred years," he says. It's the kind of story that makes him believe that there may be more hyacinths.

Sick has an interesting background. He's a naturalized Brazilian citizen. It's been eight years since he retired as curator of birds at the Museu Nacional, the country's major natural-history institution, located in the beautiful Quinta da Boa Vista Park. He was the ornithologist there for thirty years.

"Brazil has so much natural resources and wildlife, but they are destroying all . . . all," he says. "Why is it? It's their mentality—they want the wood and the gold. There are many, many reasons for this. The Brazilians don't like the forest. All the Brazilians fear danger in the forest. It's one of the things from life a hundred years ago. The Portuguese colonists on the Atlantic feared Indians, and it's exactly this mentality today for people living in the big cities. They are making the politics.

"The Portuguese came to cut down the forest for the *Pau-Brasil*." This is the wood that was so important to the colonists that it was the namesake of the country. But *Pau-Brasil* is for all practical purposes extinct. There is some in the state of Espirito Santo. They are the rarest trees.

What about replantation? Sick shakes his head, saying, "Noo. There is no interest. Brazil has wonderful laws, but nobody is interested. You can buy off local authorities, and everyone is so money hungry you can buy anything for money.

"We have a place right here, outside Rio, where you can buy the rarest birds in Brazil. If they don't have one right now, you can order one to be brought right to you in Rio." He's getting visibly upset. "Why, it's practically an official place! All the macaws and songbirds. But it's very, very expensive.

"Duque do Caxias is located in the north suburbs, and everyone knows it. It's a public market. The best day to buy any kind of animal is Sunday. Sometimes the police come there and get all the animals, but one week later they're coming back."

The professor is adamant now. "I will not hear or say anything more about this now, because they are destroying it all. It's so sad." He tenses his lips and turns from me in obvious discomfort to gaze out the window.

Sick came to Brazil fifty years ago; his first expedition was for the Berlin Museum. "I now have many Brazilian pupils," he says. "They are stronger for this [ecological] fight. Even though I've been here for many years, I am still the 'German' to the Brazilians—the gringo who is criticizing their country. After fifty years they still regard me as a foreigner.

"I first came here in 1937, right before the war. The Brazilian officials couldn't believe that I was coming here just to see birds when war was brewing in Europe. So they had me arrested and sentenced to three years in prison out on Ilha Grande, a prison island like Alcatraz. There were many other Germans who were suspected of being spies for the Third Reich. Even German Jews—can you imagine?"

Prison life must have been difficult for a man who wanted to walk the forests and look at birds. "Very hard," he says, "there were no birds around. All I could see were those little bugs on the floor . . . termites. I studied them for those three years and sent numerous specimens to a scientist friend of mine in the United States for identification. He wrote to me that among them were six that had never previously been named before."

To make matters worse, Sick was separated from his new bride in Germany for those three years and through the war. "I managed to get letters to her through the help of the king of Belgium because he was patron of the natural sciences. It wasn't until 1947 that we were reunited. At that moment I decided I would make my home in Brazil; after all, this was a paradise for someone like me—so many birds here."

I asked him to take a look down the road—what will environmental conditions be like? "There is absolutely no hope at all," he says. "The next century you'll have to look in this book [he picks up his book] to see birds. No hope. After so many years I thought . . . ah, yes . . . we'll still have the national parks. Now one national park after the other is being destroyed; they're putting roads through them . . . growing exotic plants."

What of the many new conservation groups? The professor says, "They are idealists. But how can they make change when people from abroad—North Americans, Europeans, and Japanese—are paying so much for their [despoiling] projects here?"

He seems possessed by his work, in a race to produce more before it's too late. "I have so much work, I'm not able to go out," he says. "I have my private diary from the most remote areas in South America—the Pacific Coast, isolated Amazon, Patagonia. I have more than nine thousand pages of notes."

When I say good-bye, I wonder which would be worse for the professor: staying in the urban jungle of Rio or going into the hinterlands to see his cherished, once wild places after many years?

To Market

It's been a number of weeks since Professor Sick told me about the Duque de Caxias market outside Rio. Every Sunday people can buy practically any animal found in Brazil. I simply cannot believe this, but I want to see for myself. I find that none of my friends want to go, especially early on a Sunday. Since I'm coming to the end of my time in Brazil, this Sunday will be my last chance.

On Friday, after seeing some video footage on mercury use at T.V. Globo, I hail a taxi in the middle of an afternoon rain-squall. It's getting chilly. I'm picked up by a taxi driver named Alexander, a thirty-one-year-old Carioca. He tells me he left a poor-paying office job at IBGE, the government social-statistics center. With a wife and child he's going to the streets in a cab, gambling on a better life.

Alexander is tall and lanky, with a scraggly beard and haunting, gray eyes. He's frustrated that the country is so out of control. It's raining very hard, and our body heat steams the windshield of his jalopy. The wipers don't function, but that doesn't slow Alexander's speed on the slick side streets. The traffic's bad and we talk a lot.

Alexander is a welcome confidant in the cab — sort of like a fast-moving bartender — and we get along great. I mention the wildlife market at Duque de Caxias, and he says he's been there. The market is very old; it was there even when he was a little kid. "It is very popular. The police are very impotent to stop any of this selling. It'll be good for you to see this," he says. This is my last chance — it's now or nothing. So I arrange for Alexander to pick me up at my friends' house very early Sunday.

We're both sleepy when he comes for me. The sky reminds me of Ireland; low, scudding, gray clouds obscure Sugar Loaf Mountain near Botafogo. As we head out past the airport for the suburb of Duque de Caxias, it's apparent the suburbs are the opposite of those back home. Unable to afford housing in the city center, the poor are forced by economics out to the perimeter, shuttled back and forth by crowded buses and packed trains. Alexander says robbers prey on the passengers. "To ride them is very dangerous," he says, pointing to a silvery, elevated train making its way parallel to the highway.

This rattletrap of a taxi is an old VW. There aren't door or window handles; the speedometer twitches up to 120 kilometers an hour, then smacks down to zero when we hit bumps. Idiot warning lights glow red, and Alexander has to constantly oversteer to the left to compensate for some wild shimmy in the wheels. It's early Sunday, but I'm wide awake praying that we make it.

On the way Alexander makes small talk about how I'm the

only foreigner he's ever taken to this market; the other travelers have peculiar, not crazy, requests. For example, a regular request from Germans is to go on a tour of the *favelas,* the slums lining the hills around Rio. He says they love to see the bad conditions.

It takes us about thirty minutes to reach the town of Duque de Caxias. At the town's center hundreds of cars are illegally parked on the green, and thousands of shoppers are streaming into the market. Like an idiot I've brought too much gear: two still cameras and a movie camera in a shoulder bag.

Alexander warns me that we should drive around a bit first to get a feel for the place. It's been several years since he's been here. Today only about half the market is devoted to selling animals. He warns that I should take considerable care not to pull out the camera too soon; that would draw too much attention. "There are plenty of thieves here," he says as he parks the car.

As I pull my trusty blue shoulder bag close, we get pushed into the throng. When we leave the main thoroughfare, there are a few people walking against the flow, they carry bare, wooden cages with newly purchased birds high over their heads. Lower-middle-class families are here for the outing. There are also men with hardened looks who wear clothing similar to rural people I've seen in Mato Grosso—suggesting they may have traveled there to buy or capture these animals themselves.

Lining both sides of a narrow street are stalls and open VW buses packed full of cages. There are street carts with black-plastic tarp awnings displaying bags of sunflower seeds and other bird seed, cuttle bones, cage dishes, collars, and bells—the apparatus of the pet trade. There are also fast-food vans selling fried snacks, coffee, and pop to the gawking crowd.

As we're drawn deeper into the market, we see vegetable grocers standing in front of carts hawking lettuce, beets, cucumbers . . . and screaming parrots. There's more. A small man holds a stick with an Amazon parrot leashed to it and pulls open the bird's wings for a curious onlooker. Next to him a man has a tiny monkey clinging to his shoulder and on his other arm a big, beautiful toucan with blazing colors—turquoise, banana yellow, red, and white—chained by the leg. It's the kind of toucan I saw hopping away from my camera along the Transpantaneira with Gaspar. A smaller toucanet is there, too, with bizarre zigzag color patterns on its beak.

Now we're sucked along with the crowd toward a row of card tables full of little, wooden boxes; about three boxes would fit into a shoebox. The boxes have wooden bars on them, and in each one is pressed a tiny, gray monkey. A man at one table peels a banana and jams pieces of the banana into each box. I don't think the animal can even lift its head to reach the banana. The boxes are little more than tiny, open-air coffins.

Another table holds the same kind of boxes, but in each of those is a parrot. So small are the jails that the bars prevent the birds from moving their legs. I'm getting depressed — and enraged — fast. I knew this would be bad, but this? I start to reach for my camera, and Alexander cautions silently that I shouldn't — not yet.

To the left, three tough-looking guys are handing over a fistful of cruzados novo bills. The owner is giving an Amazon parrot to them, pulling out a brown-paper shopping bag and shoving the struggling bird in. It's screaming all the while, and even though it's a diurnal animal, the bird continues to scream in the blackness of the rolled-up bag. The men look around as if to suggest the sound is coming from somewhere else.

I see a hawk shackled to a stick. Another one is caged. The owner is rasping a stick along the cage bars to show a crowd around him that the animal is vigorous. The hawk hisses with its mouth wide open and holds its wings out as far as it can in protest.

There's a flat cage. Oof. An old man bumps into me; he's carrying a watermelon-size tortoise that's upside-down and flailing its feet. My attention goes back to the flat, wooden cage, which is about the size of a home VCR and has a big, wiggling, black mass inside. As I get closer, I see it's not one animal but about thirty black birds jammed together, half of which aren't moving at all.

This is a street scene that jangles the brain. Poor kids are begging with outstretched hands. Others munch snacks, oblivious to this bargain-basement bazaar of the country's wild heritage. It's something like the weekend thieves' market in

Bangkok or the crush of people in Algiers' Casbah. Professor
Sick warned me it would be strong stuff. He wouldn't come
here for fear he'd end up shooting these people or collapsing.

We try to talk an apartment owner into letting us go up and
shoot some wide-angle pictures from his open windows into
the street below, but he fears the animal vendors will see us,
get really angry, and trash his place.

We move along. We pass a little beer shack with beat-up
folding chairs where at 9:40 A.M. a crowd is guzzling away,
finishing off their beers with shots of *cachaça.* Oglers.

More carts display parakeet cages. One is packed with eight
young Amazons; another holds about twenty tiny, iridescent
songbirds. We see vireos and tanagers and a Brazilian red-
capped cardinal—all jammed into those horribly small chambers.

And lots of monkeys. Alexander is now talking to other
vendors after I ask about different animals. "Yes," he says,
"there are more in those houses." He points to dirty, gray
concrete buildings behind the stalls. "But it's difficult for us
to go. They're suspicious of us." I want to see. "He's got *araras*
[macaws], *jaguatirica* [jaguarundi], even a small anteater," says
Alexander. Live. For sale.

I ask around for typical prices: small monkey, U.S. $9.52;
small songbird, U.S. $10; Amazon parrot, U.S. $47.62; toucan,
U.S. $79.37; macaw, U.S. $158.73; small anaconda, U.S. $63.49;
ocelot, U.S. $317.46; owl, U.S. $85.

We walk by a table where a passive Amazon parrot slouches
on a wooden branch. It looks sort of dazed. Alexander pulls
me aside and says they take a metal rod about the size of a
fork tine and jam it into the bird's ears, breaking the eardrums.
Then it's quiet.

In the damp, cold wind, two baby Amazon parrots, barely
fledged, shiver where they're chained on top of a cage. Perched
on a stick is a burrowing owl with big, yellow-and-black eyes.
It rotates its head this way and that, trying to figure this crush
of strange beings. Barging through the crowd toward us is a
man with two small, wild cats. He shoves his way past and is
gone before I can catch up.

We come to the concrete wall abutting the train station; I
can't stomach much more. I motion to Alexander—let's go

back. I pull out my camera, take off its case, and slide it into a red nylon camping bag. I estimate the exposure and begin retracing my steps with the camera at waist level shooting the birds. Brown toucans? They're not even in my bird identification book. Alexander whispers, *"Muito raro"*—very rare. Photo!

I see another guy with a hawk chained to a stick. He's bouncing the hawk in the air so that it flops its wings in sheer terror like some feathered yo-yo. Photo!

Two men are holding a large toucan down on a table, trying to fix a chain to its leg, and the bird is frantically flapping its wings with everything it's got, letting out a high-pitched scream, defecating and vomiting at the same time. Photo! Then one of the men, visibly angry, dumps the hapless, fabulously beautiful creature into a sack.

Black-and-orange orioles with blue eyes—the kind I saw at Poussada Caiman—are jammed together into a small canary cage. Photo! The men stare, paralyzed with surprise, as I shoot and move on.

A few of the vendors start to notice me and talk to each other. I lift the camera out of the bag, hold it aloft, and shoot, scanning the entire market. Photo! Turn. Photo! Turn. Photo! I wish the damned thing was an Uzi.

Now Alexander is watching in horror as I step up onto a box and take pictures in a place that is never photographed. Everyone can see me. He yanks on my jacket. "Vitor . . . go . . . go," he says. "We must leave this place. It's dangerous for you."

We shove our way past the crowd, taking a circuitous route back to the taxi. Tasting cotton in my mouth, I suggest that we leave the market, go get something to drink, and talk.

Alexander says, "You don't realize that Duque de Caxias is one of the most dangerous places in Brazil. It's more violent than Beiruit. It's true. They take about fifty dead bodies out of here a day. Thieves, murderers, the destitute live here crammed together in *favelas.* The politicians just look the other way. There's no infrastructure . . . the same as in the Pantanal. It's a wilderness."

Over fresh orange juice and hot bread at a little bistro, we talk about the corruption and total lack of control at the market. I buy Alexander a cheese omelette, but I don't have the stomach.

"One of the other birds was very calm," says Alexander. Had its eardrums been broken too? "No," he says, "it's blind. They took a flame to its eyes to ruin its cornea. That's why it's so tame. People don't realize these things until they get the birds home. Within a week many of these animals are dead."

We estimate that there were several thousand birds at the market this morning. More critters, some obviously rare, are sold behind closed doors. Alexander says today is a bad day: it's fall and it's raining. What more could they have on a "good" day?

Some of the animals come from the Atlantic forest area near Rio. In fact, I've been told that a number of thieves work the grounds of the Jardim Botānico (Botanical Gardens), where there are many toucans. The guards there have no arms and simply look the other way, or the collectors go into sections of the gardens where visitors seldom venture. They invade nests for the young or smear an incredibly sticky material on the limbs so the birds can't fly off. The animals are exhausted from their struggle. How many die from struggle, shock, or starvation before one reaches the market? And, how many die after they're purchased?

More animals are taken from the Amazon, Pantanal, and the northeast. This desperate trade is selling off many of Brazil's wildlife jewels from this incredible, troubled, tropical kingdom.

"Police never come here; it's too dangerous," Alexander says. "There's a very good chance that many of these people selling animals have pistols too." When the police do make an occasional raid, the vendors run, disappearing like mice into the nooks and crannies of the streets and houses. The eighteenth-century *bandeirante* spirit of profit from the wild lives on.

The temperature is dropping to around 15°C (59°F). A real antarctic storm has blown in, with a fierce southeaster that churns the blue Atlantic to a foaming green. Heavy, cold rain beats against the taxi window on the way home. With any kind of luck it will wash out that market and perhaps put a few of those suffering creatures out of their misery.

Alexander slows for a second as we pass a church; he genuflects, then floors the pedal. On his portable radio a *chorinho* tune is playing. A mournful song for a very sad day.

Index

Index

/

BOLIVIA

Mato Grosso

Cuiaba
Pocone

Transpantaneira
Hwys.

Pantanal National Park

Corumbà

Coxim

Campo Grande

Mato Grosso
do Sul

PARAGUAY

ARGENTINA

ASUNCIÓN

BUENOS AIRES